THE TRAIN
ROBBERS

THE TRAIN ROBBERS

Piers Paul Read

W H ALLEN · LONDON
1988

Copyright © Piers Paul Read and W.H. Allen Publishers Inc., 1978

First published 1978 by W.H. Allen & Co. Ltd
and The Alison Press/Secker & Warburg Ltd, London

Reprinted in August 1988

Printed and bound in Great Britain by
Mackays of Chatham PLC, Chatham, Kent
for the Publishers W.H. Allen & Co. Plc
44 Hill Street, London W1X 8LB

ISBN 0 491 02063 5

Contents

Acknowledgements

I am most grateful to those who have helped me with this book — particularly to Julian Shuckburgh who first introduced me to the Train Robbers, to Catherine Caute who transcribed our conversations and typed the manuscript, and to Jane Wellesley who compiled the illustrations.

I am also grateful to those besides the Train Robbers who told me their side of the story — especially their wives, their children, Mrs Rene Boal, Mr David Boal, Mrs Florence Mills, Mrs Mary MacDonald, Dr Ian Holden and ex-Detective Superintendent Malcolm Fewtrell who kindly lent me his comprehensive archives, and whose own book with the same title as my own is an essential source for the police investigations of the Great Train Robbery.

P.P.R.

List of Illustrations

Maps

Sources of Illustrations

The publishers are grateful to the following for permission to reproduce copyright photographs: Bildarchiv Preussischer Kulturbesitz, 1; Keystone, 2, 14, 19, 24 and 25; Daily Telegraph, 3, 6, 8, 11 and 13; Press Association, 7, 9, 10, 15, 16, 17, 18, 20, 21, 22 and 23; Associated Press, 12; Tara Heinemann, 26, 27, 28, 29, 30, 31, 32 and 33. The maps are by the Robert Clarke Studio.

Principal Characters and their Associates

(Train Robbers are in capital letters, invented names are in italics)

Characters	Wives/girlfriends	Associates
The First Firm		
BUSTER EDWARDS	June	*Derek Glass*
		Gus Brown
		Bernie Carton
BILL JENNINGS		
GORDON GOODY	Pat	
CHARLIE WILSON	Pat	*Joey Gray*
ROY JAMES		Micky Ball
BRUCE REYNOLDS	Franny	*Harry Booth*
JOHN DALY	Barbara (Franny's sister)	Mary Manson
JIMMY WHITE	Sheree	
ALF THOMAS		
RONNIE BIGGS	Charmian	*Stan Agate*
JIMMY HUSSEY	Gill	
The Second Firm		
TOMMY WISBEY	Rene	
FRANK MUNROE		
ROGER CORDREY		Bill Boal
BOB WELCH	Pat/Jean	

The Information

Brian Field
Mark
The Ulsterman
Lennie Field
John Wheater

The Germans

Horst
Karl

Sigi
Klaus
Hanne Schmidt
Annaliese von Lutzeberg
Otto Skorzeny

The Police

Detective Superintendent Malcolm Fewtrell, head of
    Buckinghamshire CID
Commander George Hatherill, head of CID at Scotland Yard
Detective Superintendent Gerald McArthur
Detective Sergeant Jack Pritchard
Detective Chief Superintendent Tommy Butler, head of the
    Flying Squad
Detective Superintendent Frank Williams, his deputy
Detective Superintendent Maurice Ray, second in command
    of Dept C3 (Fingerprint Department)
Dr Ian Holden, Metropolitan Police Forensic Science
    Laboratory

Introduction
OTTO SKORZENY

Towards the end of April 1976 a tall well-dressed South African walked into the offices of the London publishers W. H. Allen and Co., and offered to sell them the confessions of the celebrated Great Train Robbers. Thirteen years before they had stopped an overnight mail train from Glasgow to London and robbed it of more than £2,500,000 — the equivalent today of £8,800,000. Those who were initially caught and convicted had been sentenced to thirty years imprisonment: two were still in jail, and one remained a fugitive in Brazil; but seven of the thieves had been released on parole and were prepared to tell their full story for the first time.

Reluctant to sign up the thieves without an author to write their story, the publishers invited me to come to London and discuss the project with all concerned. A lunch was arranged in the penthouse flat on the top floor of their offices, and it was here that I was introduced to the seven Train Robbers. At first there was little to be made of them: some were tall, some were small and most were of an indeterminate middle-age. I moved around the room, talking to one and then another. I identified Gordon Goody, the mysterious hero of Peta Fordham's book on the Train Robbery, who had a huge body and straggly hair, and sat on the black leather sofa studying us from behind dark glasses; then Roy James, the racing driver, who was small with a plaintive expression on his face. Buster Edwards and Jimmy White both brought back feeble memories of wanted posters from the early 1960s: Buster Edwards was small but upright with dark features and a pigeon chest; Jimmy White was older than the rest — his head balding, his eyes and voice slow and tired. Tommy Wisbey looked like a boxer; Roger Cordrey was conspicuous only in the anonymity of his appearance. Jim Hussey was huge and looked more like a thief than the others, but the only one to strike me as slightly sinister turned out to be their South African agent, Gary van Dyk.

This first meeting was intended to enable the author to meet his subjects and the subjects to meet their author; and towards the end of lunch, as we were drinking coffee, Gary van Dyk and Buster Edwards suddenly took their leave for another more urgent appointment. I was left with the rest who a little later also departed. The lunch was over and I was taken down in the lift to the offices of W.H. Allen, where the publishers asked me whether I felt inclined to write the book.

I was undecided. Other books had been written on the Great Train Robbery and I wondered whether there was enough that was new to justify another one. I also doubted that the Train Robbers would be sufficiently candid to enable me to depict them as convincing characters, and whether they would remember details of what had happened so long ago.

The publishers agreed that these were things I should consider, but added that there was something else I should know. There was a Mr Big behind the crime — a man who had financed it and had received in return a million pounds of the stolen money. He was Otto Skorzeny — the officer in the Waffen-SS who had commanded the German commandoes during the war, and had rescued Mussolini from the Gran Sasso where he had been imprisoned by the government of Marshal Badoglio. Skorzeny had put up £80,000; one of his men had been at their hideout, Leatherslade Farm; others had abducted Charlie Wilson from Winson Green prison. They had arranged for Buster Edwards to leave the country and have his appearance changed by plastic surgery. Skorzeny himself was now dead but his organisation was still intact — indeed Buster Edwards and Gary van Dyk were at that very moment meeting with one of Skorzeny's subordinates at the Dorchester Hotel to ask if they could name her former chief.

My reaction to this news was one of mixed excitement and scepticism. I knew that though Skorzeny in his life time had presented himself as an audacious but honourable soldier who after the war had gone into business in Spain, he was suspected to have been the founder of ODESSA—the world-wide organisation of former members of the SS. The idea that these old Nazis had sustained themselves through crime struck me as an extraordinary story which should certainly be told to the world.

On the other hand if the Train Robbers had reckoned that the publishers, like the public, were tired of their old story, then they could not have invented a more piquant sauce to spice up the reheated stew. I was well aware how skilled and experienced thieves could be in fabrication, and I realised that it was not impossible—given the facilities of prison libraries and the time spent alone in a cell—for the Train Robbers to have invented the whole story.

In the days which followed I had further meetings with Buster Edwards and Jim Hussey—the two who had had the closest links with the Germans. The principal indication that the story was true was Buster Edwards's reluctance to tell it. Although Jim Hussey had been the first to make contact with Skorzeny's organisation, Buster alone had been to Cologne after the robbery and knew the full story of their German partner. His wife June was the only person to have met Otto Skorzeny himself; and because they both felt grateful for what he had done to help them, they were loath even now to betray him; for when in the Dorchester Hotel Buster had asked for permission to name him, the representative of Skorzeny's organisation—a woman called Hanne Schmidt—had refused point blank, saying that in Germany Skorzeny was revered by many as a national hero and his name could not be linked with a common crime.

It was Gary van Dyk who goaded Buster on to tell his story, saying quite rightly that the publishers, having scented a sensation, would not now pay for anything less. He persuaded Buster that he owed it to the rest of the gang, all now apparently penniless, to help them find their feet by earning enough from the book to start some legitimate business. Buster eventually agreed, and June at his request agreed to tell her side of the story.

June Edwards finally convinced me that the story was true. She was, first of all, such a direct, instinctive woman that it went against any reasonable appreciation of her character to believe that she who had suffered so much from crime should enter into a substantial deception. More convincing still, she let slip a detail in her story which by chance was the first fragment of evidence we could hope to corroborate. She described how at lunch with Skorzeny in Madrid she had met an editor of *Reader's Digest* who could speak a number of Chinese dialects. As it happened one of the publishers knew the man and was able to confirm that he had indeed been a friend of Otto Skorzeny.

Convinced by this that the Train Robbers' story was true, I agreed to write it and in the summer of 1976 started my research.

Part One **Robbery**

1. The First Firm

Two years after the end of the Second World War London remained pitted by the marks of the German bombs, but life itself had returned to normal. Certainly the brief friendship between the social classes which had been brought on by the Blitz had disappeared with the danger: the rich had returned to the fashionable residential areas of Mayfair and Kensington while the poor continued their hard life in the slums south of the river.

June Edwards, then June Rothery, was a small girl of fifteen, with dark skin, black hair and fierce brown eyes, who crossed the Thames each morning from south to north to work in the warehouse of John Lewis in Oxford Street. She returned home promptly each evening, because her parents were strict, but on Sunday afternoons she would go with her girl friends to the Regal cinema in Kennington. One Sunday in 1947 they were waiting for tickets when a group of boys about sixteen years old sauntered along the street towards them. One in particular caught her eye: he was not tall but had a slim figure and a proud, handsome, somewhat scornful face which immediately attracted her. When the boys stood in the queue behind the girls, June glanced back furtively at the one she fancied; and after they had bought their tickets, the girls dawdled in the foyer, followed the boys into the auditorium and sat in the row behind them. Throughout the film they chattered and giggled so much that the boys could not but notice them; and after the film the two groups paired off in the street, June with her handsome boy.

Buster Edwards had charm and good looks but he was not the kind of young man a conscientious father would choose for his daughter. Like June he had been born in South London and had grown up at its heart around the Elephant and Castle. As a child he had roamed around in gangs of little delinquents, and when war was declared he was evacuated to Devonshire where he was caught pinching apples from an orchard. After the war he returned to London and at the age of fourteen left school. His first job was as a fitter's mate in a garage; he moved on to work for a coal merchant, then a waste-paper business, and ended up in a sausage factory. Meat was still rationed: Buster would pilfer the pork and take it back to his family and friends.

When he first met June, he was only a year older than she was. He was as eager to impress her as she was to impress him; he wanted some smarter clothes, and in particular he wanted a brown suit which he saw in a shop window. His father would not lend him the money to buy it, so late one foggy evening he took a brick, smashed the glass and ran off clutching the suit still pinned to the dummy.

From that early age Buster and June saw each other almost every day, but it was not until Buster was conscripted into the Air Force for two years that June made up her mind to change their adolescent romance into an adult marriage. She saw an attractive engagement ring in the window of a jeweller's shop, paid a deposit on it, and wrote to Buster at the RAF camp to tell him that they were engaged. He received the news in the base prison where he was serving fifty-six days detention for stealing cigarettes from the Sergeants' Mess.

When Buster came out of the Air Force, he and June were married in Lambeth Parish Church, and their first home was a room above Buster's parents' flat. Buster found work as a window cleaner: it was boring, menial labour and was poorly paid, but without contacts or qualifications he had little choice. Poverty was humiliating for the young husband, but wealth seemed the remote preserve of those who spent it so lavishly north of the river in the jewellers, tailors and department stores of Bond Street and Knightsbridge: south of the river only the black-marketeers and street-corner bookmakers seemed able to raise themselves from the general penury of the Cockney working-classes. Buster tried some back-street bookmaking, but met with no success and went to work in a flower shop.

June was happy with whatever Buster chose to do, and her family too had grown fond of their cheerful and charming son-in-law. One of her relatives in particular took a shine to the young man who had married June, and used to take him out on a Saturday night to a pub in Vauxhall called the King's Head. There they would meet with a group of his friends who were always well-dressed, and pulling pounds from their pockets to pay for the drinks, yet who never seemed to be working. When Buster asked what they did for a living, he was told with a laugh that they were "at it"; and in the weeks which followed, through the smoke of the black-market cigarettes, and over the sound of the bar-room piano, he learned just what this meant.

They were all professional thieves. Some of them specialised in ringing cars — stealing them, changing the licence plates ("ringing the change") and selling them again; some in kiting (passing forged cheques); some in hoisting (shop-lifting) or screwing—breaking open shops with butchers' price tags or skeleton keys. There were also the creepers (cat burglars), heavies (thugs), and the bottle mob (pickpockets) as well as more ambitious thieves who nicked dough from jugs (stole money from banks) or blew Peters for Tom (broke open safes for jewellery). They all seemed to know one another, and with the proper introduction they were happy to welcome a new recruit.

Besides crime itself, there was no qualifying exam or initiation ceremony, but once it was known that you were at it, you were a member of an exclusive club of fellow thieves whose premises were dispersed between certain South London pubs, clubs and His Majesty's prisons. Some rules had to be obeyed: to lose one's bottle (one's nerve) brought contempt and relegation; to grass (talk to the police) was treason for which the punishment was maiming or death.

There were also certain conventions for survival: a successful thief had a law-abiding auxiliary—a sleeping partner whose identity was unknown not just to the police, but also to his fellow thieves, who would act as a front in all legal transactions. That the thief himself was at it could not be too well concealed; for it was an adage that a thief is only as good as his information and for that he depended upon the approaches of a vast fifth column of dishonest men in responsible employment as caretakers, security guards, postmen, policemen or bookie's runners who fed him intelligence of where and how the "prize" could be stolen.

Buster was delighted by the total and consistent lawlessness of his new friends. They ignored all the bureaucratic regulations of the state — licences, permits, taxes, insurance and of course the laws of property. They gave nothing and expected nothing in return. The only authority they recognised was that of a "name"—the leader of a group or gang more ruthless or successful than they were themselves. Buster, too, though generous and warm-hearted by nature, had an exaggerated admiration for those qualities of dare-devilry and bravado which in grown men were often the symptoms of retarded, even psychotic, personalities; and to prove himself in terms they would understand, he too was prepared to go against the grain of his amiable nature and "do what had to be done".

He started his career modestly with a set of skeleton keys, obtained from an old thief in the King's Head. On an evening, after the shops were shut, he would dress up in a white overall and with a couple of friends remove the contents of a chosen shop. Occasional passers-by might seem suspicious, but no one ever interfered, and by night-fall he would have sold the clothes, cigarettes or televisions to a "fence" for a third of their retail price. As time passed he became more ambitious and started blowing safes — not just to make more money but to cut a better figure among his fellow thieves.

More often than not these thefts were a fiasco: the safes were too strong, or their doors would jam, or the information would turn out to be wrong. The risk was disproportionate to the return, but theft like gambling feeds on the fantasy that next time it will be different; and even after a series of unsuccessful robberies, Buster did not starve because June still had a job. She had moved on from John Lewis's warehouse to a factory which made babies' bibs; then to a shoe shop, followed by a tobacconist's until she finally settled down to running a tea trolley on Waterloo Station. She enjoyed this work because it brought her in contact with different people and earned enough to keep them alive when Buster and his friends bungled one bit of business after another. She and Buster still had to dodge the milkman, or hide behind the three-piece suite when the rent collector came to the flat, for when Buster had a successful "tickle" he would take June and her family out on a binge rather than pay the bills.

Buster had become a thief to escape emasculation as much as poverty. All around him men were ground down by the harshness of their lives — the humiliation of monotonous, mechanical labour for a wage which barely sustained them — while he led a life which fulfilled his cunning, audacious nature and remained debonair and free. This helped June accept his chosen profession. Home cooking and heavy drinking had made the slim young man she had spied walking towards the Regal cinema in Kennington fat and greasy, but he still had his sense of humour — everything was a joke — and it was for this that she loved him. In the back of her mind June knew that thieves were caught and sent to prison, but a serious sentence for a serious crime seemed only to happen to other people, like road accidents or fatal diseases. She was happy that Buster remained young, cheerful and defiant while those around him who went straight already had the bearing of defeated, imprisoned men.

It was seven years after their marriage before she conceived a child. Partly because other women had frightened her with tales of the terrible sufferings of childbirth, and partly because of Buster's uncertain way of life, she had hesitated before having a baby — but now that she found herself pregnant she was delighted. So too was Buster who had always wanted a family of his own.

The baby was born with a heart lesion: Buster was told that he could not live for long; but could not bring himself to tell June. They called him Perry, and he died when he was six weeks old. The baby's body was brought back from the hospital in a tiny coffin, and laid out in a little shroud. For two days it lay in the sitting-room, with relatives calling to pay their respects. June seemed unable to accept that the child was dead; and had Buster not restrained her, she would have taken it from the coffin and held it to her breast.

Word had gone around about the baby's death and wreaths were delivered from all their relatives, friends and fellow thieves. There was a crowd around the grave as Perry was buried; and Buster and June returned to their flat paralysed by grief and exhaustion.

The surgeon at the hospital had advised Buster that as soon as they could they should have another child. They took his advice. June became pregnant again almost at once. She miscarried after four months, conceived again and miscarried again after five: only when she became pregnant for the fourth time did the baby stay fixed in her womb, but no sooner was this established than her happiness was threatened from another direction.

Buster had two friends called Mike and Johnny Prince, both fellow thieves. With them Buster now opened a drinking club called the Walk-In, whose sumptuous premises in Lambeth remained open when the pubs were closed. Its customers were their fellow thieves who had as little respect for the licensing laws as they had for other people's property. They particularly liked to get drunk on a Saturday or Sunday afternoon. A certain kind of girl (not so much tarts as gangster groupies) was also to be found at the club: wives were only invited at week-ends.

The three friends had only to put up a monkey apiece (£500) to get the club started; and such was the drunken generosity of their criminal customers that money soon flowed over the bar. It might even have provided an honest living if Buster and the Prince brothers had not been equally munificent in giving drinks on the house. They also drank enormous quantities of alchohol them-selves, as a demonstration of virility, and Buster, who was only five foot six inches tall, went up in weight to fifteen stone.

It was not his physical appearance, however, but his way of life which threatened his marriage. June loved him fat or thin, but she could not love him when he was not there. Before he had the club, Buster was around their flat in Faunce Street for much of the day: now he left home at eight in the morning, had breakfast at the Walk-In and stayed there until six when he would return home to put on a suit and snatch a meal. This was the only time he saw June, and since she was usually tired and he was usually drunk, they would invariably quarrel. Buster would leave again at seven and remain at the club until three or four in the morning. When he got back to his flat in Faunce Street, June was asleep, and when he rose in the morning she had already left for work.

One day, in August of 1959, just before the Bank Holiday week-end, a brewer called in at the club to sell the proprietors a new brand of beer. He persuaded Buster and the Prince brothers to take two four-gallon barrels on trial. After he had left they tried the beer themselves and liked it. One pint followed another until, by the Sunday morning, the three men had finished both barrels. To follow it up, Buster switched to Pernod, and then from Pernod to gin.

At seven on the Sunday evening, two friends of his asked to be taken home. Buster staggered out of the club into a Ford Anglia and set off in a haze towards the Elephant and Castle. As he circled the large roundabout he started to bounce off cars as if they were dodgems. He came to a halt; the two friends jumped out and ran. Buster drove on to the flat in Faunce Street and told June that he would return for her at nine and take her up to the West End.

He went to a small pub, borrowed a pound off some friends and bought a round of drinks. He borrowed another pound and bought some more drinks. Mike Prince came in and took Buster off to the King's Head where more drinks were poured down his throat. When the time came for Mike to return to the club, they set off in the battered Anglia on the wrong side of the Blackfriars Road. Buster drove straight through a set of red traffic lights and smashed into a car on Westminster Bridge. Mike kicked Buster out of the car, moved into the driver's seat and drove away.

Buster staggered to the club on foot. Remembering that he had made some promise to June, he telephoned her to discover that she was waiting impatiently for him to fetch her. He staggered out of the club, climbed into another car, set off down Lambeth Walk, and almost at once he crashed into another car. This accident was witnessed by a police constable on the street corner. "Hold on a minute, mate," Buster said to the policeman. "I've just got to have a piss." Fumbling at his fly-buttons he went to the corner, and once round it he ran. He reached Faunce Street, and changed his shirt and suit while quarrelling with June. Seeing the state he was in, she refused to go out with him; so he left the flat alone and drove to another drinking club, the Shirley Ann, which was run by the Richardson Brothers.

At two in the morning, after two more hours of heavy drinking, he drove back to the Walk-In. He stayed there until four, and then picked up a van to drive himself home. He was only half-way down the street before he drove it into a parked car. He staggered out and walked home, but this time his luck had run out because the van was registered in the name of the Walk-In and shortly afterwards Buster was served with a warrant for his arrest.

He was brought before the magistrates at Old Street: his whole drunken rampage was reconstructed by the police, and Buster expected to be sent to prison, but he escaped with a £50 fine and a two-year ban on driving. He paid the fine but ignored the ban, and two weeks later Old Bill (the police) pounced on him as he sat in a stolen car outside his flat in Faunce Street.

In the seven or eight years of his criminal career this was the first time that Buster had faced a serious charge. His friends advised him to see a young managing clerk in a solicitor's office called Brian Field. He retained an able barrister, Lewis Hawser, who

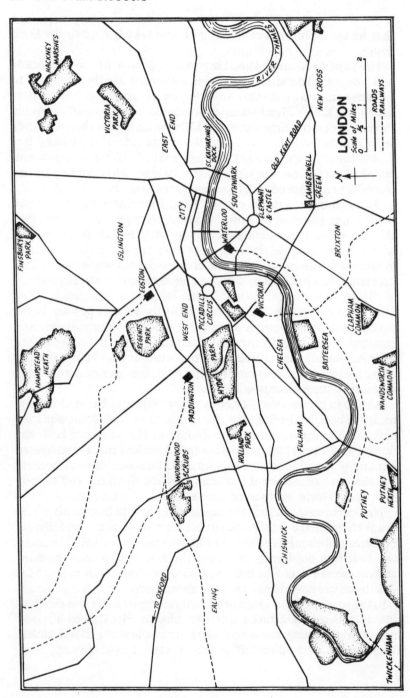

had a high reputation among thieves. Buster's defence was that he had borrowed the car from a man he had met in a pub, and when the case came to court June took the stand to swear in a trembling voice that she had witnessed the transaction.

Buster was acquitted by the jury of stealing the car, but he was convicted of driving it while disqualified. He was sentenced to fourteen days in Brixton prison: it was his first experience of a civilian gaol.

The fourteen days gave Buster time to sober up and ponder his way of life. In one sense he was happy — he was "one of the chaps", leading a chaotic, anarchic life which he enjoyed—but it was quite clear that even though June was pregnant, his marriage would not last much longer if he did not change his ways. A divorce was inconceivable: the bond with June, which had existed since they were little more than children, was more important to him than anything else; so when he returned from Brixton prison, he told Mike and Johnny Prince that he wanted to pull out of the club.

It turned out that they themselves had had doubts about its future, because the police were only waiting for an excuse to close it down, but it went against the grain in all three of them to do Old Bill's job for him by closing it down themselves. They therefore agreed that at the right moment they would smash it up or burn it down and claim the insurance.

Shortly afterwards a Welshman was introduced to Buster with inside information about the movement of coalminers' wages. He told him that on a Wednesday night the wages for eight collieries in Wales were held in certain offices of the National Coal Board with only one nightwatchman to guard them. The information proved wrong: they broke into the offices to find three security guards and were lucky to escape. They ran from the colliery and drove back to London at top speed. On the motorway near Reading the first of their two cars had a blow-out and went out of control: and though Buster and his friend were both thrown clear, they were badly injured and lay groaning on the back seat of the second car which picked them up and drove them to London.

When June saw Buster she was appalled. He was gashed across his scalp and had blood all over his face. They did not dare call a doctor or go to a hospital for fear (not so far-fetched) that the police might connect the accident with the attempted robbery in Wales, so June washed the wounds herself; but by the Thursday evening his head had gone septic and it became imperative to have proper medical attention.

At the Walk-In, where Buster went with his suppurating head covered with a cap, Mike and Johnny Prince saw their opportunity to kill two birds with one stone. Buster wanted a convincing explanation for his injuries; they all wanted to smash up the club and make it seem like the work of a rival gang: so that night at eleven they closed early and started a deliberate, destructive debauch. No bottle or glass was left unbroken; no table or chair intact. When everything that any of them could see had been smashed and smashed again, it was time for Buster's solo performance. An ex-boxer who had been their bouncer slapped Buster's scalp to open up the wound. Blood and pus dribbled over his face. He pranced around the room, shaking his head from side to side, flicking his blood all over the furniture and floor. The others tore their own clothes and slapped blood on their faces until the scene was set to call the police.

The uniformed officers arrived and swallowed whole the story of a rival gang; all the evidence seemed to suggest that Buster and the Prince brothers had paid the price for refusing protection. An ambulance was called and Buster was driven to Lambeth Hospital to have his head disinfected and stitched up.

The next morning he was summoned back to the Walk-In for a visit from the local CID. The Detective Inspector who came along was a tough man with a pitted, pudgy face who had been newly appointed to Kennington Police Station. His name was Frank Williams. He already knew enough about life in South London to have doubts about the story told to his uniformed colleagues, in spite of the overturned juke-box, the splintered tables, the torn carpets, broken bottles and in the centre of it all Buster Edwards, his head swathed in bandages, his face and body blue with bruises.

"This is a get-up," said Williams.

"A get-up?" said Buster. "Just look at the kicking they gave me," and he drew open his shirt to reveal more bruises.

"Where does all this blood come from?" asked Williams.

"Don't think we let them go without doing something to them," said Johnny Prince. "They got well seen to, I can tell you."

"Who was it, then?"

"I'm sorry, Mr Williams," said Buster. "You know we can't name names."

The Detective Inspector had to leave with his curiosity unsatisfied; but he was to see more of Buster Edwards. The insurance company paid up for the club. Buster returned to a more stable domestic life. On 9 December 1960, June gave birth to a healthy girl whom they named Nicolette, and to provide her with everything a baby could possibly want, Buster and his friends robbed Mothercare.

In the first months of 1961, the small firm composed of Buster Edwards, and two friends, Bill Jennings and Gus Brown, teamed up with a strange and slightly sinister thief called Gordon Goody. He was a huge man with a thin face and a crafty smile as if the head of a fox had been grafted onto the body of a bull. On one of his arms, beneath his bulging biceps, were tattooed the words "Hello Ireland" and on the other, "Dear Mother"; for though Gordon was the same age as Buster — in his early thirties — he lived in Putney with his Irish mother.

He had been to prison twice — on the first occasion for robbing and beating up an older man, a homosexual who had made advances to him, for which he also received twelve strokes of the birch; and on the second for robbing a jeweller in Ireland and resisting arrest. He was a solitary but successful thief, with a magpie's fascination for gold, silver and precious stones. His avarice was well-known among his fellow thieves; he was also thought to be lazy and idiosyncratic, but he more than made up for these failings by a splendid reputation for dedication and reliability as well as a growl and a glance which terrified his victims into acquiescence.

Off the job he was something of a dandy, wearing tailor-made suits and shirts from Jermyn Street. Unlike Buster, he avoided the pubs and drinking clubs where the chaps were to be found, preferring to see straight people in quiet Putney pubs or glamorous girls in smart West End restaurants. He liked women, and women were mesmerised by his aura of sinister and suppressed brutality.

With Gordon in their team, Buster, Bill Jennings and Gus Brown now robbed an occasional bookie and did the odd wages snatch — but these thefts had become so common by the late 1950s that the bags had been fitted with alarms, purple dye and metal legs which sprang out to a length of fifteen feet. They were finding it increasingly difficult to make a dishonest living, when an Irishman who had once told them about a dance hall in

Willesden introduced them to a compatriot with inside information about a bank in his home town of Cork. The money from all the other banks in the town went into its vaults prior to its despatch to Dublin; yet the premises, so the man said, were deserted at night and the door only secured by a single lock. Buster and Gordon showed an interest; they imagined the Irish police to be sleepy and incompetent, and the vaults as easy to open as a tin of baked beans. Without wasting any time, they flew to Dublin, hired a car and drove down to Cork.

They found the bank without difficulty, but before breaking in to examine the vaults they had to make sure that there was indeed no guard or watchman left there at night. Choosing a restaurant which looked over the river towards the door of the bank, they booked a table by the window for an early and leisurely supper. Buster was relaxed and cheerful as if he was on holiday, and he tucked into the food with a good appetite; but Gordon's foxy eyes never strayed for long from the door of the bank. Suddenly, at nine o'clock, he saw a man standing on the steps. Not knowing whether he had come out of the bank or not, Gordon dropped his knife and fork and ran from the restaurant as if he had been poisoned by the food. He crossed the bridge in time to see his quarry enter a pub. Gordon followed him in and sat drinking for an hour and a half until the man left the pub, walked back to the bank and let himself in with a latch-key.

The presence of this caretaker was not an insuperable obstacle to robbing the bank, because they could always tie him up on the night, but it did show that their information was unreliable and made it all the more imperative to enter the bank and examine the vaults. On the second evening, while the caretaker was at the pub, they let themselves into the offices next to the bank, and from a window on the fourth floor climbed onto the roof. They went to the sky-light, prised it open, tied one end of a knotted rope to an iron bar and lowered the other end into the dark interior. Gordon, who was in better condition than his fat friend, volunteered to climb down: he started well enough, but then his gloves started to slip on the rope. As they hit the knots they burst apart and Gordon landed with a crash on the floor with dust falling gently around him like snow.

He stood quite still and listened. There was no sound. He flashed his torch up to Buster who pulled up the rope, closed the sky-light and made his way back over the roof. Gordon crept from one room of the bank to another until he found the vaults. He took from his wallet a razor blade and slipped it between the frame and the doors of the vault to measure their thickness. It was insignificant: they would be easy to cut open.

He left the vaults and, having discovered the room where the caretaker would be sleeping, he returned to the main concourse. There he saw that all the tables and desks were covered with the dust that had floated from the sky-light. He took off his jersey and started to clean them, and only when he felt sure that he had removed all trace of his presence, did he let himself out of the front door and join Buster in a pub.

The following morning they rented a cottage a few miles outside Cork which was to be their base for the operation. They then drove north to Connemara and arranged to rent a second cottage where they planned to take the money and bury it after they had robbed the bank. From there they drove to Dublin, returned the cars and flew back to London.

The chief problem which faced them now was the transport of their cutting equipment — the generator and a valuable oxyarc — from London to Cork. If they carried it with them, and it was discovered at the customs, it would be highly compromising; they therefore packed it in crates and shipped it via Fishguard under an assumed name. They were confident they could steal the oxygen cylinders and the explosives they might need from quarries in Ireland itself: detonators would be more difficult, so Gordon concealed some in the frame of a racing bicycle and crossed to Dublin with the appearance of a young man on a cycling holiday.

Buster followed with Gus and Bill; they too were disguised as tourists and carried fishing-rods. They took the train from Dublin to Cork where Buster hired a car, giving the name of Furness and a false address. The four of them met up in the cottage, and in the next few days secured gelignite from a quarry and oxygen cylinders from a building site. They now had everything they required for the robbery except for the transformer and the oxyarc which had still not arrived at Fishguard.

It was eight days before their crate arrived, by which time the insurance had expired on the hired car. It was not something that would be noticed by Buster, but the conscientious proprietor of the car hire firm tried to make contact with his customer through the address he had been given in London.

On the afternoon before the robbery, the four thieves drove

into Cork so that Gordon could collect a suit from the cleaners. Buster dropped his three friends in the main street, arranging to meet them an hour later at the bus station. As he parked the car the man from whom he had hired it came up to him: Buster remained quite calm, and from the man's manner it appeared that nothing very serious was wrong. "Ah, Mr Furness," said the Irishman, "I'm so glad you've extended your holiday, but I wonder if you wouldn't step into my office for a moment for the insurance . . ."

Buster followed him obediently, and stood at the counter waiting for a new certificate. Suddenly two enormous plain-clothes policemen came in behind him. They asked him for his name and address. Buster could do nothing but give the same false name and false address which he had given to the car hire company.

"We've checked the address," said the first detective. "It doesn't exist . . ."

Buster began to stutter an explanation but the detective interrupted him. "Save your breath. We know what you're up to, and we're going to get you for it."

He was taken to the police station where he asked to see a solicitor. They handed him a list of those practising in Cork; Buster ran his eye down the column of O'Reillys and O'Malleys until he saw a solicitor called Mayer. "I'll have him," he said.

The solicitor duly arrived, and when Buster was alone with him, he asked what he could do to get out of it.

"We're due before the Magistrate at 2.15," said the lawyer, "but I dare say that for fifty pounds for me and fifty for the sergeant, something could be arranged."

Buster had the money on him, and he handed it to his solicitor who slipped out of the interview room and returned a few minutes later to say that Buster was free to go.

Behind him came the detective. "Get out of Cork," he growled at him. "Get out of Ireland. If you're ever in Ireland again I'll nick you so fast you won't know what's happened to you."

In the street Buster thanked his solicitor and walked by a circuitous route to the bus station. Gordon was waiting for him with the two others: he glanced at Buster who shook his head. The two stood side by side studying the time-table as if they were strangers.

"They're onto me," said Buster in an undertone. "I've got to get out of town."

"Any future for us?" asked Gordon.

"None at all. Clean up the cottage and get back to London."

While Buster waited for a bus to take him to Dublin, his three friends took a taxi to their hide-out where they broke up the transformer and sank it, together with the gelignite, detonators and oxygen cylinders, in a swamp by the sea. When it came to the oxyarc they could not bring themselves to throw it away, so Gordon wrapped it in plastic sheeting and hid it in a disused quarry a mile or so from the cottage.

Despite this run of bungled business, Buster had maintained a reputation among the "chaps" as a reliable thief; and soon after his return to London he joined another firm, who claimed to have an expert at fixing alarms, in an attempt to rob a bank in the West End. This bank had one advantage over any other: there was a side entrance which opened into the foyer of an office block. If the thieves waited until the offices had closed and gained access to them, they could then pick the lock unobserved from the street.

In the middle of the morning they sent along a crooked locksmith who in front of the busy passers-by changed the lock on the door to the office block. That evening the thieves let themselves into the foyer and set to work on the door to the bank. They entered it without any difficulty, and the expert supposedly doctored the alarms; but as the safe cutter started with his torch, one of the gang who was on watch upstairs came down to report that a group of policemen was coming in through the front entrance to the bank. Buster stopped the cutter. "It looks a bit naughty," he said. "We'd better get out of here," and picking up a gemmy he led the group of thieves up the stairs where with terrible screams they rushed at the policemen and bank officials who fled into the manager's office.

There were more police in the street, and a group of passers-by who had stopped to see what the fuss was about. Buster came out first and stood snarling with the gemmy in his right hand while the others sneaked out behind him. A man tried to grab hold of Buster: Buster hit him with the gemmy and broke his arm. The police knew better: they bided their time. When his friends were all away Buster turned and ran after them, turning right and then right again to where they had parked two stolen cars. The police ran after them, and as the thieves all piled on top of one another in the first car a clever constable put his hand through the open window and removed the ignition keys.

They were surrounded once again, but once again they fought their way out of the car and made for the Ford Zodiac a little further down the street. This time they got away, but they did not make for home because they had been wearing no masks and it was possible that some had been recognised. Buster was dropped off at his sister-in-law's, promising to meet the others the next day at a pub in Sloane Street. From there he telephoned June and told her to destroy all the photographs she had of him, including the one in his passport.

The next day he set off for Sloane Street to keep his appointment with the other members of the gang. He arrived late, to find two squad cars parked outside the pub. They had been grassed. Buster drove off towards Chelsea Bridge and did not stop until he had reached Pevensey Bay on the south coast. There he took a room in a small hotel and telephoned London. Half the gang had been arrested, including his friend Gus Brown and the youth who had failed to fix the alarms. The latter had apparently turned Queen's evidence and had given the police the telephone number "of a man called Buster" which had led them to Faunce Street. There was a warrant out for his arrest.

Buster went underground. He adopted the name and persona of a straight friend of his called Derek Glass who on several occasions had acted as his front man. In Pevensey Bay he rented a flat and used it as a base from which to travel to London.

There, in the pubs and drinking clubs south of the river, Buster asked if "anyone knew anyone" in the West End CID. In a short time he had found an intermediary called Fat Bill who went off to find out if "anything could be done". He brought back word that the charge could not be dropped, but for £1,500 it would be forgotten. The price was reasonable, but after his sequence of failures Buster possessed nothing like that sum of money. He needed work urgently — not just for this expense, but to hire the best barristers for Gus Brown.

To tide himself over he went on a quick wages snatch with the rump of the other firm which had joined him on the West End bank job. He drove with two others in the back of a van to a railway siding, and returned with £4,500 of railwaymen's wages. It was better than nothing, but hardly enough, and it reminded Buster of a similar robbery he and Gordon had once planned but never carried into effect.

The prize was again railwaymen's wages, paid out from an office to all those who worked in the sidings and marshalling yards of the Western Region. Buster telephoned Gordon from Pevensey Bay and the two men met together in London. The plan was still fresh in their heads and they agreed to go ahead. Buster brought in Bill Jennings and Gordon invited a fourth man called Charlie Wilson who had an excellent reputation as a thief.

The money for the railwaymen's wages was delivered by a security van to a single-storey office built next to some sidings. The clerical staff always bolted themselves in while they sorted the money into wage packets, and then paid it out at a small window. Late on the night before the delivery was due, Buster and Gordon let themselves into the deserted office with a skeleton key. They examined the bolt and saw that it ran through the jamb of the door into the concrete of the wall. They therefore unscrewed it from the door, cut the screws short, cut off the end of the bolt so that it only just went into the clasp and put everything back into place.

The next day they returned in full force with Gordon at the wheel of a stolen van. They waited in the street outside the entrance to the siding until they saw the security van depart; then while Buster, Bill and Charlie Wilson pulled down their stocking masks and drew out their coshes, Gordon drove down to the office. One kick threw it open. Inside there were five men and one woman: the men dived straight to the ground but the woman came flying at them. Buster held her and they fell on the ground in a struggling, screaming ball while the others packed the bundles of bank-notes into a hold-all. As they left they locked the door behind them and broke the key in the lock.

When they counted the money in the hold-all, it came to £26,000. From Buster's whack, £1,500 went to the West End police officer; and £1,000 towards the legal expenses of Gus Brown. When his trial came up at the Old Bailey, Gus was defended by Lewis Hawser. The jury returned a verdict of Not Guilty.

Charlie Wilson, who was part of the firm for this successful raid, was a humorous, warm-hearted man who lived with his wife and three daughters in Clapham. He was tall and strong, like Gordon, and bright blue eyes.

He was a Battersea boy, but unlike the others had started stealing late in life. He then went far and fast, and what was particular about him now were the bonds of loyalty and friendship he had forged with certain violent and unscrupulous gangsters who ran the protection rackets in London's West End. Charlie, who saw everything in black and white, was quite uninhibited about the methods he used to pursue both his own interests and those of his friends; many thieves had friends, but few could rely on them to blow off the head or the legs of an adversary with a sawn-off shot-gun without asking the reason why.

Charlie had acquaintances in Middlesex who knew he was "at it", and like many outwardly honest people, they admired him for it. One day, in the autumn of 1962, they invited him out to their home where they introduced him to a man who worked in Comet House at London Airport — the administrative offices of BOAC. They were left alone in the sitting-room where this man slyly mentioned that he knew details of the movement of wages for the entire airline staff.

Comet House was a modern block on the south side of the airport — separated from the passenger terminals by the runways themselves. It was the largest of a complex of offices, warehouses and service hangars strung out along the south side of the airport about fifteen miles from the centre of London. A wide road leading out of London to the South West ran along the perimeter; and on the other side of the wire fence there was another small road for airport vehicles.

A few hundred yards from Comet House, also within the precincts of the airport, was a branch of Barclays Bank; and it was from here that each Tuesday morning a box was brought to Comet House containing the wages for the staff—estimated to be between three and four hundred thousand pounds. It was carried in a van by two security guards who were followed by three cashiers; and although the distance from the bank to the office was short, it was sometimes escorted by a police car.

Charlie's informant had envisaged stealing the money from the vault in the bank. Charlie, when he returned to London, discussed it with Gordon and decided in favour of a snatch, and together they started to recruit a gang of the best thieves in London. Gordon brought in Buster, who had moved back to London from Pevensey Bay and was living with June and Nicky at 214 St

Margaret's Road, Twickenham, as Mr and Mrs Derek Glass and daughter.

The two men drove out together to London Airport on a Tuesday morning, respectably dressed in sober suits, and strolled into Comet House as if they worked there. While Gordon waited in the foyer, Buster took the lift to the top floor and there went to the men's cloakroom. Standing at the urinal, he found that he could see the entrance to the bank. He waited until he saw the security van draw up at the door; and when it left again, he timed its short journey to Comet House. Down in the foyer, Gordon saw the heavy box containing wages unloaded from the van onto a trolley, and wheeled through the door to the lift by two security men. There they waited for the lift to descend, and take them up to the cashier's office on the first floor.

As the two thieves returned to their car, Buster noticed two youthful chauffeurs lounging in the front seat of a sparkling Jaguar. He recognised them at once as two of the chaps.

"It's Roy and Mick," said Gordon. "They'll be driving for us."

"Well if *I* can see they're grafting, it'll be clear as day to Old Bill."

The first meeting of the firm which had been formed for the Airport Robbery was held at Buster's flat in St Margaret's Road. Besides Gordon, Charlie and Bill Jennings there were the two drivers, Roy James and Micky Ball, and a man who was always the dominant personality in any group he worked with — Bruce Reynolds.

Unlike his friends, Bruce did not look like a thug or a thief; he was tall and had the bespectacled, intelligent face of a handsome school teacher. Buster had first met him at the Richardsons' club, the Shirley Ann, and had worked with him once or twice since; but Bruce, although he came from a similar background, avoided the pubs and clubs of South London, and preferred to be seen in the Ritz, the Savoy or the Dorchester.

Unlike Buster whose chief quality was cunning, Bruce had both intelligence and imagination, neither of which had served him well in his chosen profession. Coming from a respectable, working-class background—his father was an active Trades Unionist and Socialist at the Ford Factory in Dagenham—he had since childhood been propelled by an intense romanticism—first to be a naval officer, then an ace journalist, then a new Pasteur; but a week or two on the bottom rung of the ladder had always been enough for him, and with the right contacts from his childhood (he had played with Charlie Wilson as a boy) he had started at the age of seventeen to rob shops for which he was eventually arrested and imprisoned.

He had been in and out of prison ever since, each sentence earning him promotion, until he now led a small gang of his own which specialised in top class crime. He saw himself as Raffles, the gentleman thief, and reality and fantasy were nearer now than ever before. He had married a sixteen-year-old girl, drove an Aston Martin, dressed elegantly, ate at the best restaurants, took holidays in the South of France and let it be known that he had been the youngest major in the British Army.

The two chauffeurs, Roy James and Micky Ball, had reached the same stage in their careers. Both working-class boys from Fulham, they had made up for their small stature with an exceptional talent for driving. They had started at the wheel of stolen Jaguars for smash-and-grab, had both been in and out of prison, and had now progressed to a more lucrative line in creeping (cat-burgling). Shortly before this meeting at Twickenham they had returned from three months on the Côte d'Azur where, having spent £30,000 they had brought with them, they committed two spectacular thefts of jewellery—one collection worth £62,000 and another from a woman whom they had followed back from the Monte Carlo casino, worth £80,000.

This was the nucleus of the gang formed to rob Comet House, and the feeling among them was optimistic: the forecast of a prize worth two or even three hundred thousand pounds seemed quite plausible, given the size of the airline's staff. They had all been to Comet House, had studied the possibilities and now contrived a plan.

For the robbery itself they had agreed upon a snatch: the heavies (thugs) would enter the building disguised in bowler hats and City suits, and hide in the men's lavatory on the top floor until they saw the van leave the bank; then they would descend in the lift and burst out on the security guards as they waited in the foyer. Roy and Micky, dressed as chauffeurs, would be waiting with the two Jaguars in the car park. The money would go in the first; the heavies in the second: and instead of leaving through the main entrance, as might be expected, they would storm along the perimeter road, drive through one of the gates in the perimeter fence and disappear into Hounslow.

Gordon took charge of the gate in the perimeter fence which was secured by a chain and padlock. He drove a friend to various ironmongers in his own Jaguar, and sent him in to ask for bolt-cutters: they were not easy to find, but he ended the day with two different pairs, and the night before the robbery drove out to the Airport with Buster and cut the chain.

Bruce arranged for a flat where they could all meet up after the raid: it was in Norbury and belonged to an older thief called Jimmy White, an ex-paratrooper whom Bruce used as his Quartermaster Sergeant. He also brought in a friend called Harry Booth, and his brother-in-law, John Daly, as a reserve driver.

On Tuesday 20 November, they were ready and had taken up their positions in and around Comet House by nine in the morning. Roy and Micky, wearing chauffeurs' uniform, sat in the driving seats of the two Jags; behind them, wearing City suits and reading *The Times* and the *Daily Telegraph,* were Bruce and a friend of Gordon's, Denis Marlowe, as if waiting for some important appointment. Each carried a rolled-up umbrella in which the stems had been replaced by an iron bar.

Up on the fifth floor of Comet House, dressed in suits and wearing various hats to cover their rolled up stocking masks, were Gordon, Charlie, and Harry Booth. Bill Jennings waited by the lift for a signal from Buster who stood at the urinal watching the entrance to Barclays Bank. He saw the van drive up, the money loaded — and was about to give the signal when to his dismay a police car drew up and prepared to provide an escort.

"Oh God," he moaned. "It's Old Bill."

Down in the car park, Bruce and the others also saw the police car and knew that the job would be off. The two Jaguars slipped out of the car park and set off back to London.

They all knew that the van was occasionally escorted, and so were not upset by the postponement of the raid; they had only to be patient and keep their nerve. On the Friday night they drove out to the Airport to check the gate, and found that the chain had been replaced. This alarmed them, because any intelligent security officer might deduce that a raid was planned: so rather than confirm his suspicions by cutting the chain a second time, they went to the old metal-smith in Chiswick who had built iron bars into their umbrellas, described their dilemma, and on the following night returned to the Airport with a false link for the chain. Outwardly it was identical to the others, but he had cleverly contrived it so that it would pull apart. They cut the chain again and then joined it with this false link.

On Tuesday 27 November they went once again to Comet House. By nine they were in position — Roy and Micky with Bruce and Denis in the Jaguars; the rest on the top floor. Each had his own particular disguise: Buster and Bill wore pin-striped suits and bowler hats. Gordon had dyed his hair black, wore a check cap and a false moustache. Each had his own particular cosh concealed in a special pocket in the lining of his trouser leg: Buster's was a foot of 1¼-inch pipe-spring, filled with lead and bound with tape. Charlie had a length of cable, again bound with tape, and Gordon a truncheon he had bought in Madrid which was surplus stock from the Guardia Civil.

Gordon, Charlie and Harry Booth washed their hands, combed their hair and straightened their ties to distract the old cloakroom attendant, who seemed curious that Buster should stand so long at the urinal. Buster saw the security van move away without an escort, zipped up his trousers and signalled to Bill to call the lift.

The lift arrived. Bill turned down the switch to hold it, and the others filed out of the cloakroom past the baffled attendant while Buster went to the window overlooking the entrance to wait for the van. He looked at his watch: the van should have arrived, but there was no sign of it. There was a constant, unnerving ping as people on different floors rang for the lift. Bill came out of the lift to ask Buster what had happened.

"I don't know," said Buster. "It should have been here by now."

As he spoke, they saw the roof of the security van below. They rushed back to the lift; Bill moved the switch and pressed the button for the ground floor. It started to descend but stopped on the third floor. Five faces, afraid of being identified, turned to the wall, but there was no one there; apparently those who had called it had grown tired of waiting. The doors closed, the lift continued. It stopped again on the first floor; again there was no one there. The doors closed, the lift descended and five pairs of gloved hands reached under their hats to pull the stocking-masks and balaclavas down over their faces. Their coshes were whipped out of their trousers as the lift stopped and the doors opened on the ground floor.

They stormed out. Harry and Bill had one job only — to seize the large black box containing the wages. As they did so Gordon and Charlie attacked the two guards who were holding it. One was caught by a cosh behind the ear and went down like a sack of potatoes, but the other dodged the first blow and darted to the door. Between him and the entrance stood Bruce and Denis; a crack across the head with a steel umbrella and he too went down.

It was now the turn of the clerks. Two fell flat without a murmur, but one stood still, grinning, as if paralysed with terror. Buster smashed him on his head with his new pipe-spring cosh: the skull seemed to split open and the man fell with blood flowing from his scalp.

Harry and Bill were already at the door with the box. The two Jags backed towards them: they ran to the first, which was driven by Micky, while behind them, running backwards, came the others—their coshes ready, their eyes on the door. In a moment the money was in the boot of the first car: Harry, Bill and Denis got in and it drew away: the others jumped into the second, driven by Roy and then they too were away.

They sped out of the car park, onto the narrow perimeter road, and along the inside of the fence until they came to the gate. There Buster and Charlie leaped out of the cars, both holding a pair of bolt-cutters. While Charlie stood ready to protect him, Buster went to the gate. He could not find the false link so he lifted the bolt-cutters and cut the chain. He pulled open one of the gates while Charlie dragged back the other.

Micky's car with the money was first out onto the main road; there he hesitated because behind him a little Austin A40 was reversing to block off Roy. Roy swerved, grazed his wing, but was past and accelerated up to the traffic lights, overtaking Micky as he did so; and just as he reached the lights, they changed from green to red. Micky was behind him. There was every chance that if Roy went ahead Micky would be caught by the cross traffic, so Roy swung across its path. A petrol-tanker, which had moved forward on the green light, was forced to stop and behind it the whole tide of traffic driving out to the West. In a moment Micky had swung round and was off with Roy now close behind him.

They drove fast to the change-over garage; there they transferred the money to the Mini van and Micky Ball set off at once to drive it across London to Norbury. The Jags were abandoned with the bolt-cutters lying on the back seats. Roy had a motor-bike which would not start, and Gordon who had meant to ride with him left on foot for the nearest underground station. He returned home to remove the false moustache and make-up. Buster, meanwhile, took a bus to Vauxhall, picked up his own car and reached Jimmy White's flat just as news of the robbery was being broadcast on the radio. The others were already there, waiting for his arrival before opening the box. They took out the bundles of bank-notes and counted them. The prize came to £62,000—a fraction of what they expected. London was in an uproar at the audacity and brutality of the Airport Robbery: the thieves themselves were disappointed.

The police moved quickly against the gang of "City Gents", as they were called by the popular press. Detective Superintendent Osborne and Detective Inspector Field, who led the CID in London's T Division which covered London Airport, were momentarily baffled; but Scotland Yard's Flying Squad, the autonomous band of rough and sometimes dubious detectives, knew at once which gang must have performed such a well-planned and well-executed theft. Roy James and Micky Ball were the only drivers capable of that getaway; and certain officers remembered little details they had noticed before — theatrical make-up in Gordon Goody's flat which they had raided recently for stolen jewellery; or the umbrella and bowler hat in the back of Micky's Mercedes. They knew that Roy and Micky worked with Gordon and Charlie, and that very night they started to look for them.

By the following morning they had already pulled in Charlie, Gordon, Roy, Micky and a friend of Charlie's called Joey Gray. They held an identity parade at Cannon Row Police Station, but no witness to the raid could identify the suspects. Since no other incriminating evidence had been found in their homes, the police had no alternative but to release them. Gordon, insouciant as ever after this narrow escape, now went abroad. He flew with Gus Brown to Gibraltar and then crossed to Tangier. Bruce and his wife Franny had already fled to France where they remained in a villa near Cannes until word came from England that Bruce was in the clear.

The police still intended to bring charges against the four original suspects. While Gordon was in North Africa, Detective Inspector Field re-examined the witnesses' statements and sifted out seventy who claimed to have had a good view of the City

Gents. By the second week of December he was ready for another identity parade: Gordon had returned from Tangier and together with Charlie, Roy and Micky he was taken to Twickenham Police Station. They were all dressed in bowler hats and false moustaches and lined up with similarly dressed strangers who had been brought in off the street, while the witnesses filed past.

Then they were told to change into workmen's overalls because the police had found the ironmonger who, having sold a pair of bolt-cutters to Gordon's friend, had followed him out to Gordon's car and taken the number. He identified Micky as the friend, and since Micky was also identified as one of the heavies in Comet House, he was immediately arrested and taken off by Inspector Field in a squad car to Harlington Police Station. In the car Micky broke down. Realising that he had been mistaken for Bill Jennings who looked something like him, and afraid that he would be blamed for the blood and violence, he burst into tears, confessed that he was guilty, but begged the inspector to believe that he had only done the driving.

Later that week there was a second, and then a third identity parade, in which both Gordon and Charlie were identified by witnesses to the crime. No one had recognised Roy, so he was released, but Charlie and Gordon were charged. Unlike Micky Ball, neither made a statement. They were both too controlled to give anything away: they knew that a charge was not the end of the game, but just the start of another round.

Some months before, in a night-club in Soho, Gordon had met Brian Field, the young managing clerk who had arranged Buster's defence when he was caught with a stolen car. Gordon had been immediately impressed by Field's plausible manner and glib tongue. He was a young man of medium height, with a round face and an ingratiating manner which at times amounted to charm. He had a pretty German wife called Karin, and shared Gordon's taste for a life that was fashionable, elegant and expensive. But beyond all these qualities what attracted Gordon to Brian Field was one other which was paramount: Brian Field was bent.

To a practising, professional thief an honest solicitor was useless. What was needed was a man who could concoct false alibis and hand out "drinks" (bribes) to witnesses and policemen. Brian was only twenty-eight years old, but already he seemed to know his way around; and although prior to the Airport Robbery he had had no opportunity to demonstrate his professional talents, he had gone so far as to describe to Gordon the contents and layout of a country house near Weybridge where his wife had once been *au pair*. And while his employer, John Wheater, remained muddled in both his legal practice and his personal finances, Brian drove a dark blue Jaguar and had a pleasant house near Pangbourne where Gordon had been to visit him on summer week-ends.

Now Brian had the chance to prove his abilities and he moved quickly. The first step was to get bail which normally, over a robbery of this kind, would have proved impossible: but Charlie's gangster friends had been at work, and when he and Gordon were formally charged at Uxbridge Police Court bail was given. Micky Ball, who was pleading guilty, was taken to Brixton Prison.

The second step was to concoct an alibi. On the morning of the robbery Gordon was to have gone up to Jermyn Street to visit his shirt-maker; he was to have gone into a coffee shop and there inadvertently have bumped into a Mr Simon Blatchley, company director, causing him to spill coffee on his trousers. He also prepared to discredit one of the witnesses who said he had seen Gordon from the top of a bus on Western Avenue, getting out of a Jaguar. Gordon hired a double-decker bus and went with a photographer to take photographs of the Comet House car park to prove that the man could not have seen him.

The trial in due course opened at the Old Bailey, and at the end of the prosecution case Charlie was acquitted upon the direction of the judge. Two witnesses swore that they had seen him, but in different places at the same time. Gordon's defence, however, did not go so well. The alibi was too obviously contrived to be believed, and the witnesses were quite confident that Gordon had been there.

Towards the end of the trial, Gordon decided to try to bride the jury. From his place in the dock he had studied the faces of each of the twelve men, and picked on one that looked weak. At the end of that day he pointed the man out to some friends and they followed him but lost him in the crowded street. The next day Gordon tailed him himself to a house off the Finchley Road. He returned later that night with Buster in the silver Jaguar and knocked at the door. There was no reply.

The next day was the last day of the trial. Gordon got up early, took leave of his mother, and drove back to the Finchley Road. Shortly after nine he saw the man come out of his house. He let him walk a little way along the street, then drew up beside him and offered him a lift.

Without realising who it was behind the wheel, the man got in.

"Fancy seeing you here," said Gordon. "Going to court, I suppose."

Only then did the juror recognise the prisoner who had faced him in the dock. He did not seem perturbed, and as they drove towards the Old Bailey they chatted about the trial. Gordon asked him what verdict he thought it would be.

"Between you and me," said the juror, "I've done some bird myself." (I've been to prison myself.)

"Well, if you bring in a verdict of Not Guilty," said Gordon, "there's a little present for you in there." And he pointed to the glove compartment of the car where he had placed a packet containing four hundred pounds.

"I don't want that, mate," said the juror.

"Will you guarantee to vote my way?" asked Gordon.

"If you like."

"Will you shake on it?"

"O.K."

They shook hands.

Near to the Old Bailey there was a multi-storey car park where Gordon parked his car. There he parted with the juror, and they went their separate ways to the same court-room.

The judge completed his summing-up that morning. He sent out the jury to reach their verdict, reminding them that by law their decision must be unanimous. Several hours later the jury returned and the foreman reported that they were unable to agree. They were sent out again but again they returned: they could not return a unanimous verdict. The judge had no alternative but to order a retrial.

Micky Ball, who had pleaded guilty, was sentenced to five years in prison. He sent out word to his friends that he did not want to escape: he would serve his time.

Gordon had had a narrow escape, and though paying through the nose to Brian Field he no longer felt inclined to rely on the skill of his counsel, Lewis Hawser, or the good will of the odd juror. He had to attack the evidence.

The witness who said he had seen him from the top of a bus was more or less discredited by the photographs they had taken; but there were other points to the prosecution's case which might well convict him. The ironmonger still swore that it was Micky Ball who had bought the bolt-cutters and then climbed into Gordon's car. It was difficult to explain the stage make-up found in his flat; and another witness was quite emphatic that it was Gordon who had hit him in the foyer of Comet House.

To deal with the make-up, Gordon found the owner, an actor and stunt-man, who could confirm that it was his, and that he had left it in Gordon's flat. The evidence of the ironmonger was more complicated and involved more risk. The bolt-cutters used to cut the chain in the gate to the perimeter fence had been left in the stolen Jaguars and recovered by the police. The chain itself had been sent to the forensic science laboratories at Scotland Yard and an expert had taken the witness stand to swear that in his opinion the chain had been cut by these bolt-cutters. The ironmonger would swear that Micky Ball had come into his shop and bought just such a pair of bolt-cutters; and that he had left in a silver Jaguar which was traced through its registration to Gordon Goody.

Since Micky had pleaded Guilty, Gordon was heavily implicated by this evidence if it was proved: he had the advantage, however, that it was not Micky who had asked for the bolt-cutters. He therefore persuaded the friend who had gone into the shop (and did look like Micky Ball) to be prepared to come into court dressed in workman's dungarees.

The evidence of the last witness was more difficult to deal with. Throughout his evidence in the first trial, this man had smiled amiably at Gordon as if he bore him no malice, yet he remained quite emphatic that the man wearing a checked cap who had hit him was the prisoner standing in the dock; so that even if Gordon, or one of his friends, was to find him and persuade him to change his evidence, there was little he could do without arousing the suspicions of the police.

Then Gordon came up with an ingenious solution. The checked cap which he had been wearing had fallen off in the mêlée in Comet House and was now in the possession of the police. At a cost of two hundred pounds, this cap was replaced by an identical cap three sizes larger. All that remained now was for the witness to swear that the face went with the cap—that if Gordon had not worn the checked cap, he could not have been the man who hit him.

Early one Sunday evening, Charlie and Gordon drove down to see Buster in Sunbury-on-Thames where he was staying with Derek Glass. Buster came out to their car. "We want you to do us a favour," said Charlie. "I'd do it myself but I can't, because I just got off."

"What is it, then?" asked Buster.

"There's a witness," said Gordon. "When he looks at me he smiles. I think he'll do a deal. We want you to go down and see him."

"Leave off," said Buster. "How can I do that?"

"I need help, Bus," said Gordon; so Buster climbed in the back of the Jaguar and the three of them drove off to Harrow where the witness lived. They explained to Buster that all the man had to do was to swear emphatically that only if Gordon was wearing that cap was Gordon the man who had hit him.

They dropped him at the bottom of the street. "If there's any commotion," said Charlie, "we'll be here."

Buster walked up the street and knocked at the door. It was opened by a young woman.

"Can I have a word with your husband?" Buster asked.

"Come in," she said, "He's out the back."

Buster went into the house. The door was shut behind him. The woman called her husband who came in from the back yard. In his hand was a hammer.

He led Buster into the sitting-room and the two men sat down.

"Er . . . I'm a friend of Gordon Goody's," Buster began. "He . . . er . . . saw you smile at him in court and thought that perhaps you might . . . er . . . be prepared to help him."

The man looked at Buster for a moment without saying anything. Then he stood up and went towards the telephone. "I'll just call my brother," he said.

Buster too got to his feet. "Don't go near that 'phone," he said.

His host turned to him and smiled. "Don't worry," he said. "We were expecting something like this."

He dialled a number, spoke to his brother and rang off. "I'd like you to talk to him," he said to Buster. "He'll meet you in five minutes in the pub round the corner. He'll be wearing a white mac."

Buster left the house and walked back up the street to where Gordon and Charlie were waiting for him. He told them what had happened, and asked whether he should meet the man or leave

now while there was time. They said it was up to him, but if he
went to the pub they would "mind" him, watching to make sure
he escaped. Buster decided to take the chance. He went to the pub;
they followed in the car and waited outside. He ordered a gin and
tonic, and a few minutes later a man in a white mackintosh came
into the pub: it was evident at once that he was the brother of the
witness. He recognised Buster as easily. "Jump in the motor
outside," he said. Buster swallowed his drink, went out of the pub
and got into the car which was waiting with the door open.
"Please God," he said to himself, "that Charlie and Gordon
follow me everywhere."

"Look," the brother said to Buster as they drove off, "we
don't want any trouble from you people. We don't want to be
hurt."

Buster reached into his inside pocket for a packet containing
two hundred pounds. "We thought," he said, "that for a little
drink, your brother might add something to his evidence."

"We don't want money," the other man replied. "We just
don't want to get hurt."

"Nothing like that is going to happen."

"Just tell me what you want him to say."

Buster explained about the cap. The man agreed that his
brother would meet with Gordon to rehearse his lines; then he
dropped Buster off at a corner where a minute later he was picked
up by the silver Jaguar.

At the second trial, all went according to plan. The actor gave
evidence that the make-up was his. The forensic expert from the
Home Office laboratory at Scotland Yard solemnly pronounced
that the chain had been cut by the bolt-cutters which had been
found in the car; and the ironmonger swore that Micky Ball had
asked for just such a pair of bolt-cutters in his shop on the Euston
Road. But when it came to cross-examination by the defence, the
friend of Gordon's who had asked for the bolt-cutters was seated
in the court wearing dungarees. When he saw him the ironmonger
hesitated, and then collapsed. He was no longer sure about Micky
Ball.

The friendly witness gave the same evidence as before. Gordon
Goody, wearing the checked cap, was the man who had rushed at
him from the stairs and hit him behind the ear. And if Gordon
Goody had not been wearing that cap? Then it could not have
been Gordon Goody. The cap was produced. Gordon was asked

to try it on. It was handed up to the dock. He put it on his head; it fell over his ears and eyes.

As the trial came to an end, the jury retired and shortly returned with a verdict of Not Guilty. Gordon was elated. Hands stretched out to congratulate him as he left the dock. He came down into the well of the court, and as he passed the prosecution benches he saw the chain which had bound the perimeter fence. The prosecution counsel, who was gathering up his papers, smiled at Gordon and congratulated him. Gordon picked up the chain, and said: "Your expert isn't much good, is he? He never even noticed this." And before the eyes of the barrister he broke apart the artificial link which they had prepared but never used. Then with a scoffing laugh he left the Old Bailey a free man.

2. The Information

The £6,000 whacks from the Airport Robbery were soon spent, and by the middle of January 1963 the whole gang except for Micky Ball was back in London and ready to return to work. Their success at both stealing money and escaping the consequences had given them the confidence to take on anything at all: it had also earned them the reputation of one of the strongest firms in London, and as result some good information came their way.

It all involved trains. The same Irishman who had told Buster about the bank in Cork reported heavy boxes, thought to be the wages for railway workers at Swindon, being loaded onto the Bristol express at Paddington. Gordon had information about shipments of gold bullion from the Union Castle liners at Southampton; and Bruce knew of mail bags which came off a train under police supervision at Weybridge station in the early hours of the morning.

They set to work planning all three projects at once. Buster and Gordon went to Paddington and followed the boxes onto the Bristol express. They got off at Swindon and saw them unloaded again under equally tight security: the only way to take the money would be to stop the train between stations by pulling the communication cord. At a meet in Battersea Park it was agreed to have a trial run. Lots were drawn with blades of grass to decide who should go on the train and Buster picked the shortest. Bill volunteered to go with him, and Gordon and Gus Brown to pick them up at a disused factory which bordered the line at West Drayton on the outskirts of London.

They planned it carefully, making frequent trips to Reading,

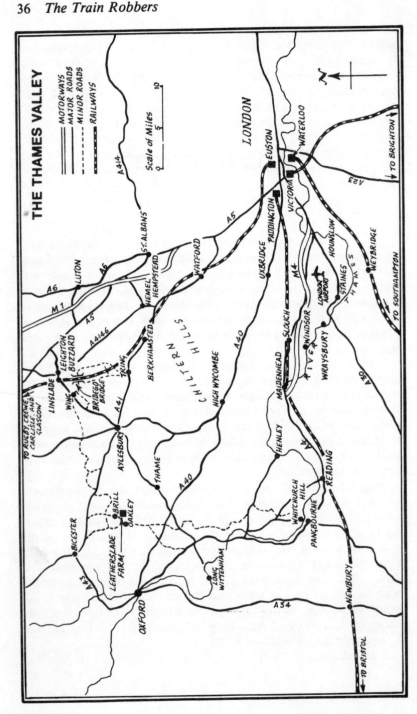

until the day came for the dummy run. Then Gordon departed in his Jaguar to keep the rendezvous, while Buster and Bill took the train. Bill shut himself in a lavatory. Buster waited outside. When they reached the signal box at Hayes and Harlington, Buster banged on the door and Bill pulled the communication cord which automatically released the vacuum and applied the brakes to the whole train. There was a screeching of steel on steel as the train decelerated: when it stopped they both jumped down onto the track, and found themselves exactly alongside the factory. In a moment they were over the fence through the factory and into the lane where they were picked up by Gordon and driven to London.

All seemed set for another success, and a date was fixed for the robbery. This time Gordon's friend, Denis Marlowe, drove a van to the disused factory while Gordon, with a crow-bar concealed beneath his mackintosh, came on the train. With him were Bruce, his friend Harry Booth, Buster, Bill, Gus and Charlie. As before, Bill locked himself in the lavatory while Buster stationed himself outside the door: the others remained in their seats until the train had left Paddington: then, as it gathered speed and clattered through Ealing station, they rose one by one and walked down the corridor towards the guard's van at the back of the train. Gordon took the crow-bar from beneath his mackintosh, smashed through the lock and leapt into the van with the crow-bar raised to threaten the terrified guard.

"Down on the floor," he growled.

The guard fell flat on his face. Charlie moved across to the wooden boxes which were chained to the wall of the carriage, and freed them with a pair of bolt-cutters.

Back along the corridor, Buster saw the signal box at Hayes and Harlington and banged on the door of the lavatory. Bill pulled the communication cord but nothing happened. He pulled it again but the train continued to hurtle along at sixty miles an hour. He came out into the corridor and together with Buster ran along to the guard's van. There the others had opened the side door and were ready to unload the boxes when to their horror they saw the first buildings of the factory premises where Denis was waiting for them glide past before their eyes. Buster grabbed a large wheel which looked like a manual brake and started to turn it: the brakes engaged. Again there was the loud noise of scraping steel on steel and slowly the train came to a halt three quarters of a mile beyond the factory.

All they could do now was run. Some, reluctant to abandon the money, seized one of the boxes which though wood on the outside were lined with lead and were a dead weight even for two men to carry. One by one the boxes were abandoned. First Buster who was obese, then Bruce who was fit, dropped them on the track. Charlie carried his as far as a pig farm which was next to the factory, but as the farmer came out of his house with an Alsatian dog, he dumped it in the hedge.

"The train's stopped," Buster said to the farmer. "We've got to get help."

They all jumped the hedge, and ran through the farm towards the factory. They were afraid that Denis might have driven off, but when they reached the lane the van was there: Denis backed down, picked them up and drove off towards London. Only Gordon, with his strong arms and even stronger love of money, had come away with a box. They opened it and found seven hundred pounds.

Undeterred by this failure, the same gang started to work on the two other projects—the mail bags at Weybridge and the bullion at Southampton. Bruce favoured Weybridge because the station in this wooded suburb of London was set in a cutting which made it suitable for an ambush. They would have to tackle three policemen and at least as many Post Office workers loading the van, and the thought of such a heavy bit of business daunted the others: their only real advantage would be surprise, and the probability that the Post Office men would not put up much of a fight, but the scuffle with the policemen could be ugly and the penalties if they were caught severe.

Bruce, living out his fantasy as a paratroop commander, proposed a plan whereby the heavies would hide in the taxi-drivers' hut near the station and then pounce upon the police car wearing gas-masks and crash helmets. One would snap off the radio antennae while another would stick a nozzle through the window and release a cloud of flour and pepper from two cylinders of compressed air. Jimmy White—Bruce's Quartermaster Sergeant—prepared the equipment and stored it with two stolen Jaguars in a lock-up garage, but the day before they were ready to move the project had to be postponed: the garage was broken open and the Jaguars with all the equipment were stolen.

While Bruce had been planning this robbery with Roy and Jimmy White, Gordon and Buster had pursued the bullion. They saw it come off the boat at Southampton and loaded onto a special coach at the back of the London train, supervised by a Bank of England official in a beige mackintosh. They watched it unloaded at Waterloo station into dark-blue armoured vans. There was no question of stealing it at either end: if they wanted the gold they would have to stop the train, but even then it would be heavy and difficult to transfer onto a lorry.

Gordon suggested putting a bomb in the coach, timed to blow up at a certain stretch of the line. Then it would be up to each one of them to grab what he could and run. It was an idea which appealed to him because he was fit and strong; less to Buster who was unhealthy and overweight: and it went against the grain for all of them to "nause" such a bit of business when time and thought might bring them the whole prize.

Shortly after this trip to Southampton in January 1963 Gordon was telephoned by Brian Field, who asked him to come to the Old Bailey the next day. Gordon kept the appointment at these familiar courts of law, and in the main concourse, amid the gowns and wigs, he recognised the podgy face of Brian Field with its ingratiating smile. Brian shook Gordon by the hand and then put his arm around his shoulder to lead him aside. When he was sure they were out of earshot of anyone else, he told Gordon that someone had come to him with information about the movement of very large sums of money. They wanted to make a contact with a firm that was strong enough to take it, and Brian wanted to know if Gordon and his friends would be interested.

Gordon was by now experienced enough to be wary of these stories of vast sums of money; but at the same time it was not in his nature to turn anything down without further investigation. He told Brian Field that he was certainly interested, and said he would discuss it with one or two of his colleagues. They arranged to meet again the next day at Brian's office at James and Wheater. Field went back into court and Gordon returned home where he immediately telephoned Buster. They met at Twickenham. They discussed the risks — the possibility of "a ready-eye" (a police trap) — but Brian Field had already proved his reliability with information so they agreed to look into it further.

The next day they went together to the offices of James and Wheater in New Quebec Street near Marble Arch. With Brian in his office there was another man who was introduced to them as Mark. He was well-dressed, aged around fifty, and spoke with a smooth accent, giving the impression of a financier or a business man. It was Mark who was to take them to meet the man with the information.

"What sort of money are we talking about?" asked Buster.

Brian hesitated. "Several million," he said.

"And where is it?" asked Gordon.

"On a train."

Mark drove Gordon and Buster north from Marble Arch, up through Regent's Park into the dingier areas of Camden Town and Holloway. Eventually he parked his car on the Seven Sisters Road and led them both into Finsbury Park. They wandered along a path among the young wives wheeling their babies in the wintry sunshine until they came to a bench under a tree. There, sitting at one end, was an ordinary, slightly balding, middle-aged man. He was watching them as they approached and when they reached him he gave Mark a slight smile of recognition. Mark shook his hand and presented Buster and Gordon without mentioning any of their names.

The four of them now resumed their stroll, Gordon and Buster on either side of the man they had come to see. As they walked he started to talk in a quiet voice with a lilt that Gordon recognised at once as the accent of Northern Ireland where he had been brought up as a child. The information, this Ulsterman said, concerned the High Value Package coach on the over-night mail train from Glasgow to London. It was on this train that the banks sent their surplus money to London—money not only from Scotland but from all the towns it passed through on its way down. At the same time as this train came from Glasgow, another left London for Scotland with a fresh supply of money for those banks which were short. On both trains the HVP (High Value Package) coach was the second from the diesel engine. In it were five Post Office workers, sorting the mail.

"And how many men on the rest of the train?" asked Buster.

"Another seventy or so, but there's no one in the first coach. Only parcels."

"And how many bags in the HVP coach?" asked Gordon.

"Normally," said the Ulsterman, "there are sixty or seventy bags on the train when it leaves Rugby which is the last stop before Euston: but two days after the August Bank Holiday there could be four times as many. Anything up to two hundred and fifty sacks."

"How much in each?" asked Gordon.

"I don't know."

"What would it come to, then?"

"I can't be sure, but perhaps as much as five million pounds."

The Ulsterman asked them if they thought they could handle a robbery of that size; and although both Buster and Gordon were staggered at its dimensions—the number of men on the train, and the size of the prize—they gave him the impression of great confidence. They made an arrangement to meet him a week later in the same spot in Finsbury Park when the Ulsterman promised he would answer any further questions they might raise about the train.

Mark drove them back into London. In his presence the two thieves were silent, but their thoughts were busy. They were dropped at Waterloo where they took a train to Twickenham. From Buster's flat in St Margaret's Road they telephoned Bruce and Charlie and later that day met up with them to let them in on the information.

Bruce and Charlie were incredulous; and that very evening the four of them went to the second platform on Euston Station. There, just as the Ulsterman had promised, were mounds of HVP mail bags being loaded onto the second coach of the mail train.

They returned to Bruce's flat in Putney. They were all torn between excitement and scepticism. Like all thieves, they dreamed of the one big "tickle" that would bring them enough to retire from the game. Chimeras of the good life took shape again: for Gordon and Bruce an everlasting life of luxury and idleness; for Buster and Charlie, large houses for their wives in exclusive suburbs and private education for their children.

But how could it be done? At Euston, or any of the stations on the line, there would be the police as well as the railway and Post Office workers. Even without the police, there were the seventy sorters. The Ulsterman had suggested that they might ambush the train at one of the stations on the line, but a snatch of that kind would only win a fraction of the prize. The best plan would be to separate the engine and front two coaches from the rest of the train and stop it on the track, but they could not board the train because there were no passenger coaches, and they knew from experience that the communication cord was unreliable.

It was then that Buster mentioned the gossip he had picked up in the pubs and drinking clubs of South London about another firm which regularly robbed trains on the Brighton Line. They were said to have an expert who could manipulate the signalling system to stop a train at a chosen point. Buster knew one of these thieves—Tommy Wisbey—and he suggested now that he should ask Tommy if they could borrow their expert.

This idea caused an uproar. In normal circumstances it would be quite "out of order" to approach a rival firm who might either steal the information or leak it to the police in exchange for some favour: but Buster had worked with Tommy Wisbey, and such was the trust of his present companions that he was authorised to sound him out. He went next day to the New Crown Club in the Elephant and Castle, where among the heavy-drinking villains from south of the river he found his jovial, swaggering friend. After some initial pleasantries, he took him aside and mentioned obliquely that he and his friends had some information involving trains and would like to consult their expert.

"What expert?" asked Tommy, who spoke slowly likely a retired boxer.

"Come off it," said Buster. "Everyone knows you're doing the Brighton Line with some geezer who knows how to stop the trains."

"Hang on," said Tommy. He went to the bar, and then returned to lead Buster up the stairs to the office of the proprietor, Bob Welch. He sat there with another man, Frank Munroe, and both men looked angry.

"What's this you're saying?" asked Bob Welch. "That we're doing the Brighton Line?"

"Everyone knows," said Buster.

"Well, what if we are?" said Bob Welch, still furious that their covert crimes appeared to be public knowledge.

"The word is you've got a man who can stop trains on the track," said Buster. "Now we've got some very good information concerning trains, but we don't know how to stop them so we'd like to bring him in."

"What's the information?" asked Frank Munroe.

"You know I can't tell you that."

"What's in it for us?" asked Tommy.

"That would have to be discussed."

"This expert of ours," said Frank, "if he exists—he's his own man. He'd make up his own mind."

"Of course," said Buster.

"We'll let you know," said Frank. "We'll let you know what's on and what isn't on, but don't go around saying we done the Brighton Line because if Old Bill gets the word he may decide to do us for it."

"You know me," said Buster. "I wouldn't do that": and because they did know him—because his reputation for reliability was so strong — they let it go at that and promised to be in touch. A day or two later Tommy Wisbey telephoned Buster and they arranged to meet on the next Sunday afternoon in the buffet at Waterloo station.

When Buster entered he saw that Tommy had already arrived and was sitting at a table in the corner next to a small, unassuming, middle-aged man who glanced at him with half-shy, half-suspicious eyes. Buster sat down between them and was introduced by Tommy to Roger Cordrey. He stirred his cup of tea and started at once to describe the two different projects—steering a delicate course between telling him enough to whet his appetite yet not so much that the other firm could steal the business for themselves. He described how bullion was unloaded from "a liner at a port", and about HVPs on a train "from the north" carrying old money to the central banks in London. He said that on a normal run, according to their information, there would be fifty or sixty bags in the HVP coach, but after the Bank Holiday there would be two hundred and fifty which, he estimated, could come to several million pounds.

Roger looked at him sceptically. "And did your man tell you how much there was in each sack?" he asked.

Buster shook his head. "No. He didn't know."

Roger looked satisfied. "That shows he knows what he's talking about," he muttered.

"We're strong enough to take it," said Buster, "and we could have a go at stopping the train, but we don't want to nause such a wonderful bit of business by getting it wrong."

"I can stop the train," said Roger, in a nasal, genteel voice. "You needn't worry about that. But you'd have to meet my conditions."

"Yer, well, what sort of conditions are you talking about?" asked Buster.

"I want our firm on the job," said Roger, "and I want ten grand in advance."

Buster swallowed. "Ten grand? Win or lose?"

"Look," said Roger, "I'll be risking my liberty working with a firm I don't know. If you want me, find the ten grand and bring in the others. If you don't, we can forget it."

"How many in your firm?"

"Tommy, Frank and Bob Welch."

"Yer, well, I should think that'll be on, but the ten grand . . . I'll have to ask the others."

Buster departed and called his friends to a meet in his flat in Twickenham. When they heard of Roger's demand, they exploded. Charlie went wild, threatening to do them for extortion; Bruce was outraged but Gordon, with his eye on the ball, calmed them down and put things in perspective. "What's ten grand out of five million?" he asked. "Nothing. If this guy can really stop a train in the middle of nowhere, then he's worth the ten grand."

"He may be worth it," said Buster, "but have we got it?"

Seven pairs of eyes looked at the floor—for besides Buster, Gordon, Bruce, Charlie and Roy there were at that meeting Bruce's brother-in-law, John Daly, whom Bruce liked to work with because he thought he was lucky; and a heavy they had hoped to bring in on the Airport Robbery, Jim Hussey.

"Well I'm skint," said Buster, since no one else had answered his question.

"The truth is," said Roy, "that even if we could raise the ten grand, we aren't going to . . ."

"And ten grand won't be enough," said Bruce. "Because if either of these two jobs are going to be done, then they've got to be done properly, and that means finance. We'll need money for living while we set it up, otherwise guys do silly little jobs for pennies and get nicked like Jim in Germany."

"Too true," said Jim Hussey. "And talking of Germany . . ."

Hussey's German adventure proved the point that Bruce had made about first class thieves taking a big risk for a small return. A little younger than the others, Jim came from the same South London background and had grown into a huge man with dark hair, hooded eyes and a square jaw. Whether destined to be a thief or not, he always looked like one and he heightened his thuggish appearance by diffidently adopting a slow and stupid manner to camouflage his perceptive personality. He had first gone to prison at the age of nineteen after a battle between rival gangs around the

Elephant and Castle. On his release he had briefly worked for a scaffolding company, but by nature and inclination he was a delinquent, and soon he was stealing cars, cigarettes, Oxo cubes, razor blades—anything that could be easily taken and easily sold. He dabbled in every branch of the business — never a schemer but always a reliable partner in someone else's plan. All he asked was the feel of a thick wad of money in the hip pocket of a smart suit as he drank or played snooker with the chaps in one or other of the pubs and clubs south of the river.

In 1958, four years after his release from prison, he went north to rob a warehouse in Cheshire. The job went wrong and in the course of the mêlée Jim coshed a police inspector and left him unconscious on the floor of the warehouse. He was caught and sent back to prison for five years; he was released, in early 1962, and it was then that he started to work on and off with the first firm.

He was chronically short of cash, and at the end of September he was chatting to some of the bottle mob (pickpockets) in a betting-shop around the Elephant and Castle who invited him to join them on a trip to Munich for the *Oktoberfest*. Picking pockets is an art in itself which some other thieves despise, for it robs rich and poor alike and causes misery to individuals instead of discomfiture to institutions and insurance companies: but Jim was easy, and in his time had tried it himself. His appearance was against him—he was too tall and villainous-looking to be inconspicuous in a crowd—but the suggestion now was that he should mind the others. Jim had never been abroad, so from curiosity as much as greed he accepted their invitation and with four others flew out to Munich.

The team went to work almost at once, concentrating on the crowded trams. On the first day they stole around fifty wallets which brought in almost DM 7,000 — then worth around £650. On the second day they were doing even better until late in the afternoon when they climbed off a tram at the Bayerische Hof Hotel and found themselves surrounded by plain-clothes police with drawn revolvers. One of the pickpockets fled, but the others, including Jim Hussey, were caught.

They were taken first to a temporary police station set up for the *Oktoberfest*, then to the Central Police Station where Jim was separated from his friends. He spent five nights in a cell with a German prisoner and was then transferred to Neudeck prison on the outskirts of the city where he was placed on remand. The regulations were strict, the food was bad and Jim was shut in a cell for twenty-three hours a day with two German thieves whose language he could not speak. There was a lavatory in the cell but no heating, and the only visit he received was from the wife of one of the other thieves who left him some money to buy jam — a luxury to add to the daily diet of sausage, bread and potato.

Towards the middle of November Jim was transferred to another cell at the end of the row which he shared with a man called Horst. Horst was strong, stocky, around ten years older than Jim, and he spoke some English. Before long the two men had become friends and Horst's conversation did much to lift Jim out of the depression he had felt upon finding himself back in prison. They talked about their pasts: Jim said he was there for picking pockets, and Horst hinted that he had been imprisoned for smuggling arms. Once, when Horst was washing, Jim noticed a number on the skin under his arm: it was his blood-group, Horst explained, tattooed onto him as a young recruit in the Waffen-SS.

Although Jim was guarded about his criminal career, news of his earlier five-year sentence had seeped into the prison and Horst seemed eager to know if Jim was a big-time "gangster". Not wishing to play down this source of respect, Jim intimated obliquely that he and his friends were among the strongest firms in London, upon which Horst said to him that if they ever wanted help of any kind—either logistics or finance—he knew of an organisation that could provide it.

In the middle of December Jim was suddenly informed that a visiting magistrate had passed sentence on him equivalent to the weeks he had spent on remand. He was to be deported forthwith to England. His spirits suddenly soared. He exchanged addresses and telephone numbers with Horst, who was also due for release, and on 21 December was escorted by police to an aeroplane which delivered him back to London. That evening he ran into Buster and Charlie who gave him a "drink" of £2,000 they had put aside for him after the Airport Robbery. It enabled him to celebrate in style with his parents and his girlfriend over Christmas and the New Year.

Now, some weeks later, when Bruce talked of planning and finance, Jim remembered Horst and told the others about his offer of assistance. On the face of it this seemed even more preposterous than Buster's approach to Roger: there at least they were on their own territory; to bring in Germans would be a leap into the unknown. Charlie in particular loathed the idea of trusting foreigners, but the more sophisticated members like Bruce, Gordon and Roy, who had developed a taste for the continent, warmed to the concept of a European connection. "Anyway," said Bruce, "there's nothing to lose. At worst we waste time: at best we get some finance. Let Jim ring him and find out the full S.P." (Starting price.)

From Buster's flat in Twickenham, Jim Hussey called the number in Munich that he had been given by Horst. They had an amicable conversation before Jim got around to business; and then, since little could be said over the telephone, it was no more than a reference to what they had discussed in prison and an invitation to come to London.

Horst accepted, and Jim met him at the Airport. He drove him to the Regent's Palace Hotel in Piccadilly where Bruce and Buster were waiting, and over tea they outlined in vague terms their plan to stop the mail train. All they required was some risk capital to secure the services of a train expert and keep the different members of the firm out of trouble during the time it took to plan the raid.

Horst appeared to think that the organisation he had talked of would be interested in such an investment if the return was adequate, and if it was convinced that their firm was really capable of such an operation. He asked for some proof that they were in that league, and Bruce told him that they had pulled off the Airport Robbery. Horst seemed impressed. He agreed to report back to the organisation and inform Jim of the result.

Ten days later Horst returned to London with another German called Karl. Karl was an older man—aged around fifty—and to all outward appearances a successful businessman—plump, sunburnt and well-dressed. This time Bruce had arranged their meeting in the Ritz, and once again outlined their plans. When he had finished Karl asked how much finance he thought they would need.

"Twenty thousand pounds now," said Bruce, "and possibly another twenty later on."

"That should be possible," said Karl. "We could provide you with as much as you need, but in return we would want £2 million of the proceeds."

Bruce and Buster seemed unperturbed by this demand. They said that they would have to consult their friends, and the three men parted, having agreed to meet again in the Ritz Hotel on the following afternoon.

As they drove back to Twickenham, Buster turned to Bruce and said: "Gordon isn't going to like it."

"Like what?"

"Giving the Krauts two million."

"Who's giving them two million?"

"You are."

Bruce laughed. "That's what he thinks."

Buster saw the glint in his eyes. "You can't . . .'

"Why not?" asked Bruce. "If he's fucking stupid enough to give twenty grand to two men he's never met before, then he deserves it."

Buster brooded. It went against the grain to double-cross fellow criminals, even if he was a German; he also had the feeling that Karl was not as "fucking stupid" as Bruce thought he was. There was a meet that night with the rest of the firm, and the others were all behind Bruce—all that is except Jim Hussey who disliked the idea of swindling his friend. It was agreed, however, that they should get hold of the money and use it as planned: the question of a return for the Germans could be settled later.

That night Buster telephoned Tommy Wisbey to say that the deal was on: they would pay Roger £10,000. The next day he went back to the Ritz with Bruce and found Karl waiting for them with a brief-case. When they told him that the gang had agreed to his terms, he passed the brief-case to Bruce. "This is the first instalment," he said. "I shall return in three weeks to check up on your progress, and if necessary provide more money."

"As I told you," said Bruce, "we'll be paying out ten thousand now to secure the expert, and putting our people on a wage to keep them out of trouble."

"You will plan it well, I hope?"

"Down to the last detail."

"Like a military attack?"

"That's my style," said Bruce.

"Excellent. First class," said the German, rubbing his hands together. "Now wouldn't you like us to send some of our men to help you?"

Bruce blanched. "Er . . . thanks, but no. It wouldn't be on. I mean, the others wouldn't wear it."

Karl looked disappointed. "Very well," he said. "But if there is any trouble afterwards, then we can help. We have excellent arrangements for foreign travel . . ." He smiled. "Now," he said, "I return to Cologne. You have my number. If you need anything, call me." He stood up and shook hands with Bruce and Buster. "Good luck," he said as he left.

Bruce paid the bill and carried the brief-case out to his Austin Healey. Buster held it on his knee as they drove west. "Take a look," said Bruce. Buster snapped back the catches and carefully lifted the lid: inside were bundles of British five-pound notes.

3. The Second Firm

Roger Cordrey, the expert at the centre of the second firm, was a curious, furtive little man—quite different in character and background to the South London thugs with whom he had cast his lot. He was a florist from Brighton with a wife, three children and several respectable relatives living around Hampton Court; but he had become a compulsive gambler which had brought him to work as a thief. In a Brighton gambling club an old grafter—a man who looks for opportunities for other thieves—called Cyril had once explained to him how easy it was to take registered packets from sacks of mail lying in the guard's van on the London to Brighton trains. A little later, after a run of bad gambling luck, Roger tried for himself: he waited until the van was unattended, walked in, opened a bag, picked up an envelope and walked out again.

The contents—title deeds—were disappointing, but the ease with which they had been stolen encouraged him. He knew that all mail from London to the South Coast travelled along with bicycles, boxes of flowers and bundles of newspapers in the guard's van of the ordinary passenger trains. He started to ask questions of postmen and railway workers about the movement of mail on the trains, and partly because railway enthusiasts were so common in England, and partly because his appearance was so innocuous, Roger's questions aroused no suspicions. Indeed the people he talked to were often flattered by his interest and delighted to tell him all they knew. At one station between London and Brighton he got into conversation with a Post Office inspector outside the sorting office. "It amazes me," he said, "to look at all these bags and realise that there must be tens of thousands of letters, and yet each one is going to arrive at its destination. I can't understand how you people manage it.''

"It's quite an operation," said the inspector, flattered by Roger's remarks. "If you're interested, perhaps you'd like to see more?''

"That's very kind of you," said Roger and he followed the inspector into the sorting office. He was given a guided tour, and the whole process of sorting the mails was explained to him. It was only towards the end that they reached the subject of registered mail. "It always goes in the last bag," said the Inspector. "That and the HVPs.''

"The HVPs?''

"High Value Packages—mostly money from the banks going back up to London. The chap filling the sacks will see if there's anything to go on a scheduled dispatch—say the 3.15 to Waterloo. If there is, it comes down in a smaller bag and goes into the last sack which is marked with a pink label.'' He showed Roger the ordinary Post Office label—about 4 by 2½ inches, and then one with a pink margin of about 1 inch. "Of course that doesn't mean there are any HVPs," he said. "It just means it's the last sack of the batch.''

"But they always go in the last sack?''

"That's right.''

"Very interesting," said Roger, "very interesting to know how it's done.''

Equipped with this information, Roger decided to try again. While Cyril, the old man from the gambling club, distracted the guard on the platform, Roger popped into the van, quickly found the bag with the pink label, cut the rope at its neck, and opened it up. There were none of the smaller canvas bags which he had been told contained the HVPs, but there were plenty of registered packets. He took a bundle of the most promising, stuffed them into a hold-all and went out of the guard's van, into the corridor and then off the train.

Again the contents were disappointing and it was clearly senseless to take the risk of robbing a mail bag unless he could be sure that it would contain money. But as the Post Office inspector had explained, there was no way of knowing whether or not the sacks with the pink labels contained HVPs. Yet large sums of money did go back and forth from London and Brighton and the other prosperous towns in the Southern Region such as Lewes,

Haywards Heath or Royal Tunbridge Wells. From reading books from the public library, and chatting to people who worked in banks, he had learned that each branch works with a certain sum in cash. If, at the end of a day or a week, it has more, then it sends the surplus, often in shoddy notes, to the central branch in the City of London: if, on the other hand, it has too little it has a fresh supply sent down to make up the proper amount.

In Brighton there was a large branch of the Westminster Bank and around the corner a small Post Office with only six employees. Roger watched the bank and noticed that every Thursday morning, just as the bank opened, a car would draw up to be loaded with several of the familiar Post Office sacks. It would set off, often escorted by a police car, to the Post Office a few hundred yards away where the money was delivered. Half an hour later a mail van would draw up and the same sacks would be thrown in without any kind of escort or protection. The loaders clearly had no idea that they were handling large sums of money. All that Roger now required was a man who could tell him when these bags were on a particular train.

In the club where he had met Cyril, there was another gambler who worked as a steward on the Pullman train from London to Brighton—the Brighton Belle. Roger befriended him and pretended to be a train enthusiast. He badgered him with questions until the steward offered to introduce him to a railway guard who worked on the Brighton Line. They met in a pub. The guard answered all Roger's questions, which were so far quite innocent, and Roger slipped him five pounds for his trouble. They met a second time, talked about trains, and again Roger paid him five pounds. On the third occasion Roger took the plunge: he asked the guard if he ever knew when there were HVPs in the mail bags.

"Of course, mate," the guard answered. "You just feel them. The money's all in hard parcels like shoe-boxes. They're unmistakable."

"And could you, do you think," asked Roger with his particular, roguish smile, "ever tip me off if your train carries HVPs?"

The guard hesitated. "I should think so, yes," he said. "No one would ever know, would they?"

"Never," said Roger.

"And there'd be a few bob in it for me?"

"Of course," said Roger, lifting his hand into his pocket for another five-pound note.

Roger was now ready to start robbing the mail on the Brighton Line. All he lacked was the right kind of associate, for though Cyril was good enough to snoop around stations or distract the guard, neither he nor Roger was strong enough to put up any fight if they were caught. Cyril therefore introduced him to a London "heavy" called Frank Munroe, and the three went to work together. Frank was a professional thief, but Roger took to him because his Cockney character was such a pleasant change from the mean-mindedness of the lower middle-classes from whence he came himself. And just as Frank had no bourgeois *pudeur* when it came to lending money to pay his gambling debts, so he was equally uninhibited when it came to bashing British Railways guards and tying them up.

They started indirectly with information from the guard. He would not let them steal money from the train under his supervision, but he allowed Roger to open and examine the sacks of mail and establish a pattern for the movement of money from the banks. Then, on the same train but on a later date with a different guard, they loaded a specially prepared wooden box onto the guard's van; and at some point on the journey they distracted the guard, slipped into his van, opened the final sack, removed the HVP, transferred it to the wooden box, closed the sack again, and returned to their compartment. When they arrived at their destination, they went to collect the box; the guard helped them lift it onto the platform, and Roger tipped him half-a-crown.

The money started to roll in. On one theft alone they came away with £47,000, but it did not lead Roger to change his style of life because all of his money went on gambling losses. Frank was pleased with the partnership, and after a time his bond with Roger was such that the two of them decided to drop Cyril (who had shown himself to be unreliable) and bring in two friends of Frank's—Bob Welch and Tommy Wisbey.

Tommy Wisbey had recently come to work with Frank, whom he had known as a boy. Frank and Bob Welch had been working together for some time. Like Roger, Bob was a gambler. Tommy was excitable, and liked to play the fool, which was an asset for the work on which they now embarked on the Brighton Line. Their objective at this early stage was only to distract the guard to get at the mail. They might jam the door to the guard's van, and while the guard went to get assistance slip in to move an HVP bag from the mail sack into the box. On another occasion Bob Welch, dressed in a dark suit and a bowler hat, made out that the door to his compartment would not open: it was at a small station on a suburban train that had no corridors, so he began to climb out through the window and pretended to get stuck. The guard came to his assistance, and Bob hooked his neck with the handle of his umbrella while further down the platform Frank and Tommy slipped into the guard's van and took the money.

They could use the same trick only once. The next time, dressed in the same city suit, Bob pretended to have an epileptic fit. With Frank he chose a compartment with a kindly-looking old lady already sitting there. Six stations down the line, Bob started to moan, to roll his eyes and froth at the mouth; until just as the train drew into the seventh station he fell down backwards over the woman. Frank told her that Bob was having one of his fits, and that they must get help; so when the train came to a stop he jumped out on the platform and called for the guard. Bob then twisted and yelled and shook with such paroxysms that he ended on the floor of the train with his head hanging out onto the platform. The guard came running to see what was causing the commotion, and as he crouched to lift up the twitching, frothing passenger, found himself gripped by a fevered hand and held with his eyes to the compartment floor. Frank meanwhile, instead of running for help, had gone to the guard's van, made the change, and returned just in time to witness his friend's recovery.

The author of these stage pieces was usually Roger. He would like awake at night dreaming them up; then travel to London the next day and meet the others at the New Crown Club—the drinking club run by Bob Welch. He would never go into the bar, but would sneak past up the stairs into the offices above. There the four would relive their latest coup or rehearse the one to come, rolling on the floor with laughter as they did so. In the end, their very success made things more difficult for them. The railway police became wise to their ruses and alerted the guards: it was then that the robberies became violent. Guards who could no longer be tricked were overpowered and tied up, and trains which could not be stopped at stations were brought to a halt on the line.

Here again it was Roger who mastered the technique. From books borrowed from the Brighton public library he discovered how to tamper with the automatic signalling system and change the signals to red. There now started a succession of robberies in which Roger would stay by the track to stop the train while Frank, Tommy and Bob, their faces hidden by balaclava helmets, would storm into the guard's vans, tie up the guards and rifle the mails. It was a cruder way of doing things but more effective: nothing could go wrong. Apart ·from sending a heavy escort on every train, there was little that the authorities could do. They did take certain precautions, but the thieves learned to circumvent them. For example the use of a pink label for the final sack of mail was abandoned, and replaced by a more enigmatic system which Roger quickly learned and taught to the others.

More serious was a decision by British Railways to put padlocks on all their Southern Region trains. Normally any guards' vans could be opened by the same square key carried by any guard or railway official: now each guard would have a particular key to the padlock of his train. This was stopped, however, because it was thought to be hazardous in the event of fire or an electrical fault. Instead they reverted to the same square key, but the locks were fitted so that they could only be opened from the inside.

To tackle this Roger found a railway worker at Waterloo who obtained a work schedule—a fat time-table which recorded all the movements of Southern Region rolling-stock. With it Roger was able to discover which coaches would be used for a particular train he knew would carry money; and before the journey he would track those coaches down in one or other of the enormous sidings in South London. Dressed in a workman's donkey-jacket, he and Frank or Tommy would go to the siding, find the train, and drill a small hole from the inside of the lock on the door through to the outside. It was imperceptible to anyone who did not know it was there. Later, when the train was in commission and the money locked with the guard in the van, one of the heavies would take a brace-and-bit, attach the point to the small hole, drill away the wood, push through the square key and open the door on the astonished guard who had imagined his position impregnable.

Some of the trains on the Southern Region had no corridors: there was therefore no access to the guard's van from the train itself. To get at the money carried on one of these trains, Frank was disguised as a cripple, his face made up to seem pale and sickly, and placed in a wheel-chair covered by a rug. Tommy, as his attendant, wheeled him onto the platform at Clapham

Common and insisted upon travelling with his patient in the guard's van. The train departed; the cripple and his male nurse sat patiently in the van until just outside London, the train stopped at a signal alongside a cemetery. Suddenly the cripple rose from his chair and punched the guard on the chin with such force that he fell unconscious. At the same time his companion started sorting through the mail bags; he found the final sack of the consignment, Frank opened the door to the van and the two men jumped down onto the track carrying the sack. In a moment they were over the fence and into the cemetery. There they jumped into a car which was waiting for them and before the driver or passengers of the train had realised what had happened they swerved through the cemetery gates, onto the main road and away.

The proceeds from this robbery were disappointing. The uproar, however, was intense and for the first time since a conviction for embezzlement twenty years before Roger received a visit from the police who asked him aggressively about his interest in trains; and where he had been at the time of the wheel-chair robbery.

He reacted with the outrage that a respectable florist would be expected to show when suspected of robbing a train; and after keeping him overnight in a cell the police released him. He was pulled in again shortly afterwards to stand in an identification parade before the guard and various passengers from the train, but no one picked him out.

Although the police seemed to have no proof, it came as a shock to Roger that they should even suspect him. For several weeks he kept away from the New Crown Club; and when he did call there again it was to hold a post-mortem. No blame could be apportioned to the poor proceeds of the robbery itself; but the accuracy of the police suspicions was more serious. It showed that they had been betrayed.

Outside the firm there was only one man who knew that Roger worked the trains and that was his old associate, Cyril. It was easy to see how the police may have been led to him: at one time he too had worked the trains, and this would be marked on his record. He must have mentioned Roger—either from fear of being framed for the robbery himself, or to exchange names for a period of immunity from arrest—a kind of unofficial receiver's licence.

Grassing was the one crime that could not go unpunished, so late one night Roger and some of his heavy friends went to the house in Golders Green where Cyril was now living. They wore balaclava helmets. When he came to the door, they grabbed him and dragged him into the car. As they drove away, one held a knife to his throat while another blindfolded him. The car went south towards the river. He was told that his treachery had been discovered; that he was going to die for it; and that his only chance of living would be to confess. Trembling with terror, Cyril insisted on his innocence. The threats and protestations continued as they dragged him from the car. It was dark, and one of them brought out a torch; but Cyril, still blindfolded, was in double darkness: all he could hear was the rush of water from the nearby weir which grew louder as he was dragged, whimpering, to the edge. His hands were tied; he felt he was about to be thrown in the water when, with a croak, he broke down. He confessed. He had talked to the police. He had said nothing definite, but he had mentioned names. He told them that there were two thousand pounds stitched into the lining of his jacket; that they should take it as some recompense.

The thieves pulled him back. They felt in the lining, found the money, and tore it out. Then, while Roger turned his back and went back to the car, the others laid into Cyril with their fists and feet.

They decided now to give the Brighton Line a rest, and turned their attention instead to the registered mail on the Irish Express—a train which left Euston for Holyhead, Fishguard and Dublin. They were told that it often contained diamonds travelling to Dublin from Amsterdam.

This new bit of business required considerable preparation, for the trains of the Midland Region were not powered by electricity conducted through a rail, as they were on the Southern Region, but by diesel locomotives. To study them, Roger followed the line out of London from Euston Station until he came to a secluded stretch of country near Tring where he could climb down the embankment and examine the signalling system. He noticed at once that the signals were not operated in the same way as those on the Southern Region; but he was unable to work out what it was that automatically triggered them. He thought it must be the weight of the train on some device buried under the track; he even took some of the others to jump on the sleepers, but they failed to change the signals to red.

Eventually he came up with a quite simple solution. The signals were suspended from a gantry—a small, steel bridge—over the track. He climbed up onto the gantry, along to the signal, and opened the back. He took one of his gloves and stuffed it between the illuminated bulb and the lens of the green light. Then he took four batteries which he had brought with him and attached them with clamps to the bulb behind the lens of the red light. He climbed down again, walked back down the track and looked at the signal. The effect was exactly as if it was at red.

Later he arranged a full dress-rehearsal. At one signal he blacked out the green light and illuminated the amber one which warned the approaching train that the next signal might be at red; he then walked down the line to the original gantry, blacked out the green light again, and illuminated the bulb behind the red lens. Finally he went a little further down the track and hid himself behind some bushes near to the signal box.

Sure enough, as the train approached the amber signal it slowed down, and when it came to the red signal it stopped. Roger was delighted; these long, main-line trains with the throbbing D-type diesel locomotives were an imposing—almost majestic—sight, and quite apart from any thought of gain it was satisfying to him that he—an inoffensive little florist—should with his own wits have stopped such a powerful, gigantic machine.

He had the bonus of a comic scene between the driver and the signal man; the driver climbed out of his cabin, but instead of going to the telephone which was placed behind the signal, he walked the few yards up the track to the signal box. "What's up?" he shouted.

"How do you mean, what's up? You tell me."

"What's the delay?"

"You're the delay. Why have you stopped?"

"Why have I stopped? Because the signal's red, you daft bugger . . ."

Their preparations were now ready, and in the late afternoon of 2 January 1963, Roger set off in a van for Tring—about thirty miles outside London—where he was to stop the train and pick up the thieves with the prize. The others went to Euston, bought tickets for Dublin and boarded the train. Speaking with Irish accents, they settled down in a compartment near to the guard's van.

As the train moved out of London, the thieves went to the

guard's van and opened it with a skeleton key. It was empty. Frank quickly brought out a pair of bolt-cutters from under his coat and cut open the wire cages which contained the registered mail. The three then dragged out the bags with the HVP labels, cut them open and started to sort out those which had Dutch or Danish postmarks. Bob Welch cut them open and emptied their valuable contents into a bag; and so concentrated were they all on their task that they failed to realise that the guard and inspector had returned. "Now what the 'ell's going on?" the guard began. At once Frank leapt on him. The ticket-collector turned to run: Bob caught up with him when he was half-way down the corridor and dragged him screaming back to the guard's van. His cries were heard by some soldiers who rushed out of their compartment and stormed into the guard's van.

By then the guard lay moaning on the floor and the ticket-collector, semi-conscious and with his head bleeding, was next to him. The soldiers laid into the thieves but the thieves were ready for them with their coshes and quickly got the upper hand. One after the other the soldiers, with smashed skulls and broken arms, were thrown into the wire pen which had once held the mail.

The train rushed through Watford. A young steward from the restaurant car, delivering coffee to the compartments, reached the last coach of the train. He heard cries from the guard's van, and when he saw what was going on pulled the communication cord. The thieves, hearing the scraping sound of the brakes, imagined that they had reached the signal and prepared to jump out with their swag. They opened the door of the van expecting to see the dark night of open countryside but saw instead the orange lights of a town blurred only by falling snow. The train was at Hemel Hempstead station.

As soon as it stopped they jumped and ran. Bob Welch tried to carry the bag but knew at once that it was hopeless, and rather than incriminate himself with a handful of precious stones, he abandoned the prize. He climbed over the fence at the end of the platform, down an embankment and over a frozen field. He reached a road and found a café from which he called a cab. The driver took him to St Albans where he waited for a bus. A few people waiting for the coach stared at Bob, who was without an overcoat in the freezing, winter weather. Afraid of arousing suspicion, he began to walk towards London: he was given a lift to Harringay, where he caught the first underground back to the

Elephant and Castle. He arrived at his club to find Roger waiting there, and by midday they had heard from every other member of the gang. None had been caught: all had got home.

4. Preparations

The evening after Buster had telephoned him to say that they would meet Roger's terms, Tommy Wisbey brought Roger out to Buster's flat in Twickenham where Bruce handed over the first £5,000 of his fee. Tommy was informed that the other members of their firm would receive £100 a week on condition that they undertook no other work; but he was told nothing of the source of this finance.

Buster now gave Roger a more detailed description of the information they had at their disposal. At first Roger showed more interest in the bullion from Southampton, and was sceptical about the mail train, but neither he nor Tommy could think of a way to move the heavy gold bars in a short space of time. They returned to the mail train, and Roger told Buster that to test the Ulsterman's information he should ask him for a schedule of HVPs.

Three days later at a second meeting Buster handed him an envelope containing the official Post Office list of all HVPs coming onto the Glasgow to Euston express. Immediately Roger's attitude changed, for this proved that their informant was in touch with someone on the train itself. He now threw himself wholeheartedly into the planning of the Train Robbery. He told Buster and Bruce that they must find a suitable place on the line to stop the train—as near to London as possible yet far from any inhabited buildings. There must be a set of signals and access to a road. Tommy Wisbey drove Buster to the signal beyond Tring where they had planned to stop the Irish express, but it was placed in a deep cutting and would have involved too much time and work to carry two hundred and fifty sacks up the embankment to the road.

The two men drove back towards London following the railway through Berkhamsted, Boxmoor, King's Langley and Watford. They examined two viaducts where the line passed above the road, but one was too high and the other too near some houses. Back in London Buster went with Gordon to W. H. Smith in Richmond and bought large-scale Ordnance Survey maps covering the route of the railway from Euston to Rugby. They studied them at St Margaret's Road—noting each village, farm, cutting and embankment. They saw that after Tring the line left the cuttings which carried it through the Chiltern Hills and was lifted above the ground by embankments. Two bridges which took it over roads had buildings nearby; but a third had none.

The next day they drove down with Bruce to inspect it. After they had passed through Tring the landscape changed from wooded hills to gently undulating countryside. The main road branched away from the main line, but by crossing and re-crossing the railway they reached the bridge which they had marked on the map. They saw at once that it was perfect for their purpose.

Bridge No. 127—known as Bridego Bridge—carried the railway over a quiet country lane. The arch was only 10 feet 9 inches high, and the line ran only 15 feet above the road. The bridge itself was made of mauve brick, with slight metal railings on either side; and it was supported by buttressed walls which ran flush with the angle of the embankment.

On the western side of the bridge on one side of the road there was a copse of conifers and on the other a pond with a notice saying "Private Fishing". Next to the pond was a small area for the private fishermen to park their cars and it was here, placed as if for the convenience of train robbers, that the embankment ended in a waist-high stone wall—a perfect place to park and load a lorry.

The nearest house was a farm about a quarter of a mile down the lane. Less than a mile away was the enormous country house of Lord Rosebery at Mentmore Park, but the trees which screened the house from prying eyes obscured its view of Bridego Bridge.

Bruce set off up the track to the north, and after about half a mile he came to a set of signals suspended from a gantry which straddled the track. Thirteen hundred yards beyond it towards Linslade was the dwarf signal: both were far from any dwelling. He walked back to the bridge and the three men agreed that so far as they could see they had found the right place to stop the train.

Bruce returned the next day with Roger—each in his own particular disguise. Roger wore an old, navy-blue donkey-jacket of the kind used by most railway workers: Bruce was dressed in a paratrooper's field uniform and when they reached the area of the bridge he parked his Lotus Cortina in a field and covered it with a camouflage net.

Roger trudged up the line. He inspected the two sets of signals and agreed with Bruce that the site was right. He could certainly stop the train at the gantry: the problem would be to move it forward the half mile or so from the gantry to the bridge. They would have to uncouple the engine and front two coaches from the rest of the train and move it forward. This would isolate the seventy sorters and leave them with only the driver, fireman and six men in the HVP coach itself.

"No problem," said Bruce, "no problem at all." And Roger, whose own firm had once backed down from a similar plan he had had for the Brighton Line, was impressed by Bruce's verve and confidence.

This was the first of many trips which Roger and Bruce made to Bridego Bridge. Sometimes they came by night to identify the mail train which Bruce, by travelling up and down on passenger trains, had calculated must pass the bridge at a few minutes past three in the morning. Night after night they waited by the bridge, and always at just on three they saw the long line of pin-prick lights from the small windows of the sorting coaches, and a few minutes later the train thundered past.

The visits by day were concerned with technicalities such as the timing of Roger's route from the amber dwarf signal to the main signal on the gantry. It soon became clear that it would be risky for him to do both, and although reluctant to disclose his "trade secrets", he was persuaded to delegate responsibility for the amber signal to John Daly. He showed him and Bruce how to black out the green signal with an old glove, and then connect the four batteries to a bulb and place it behind the amber lens. When Bruce and John saw how simple it was, they were less in awe of their expert and told the others that if only they had used their own common sense, they might have saved £10,000 of the Germans' money.

Once they had agreed to Bridego Bridge, and had established that the train could be stopped nearby, three immediate problems remained to be solved over the robbery itself—the uncoupling of the second coach from the rest of the train; the breaking in to the HVP coach, and the moving of the diesel engine and the first two coaches from the gantry to Bridego Bridge.

Roy volunteered to master uncoupling. He bought a handbook on trains and learned in theory what had to be done—the actual uncoupling, and then the disconnection of tubes carrying the vacuum for the braking system and the tubes which carried steam to heat the coaches. Then he and Bill Jennings, dressed up in navy-blue boiler-suits, went to the different marshalling yards outside London's mainline stations where, passing themselves off as railway workers, they practised what they had learned from the book. Quite quickly they mastered it, and timed themselves to uncouple in the shortest possible time. Bruce's side-kick, Jimmy White, also learned to uncouple as a reserve: like Roy, Bill and John Daly he preferred not to take part in the violence which might be involved in the other aspects of the job.

To plan their assault on the HVP coach itself, they needed to examine it—to see what locks there were on the doors and measure the strength of the windows. The Ulsterman could not tell them where the HVP coach was shunted during the day—they had to find out for themselves. Bruce and Buster had noted the numbers of the different HVP coaches at Euston, so they set off to search for them in the different marshalling yards. They started with the sidings around Paddington but only found mail coaches from the Western Region. They also searched around Primrose Hill in North London, and eventually, with Gordon and Jimmy White, went out towards Wembley to the yards at Stonebridge Park. Here, again dressed in boiler-suits, they wandered among the empty carriages checking their numbers against those they had recorded at Euston; and there suddenly they found it—the entire mail train.

They climbed on at the back and walked down through the different carriages with their walls of wooden boxes in which the letters were sorted on the journey south. In the second coach from the front, they found what they had been looking for: for here were the special wire cages with padlocks behind which the sacks of HVPs would be stored. These could be easily opened with a pair of bolt-cutters; nor would the simple locks on the doors themselves present any difficulty. There were no bars on the windows: indeed the coach which carried millions of pounds up and down the country every night seemed to have no special defences at all.

The most intractable problem was moving the train from the signal to the bridge. It was only a distance of half a mile or so, but the weight and power of the huge, throbbing diesel locomotives daunted them. It would not be difficult to capture the locomotive because, as Roger assured them, the driver or the fireman would climb out of his cab and go to the telephone at the foot of the gantry to enquire as to the cause of the delay. It was then just a matter of grabbing the fireman and rushing the cab before the driver realised what was happening. The problem was how to start the engine again.

Roy was the most optimistic. He knew the procedures from studying his Railwayman's Handbook; and passing himself off as a teacher who wanted to tell his pupils about trains, he had persuaded a train driver to take him in his cab from Euston out to a siding. He was shown the speedometer, the pressure gauges and the different handles for moving the engine backwards or forwards, increasing or decreasing the power and speed, and building up or releasing the vacuum which powered the braking system of the whole train. Gordon and Bruce also climbed onto dead diesels parked in the sidings to see if they could master the controls.

After all this instruction and practice they were almost sure that they would be able to drive the engine themselves—especially Roy—but they could not be certain; and since it would be so vital to get the train from the signal to the bridge, it was not something which should be left to chance. This left them with two alternatives: either the driver of the mail train would have to be persuaded to drive it for them, or they would have to find a driver themselves and bring him in on the business. The first possibility was considered, but that too had the element of chance. What if the driver refused? How would they either persuade or coerce him? Buster suggested stuffing newspapers up his trouser legs and setting fire to them, but this might only lead him to faint with terror. In the end a vote was taken and the majority decided that they should try and find another driver.

Among those whom Bruce Reynolds still counted as his friends was a fellow convict from Wandsworth Prison, Ronnie Biggs. Since those earlier days when both had been petty thieves and ex-Borstal boys, the two had gone in different directions; Bruce went deeper into more ambitious crime, while Ronnie got caught for smaller and smaller offences ending up with another three years in Wandsworth for stealing a car.

Although Bruce now felt contempt for Ronnie's qualities as a thief, he still enjoyed his company; however half-hearted and incompetent at crime, Biggs remained an amusing and intelligent companion with the same interests in sex, jazz and Hemingway. Ronnie Biggs, like Bruce Reynolds, had named his son, Nick, after Hemingway's character, Nick Adams. He had married a teacher's daughter called Charmian, and occasionally Bruce would take Franny down to spend an evening with them drinking beer and listening to records.

In the course of one of these evenings Ronnie Biggs—who lived in Redhill and worked in the area as a carpenter and handyman—told Bruce and Franny that his son Nick was mad about trains; and as luck would have it Ronnie had been working on the bungalow of an old train-driver who had befriended him and now took Nick for rides on his shunting diesel.

"What sort of a bloke is he?" asked Bruce—as casual in his question as he could bring himself to be.

"Good as gold," said Ronnie.

"Do you think he'd ever do anything dodgy?" asked Bruce.

"He would if he could," said Ronnie. "The stories I've told him about business I've been on. 'Cor', he says, 'I wish I could have some of that.'"

"So for a few thousand quid, he might be persuaded to drive a train?"

"For a few thousand quid he'd drive a space ship."

Charmian and Franny now withdrew into the kitchen, and Bruce gave Ronnie Biggs a brief outline of the robbery they planned. Ronnie agreed to approach the old train driver, whose name was Stan, if he himself was brought in on the job as a full member of the gang. Bruce tried to persuade him just to take a "drink" for making the introduction, but finally agreed to put it to the others and meet with Biggs again in a few days time.

As he had feared, their reaction was hostile. Most of them had never heard of Ronnie Biggs, and those that had knew of his record of incompetence. Some were shocked that Bruce should have even mentioned the train to such an unreliable amateur; and to suggest that he should actually join the firm for such an ambitious robbery was like choosing a player from the fourth division for the England team. Roger's firm were actually angered by the idea, and even those who had worked with Bruce before, such as Roy James, Charlie Wilson and Jimmy White, were antagonistic—especially Roy who was so confident that he would be able to drive the train himself. He would certainly prefer to take that chance than run all the risks which would follow from bringing in Biggs and his old driver.

However, other counsels prevailed. Buster, Gordon and Roger Cordrey, who were all closely involved with the planning of the robbery, agreed with Bruce that they had to have a driver, and that if Biggs was the price they must pay to secure one then Biggs must be in on the business. They took a vote and when it was counted only Roy was against.

Bruce therefore returned to Redhill, taking Buster with him to see Ronnie Biggs and old Stan, a small man in his early sixties who winked at them with a roguish smile as if they were children planning some prank. Stan admitted to Bruce and Buster that he had never driven one of the huge D-type diesel locomotives used on the main line; but he said that he knew all about them and would find no difficulty in doing so. Bruce asked him to make sure; and a few days later Ronnie reported that Stan had been to Euston, had cadged a ride in the driver's cab of a D-type diesel, and was quite confident that when the time came he would be able to move it.

The recruitment of Ronnie Biggs and old Stan exposed the potential antagonism which existed between the two firms. Their merger was extremely unusual in a world where trust was rare. Most thieves worked only with old-established associates: here half the gang neither knew nor trusted the other half. The second firm knew quite well that some of the first firm—Charlie and Bruce, for example—would be happy to do without them; and they had the nagging fear that Roger might defect. They were also irritated by Bruce whom they found socially and intellectually pretentious. In itself this might merely have amused them, but combined with the kind of high-handedness he had shown in approaching Ronnie Biggs, it put them in a quarrelsome mood.

Gordon also irritated them—and some of those on his own side. He liked to work on his own, which meant that he neither told the others what he was doing nor trusted them to do their job. He persistently nagged at Roger about stopping the train—as if doubting his ability to do so: he questioned him closely about the danger of an accident—another train running into the back of the mail train—because he mistrusted Roger's assurances that an accident was impossible. He was also inclined to show off—as for instance when he had revealed to the prosecuting counsel at the Old Bailey the false link in the chain. Roy suspected him of boasting in advance about the train robbery; from chance remarks passed back to him from Flying Squad detectives, it looked as if they knew that some big robbery was in the offing. At one of the meetings of the train gang, Roy proposed that the job be postponed because the police seemed aware of what was going on.

The first firm had reservations about the second firm—particularly their qualifications as big-time thieves. Although Bruce and Charlie had been involved in their share of fiascos, they had the Airport Robbery to their credit and the pilfering of registered mail on the Brighton Line did not seem to them to qualify the others for such an ambitious project as the train robbery. What was really at the back of their minds was the fear that if it came to a fight—perhaps with a posse of Post Office sorters—they would not be able to rely on the second firm to stand at their side.

This antagonism reached its climax when the second firm were told about the Germans. Throughout March, April and May Bruce had had further meetings with Karl, and by the end of June had received from him four instalments of £20,000. Some of this money had been handed in a weekly wage to members of both firms; some had been spent by Bruce on "expenses"; but the more he had received, the less inclined he became to double-cross the Germans. In conversation with Karl over lunch in various expensive restaurants, he had not only come to like him but also to respect his organisation which, Karl intimated, was formed from veterans of the Second World War. Bruce became convinced that if they did double-cross the Germans, they would risk their revenge—either by betraying them to the police or through the more conventional methods of criminals. He also saw the advantage of having them on their side should anything go wrong and any of them want to leave the country. Karl had promised not only to help them escape but to open Swiss bank accounts for any of them who chose to take their money out of the country. If the thieves could arrange for a boat to take it to the mouth of the Thames estuary, Karl's organisation could handle it from there: his only stipulation was that one of his own men should be with them on the robbery to protect his interests.

When Bruce told his friends in the first firm that it was no longer "on" to double-cross the Germans, and that he had agreed that one of their men should go with them, no one objected: Buster and Jim Hussey were relieved and even Gordon saw the sense in it. The trouble came when the second firm were informed of an arrangement of which they had had no intimation before. Bob Welch and Frank Munroe exploded with fury. That £2 million of the prize should be given away to unknown Germans was the last straw: they saw it as an intolerable affront to their pride, and demanded a meet between both firms to have it out.

It was fixed for six one Wednesday evening on Putney Heath, and before they set off Bob Welch and Frank Munroe concealed sawn-off shot-guns in their mackintosh pockets. From the tone of the invitation the first firm had realised how the meet might end, and Charlie and Gordon both came with their "shooters". As soon as the two groups met Bob Welch laid into Bruce for giving away so much money. "Fuck the Germans," he said. "If we're going to have a row with them, then let's have a row, but tell them to fuck off. We've had their money. What do we care?"

"That's it," said Bruce. "We've had their money, all of us . . ."

"Eighty grand? And they want two million pounds for fucking eighty grand? Who do they think they are? We've got our liberty at stake. They're risking nothing. They don't deserve a fucking drink of two million pounds."

Bruce counter-attacked. "It's your lot's fucking fault for being so fucking greedy in the first place," he said. "If Roger hadn't asked for ten grand, we'd never have seen a fucking German. But we had to go to them; we did a deal; and now we're going to see it through."

"And where is the eighty grand?" asked Frank. "All I've seen is a lousy £100 a week."

"And all you've done is sit on your lousy arse while we've done all the fucking work . . ."

The arguments raged on, fingers twitched around triggers, and the excitable, paranoid thieves might have lost control and shot it out had not Buster intervened. Dependable and easy-going, he was known and trusted by both sides: he had brought them together and now kept them together. "Look," he said, "what's done is done. We've taken their dough, and they'd be really raving mad if we don't pay up. We'll still come away with 175 grand apiece, and it would be stupid to risk any aggravation by double-crossing them. And another thing—the Germans have promised us help if we want it afterwards. They can arrange false passports, plastic surgery and Swiss bank accounts . . ."

The second firm, most of whom had never left London, were unimpressed by these fancy facilities; but Buster's intervention made them realise that it would serve no purpose to "nause" the whole business because they "had the hump" with Bruce. A man could swallow a lot of pride for £175,000. They had made their point and the two firms now dispersed to make their final arrangements.

Though they had mastered the difficulties of the robbery itself, the Train Robbers were left with the question of what to do with the money once they had got it. Two hundred and fifty mail bags could not be easily moved or hidden: nor would the theft remain undiscovered for long.

Roy favoured a dash back to London in specially converted 3.8 Jaguars. He had already prepared a prototype with the back seat removed to make room for the money. Bridego Bridge was only fifteen miles from the newly opened M1 motorway: they could be back in London in an hour. There were objections to this: a fleet of Jaguars driving through country lanes in the middle of the night would arouse suspicion; they were now without Micky Ball, and no one else in the gang had Roy's skill at fast driving; and they were unlikely to have so much as an hour's grace before the robbery was discovered and road-blocks set up by the police. It was therefore decided that they should look for some sort of hide-out within half an hour's drive of the bridge: they could then go there with the money and wait until the immediate hue and cry was over and the road blocks lifted.

Bruce and John Daly set to work looking at the property columns of local Buckinghamshire, Hertfordshire and Oxfordshire newspapers for remote cottages or farmhouses: eventually they found a reference to a farm near Brill which was twenty-seven miles due west of Bridego Bridge on the other side of Aylesbury. On 24 June they drove out to Bicester and went to the offices of Midland Marts who had advertised the farm. Bruce, dressed in a suit and wearing horn-rimmed spectacles, asked the woman at the desk if they had any farms near Brill on their books. "You must mean Leatherslade Farm," she said and took from her file two pages of duplicated particulars. She gave them to Bruce and then asked for his name.

"Why do you want my name?" Bruce asked.

"We usually take the name," she said.

"In that case you can have this back," said Bruce offering her the particulars.

"No, no," she said. "It doesn't matter. It's just that we're joint agents for the farm, and if you were to buy it we would want to know whether you came through us or through the other agency."

"If that's the only reason you want it," said Bruce, "then you can have it. It's Richards. J. Richards."

He left the office and joined John in the Lotus Cortina. They drove out of Bicester towards Aylesbury, and then turned off on the B road towards Thame. Just after the village of Oakley they came to the track which led up the hill to Leatherslade Farm. Here they stopped the car and looked up the track to the farm. It was about a quarter of a mile off the road and, except for the barn and milking shed at the foot of the track where they now were, at least half a mile from the nearest building. Although the farm itself was built on the side of the hill which led up to the village of Brill, and would therefore have views of all the surrounding countryside and the roads which approached the vicinity, it was itself surrounded by trees and so invisible from the road.

From the particulars given to them by Midland Marts they saw that the farmhouse had a sitting-room, dining-room, kitchen, bathroom and four bedrooms. Outside was a garage and a timber and corrugated asbestos workshop. There was mains water and electricity supplied by a diesel generator. Without going any closer John and Bruce decided that Leatherslade Farm was just what they wanted.

They returned to London and reported on what they had found to the others. They discussed the best method of getting hold of the property in such a way that if it was ever identified as the hide-out it could not be traced back to them. Gordon suggested that they should leave this to Brian Field who was, after all, a solicitor's managing clerk.

Gordon went with the particulars to Brian Field who agreed to arrange for the purchase of the farm through his employer, John Denby Wheater. This bluff, inefficient ex-army officer who had turned to the law after the war was happy to leave much of the running of his office in the hands of his cunning subordinate who now brought him so much well-paid practice through his contacts with big-time thieves. Among these clients was a man who was ⁿo relation to Brian Field but had the same family name. This Heɪ.y Alexander Field had faced charges of buggery and horsedoping, and more recently of robbing a bank in Stoke. Since he intended to plead guilty to this last offence, Harry Field arranged for his younger brother, Lennie Field, to be given power of attorney; this was witnessed by John Wheater. Just over a week later John Wheater borrowed a thousand pounds from Harry Field: four days after that—on 27 May 1963—Harry Field was sentenced to five years' imprisonment.

Now, towards the end of June, when Brian Field was looking for someone who might lend his name and some money for the purchase of the farm, his eye fell on the young Lennie Field. The price asked for the farm was £5,500; but vacant possession could probably be arranged after ten per cent of the purchase price had been paid as a deposit. The proposal that was made to Lennie Field was that if he bought the farm and paid the deposit he would be given a drink of twelve thousand pounds when the job was done. Lennie, who was allowed to think that the plan was to hijack a lorry-load of cigarettes, agreed.

Two days after Bruce had obtained particulars of Leatherslade Farm, John Wheater telephoned Midland Marts and told the agent that he had a client who was interested in buying the farm. On 27 June, the two unrelated Fields—Brian and Lennie—went down to Brill. The owner's wife, Mrs Rixon, showed them around; they did not show much interest in the house but examined the outbuildings to see how many vehicles would fit into them. They were told by Mrs Rixon that another man was interested in the farm. "Well, if you send the contract to us," said Brian Field, "we'll sign it at once."

"What will you do with the farm?" asked Mrs Rixon, as they walked out into the sparse garden and looked back at the meagre, brick-built dwelling.

"Can you imagine this place with nice gardens all round?" asked Brian Field, "and a swimming-pool?"

"Oh yes," said Mrs Rixon.

"Well, if your husband lets us have the contract," said Brian, "you can start digging a hole."

He laughed, and with Lennie Field drove back to London.

In the negotiations with the Rixons which followed, Wheater first increased his offer to £5,750 to outbid the other purchaser; but when that deal fell through he reduced his offer once again to the asking price. Eventually the two parties compromised and the price of £5,550 was agreed. The contracts were exchanged with Lennie Field named as the purchaser and the conveyancing proceeded in the hands of the solicitors—John Wheater acting for Lennie Field, and a Mr Meirion-Williams acting for Mr Rixon. As always it was a lengthy process, and as the weeks passed and the August Bank Holiday approached, Wheater's letters to Meirion-Williams took on a note of urgency. "Our client is anxious to commence work on the property as quickly as possible and we would like to know when vacant possession can be granted and if he can commence work, even if it is not possible to complete the purchase by the time vacant possession can be granted."

"Our client's completion funds will not be available until the 13 August and we do not feel it unreasonable that your client should make the concession asked for. Perhaps you would let us have your client's answer as our client considers as a paramount point of importance, that he should be allowed to enter into possession for the purpose of redecoration on exchange of contracts."

On 19 July Mr Meirion-Williams replied that his client was prepared to agree. On 22 July the contract signed by Lennie Field was sent to Mr Rixon's solicitor, and the next day a cheque for £550 was sent to Midland Marts. On 29 July the Rixons moved out of Leatherslade Farm, and Brian Field was able to tell Gordon that it was now at their disposal.

The full strength of the combined firms which came together for the Train Robbery was fifteen men. It consisted of Buster Edwards and his friend Bill Jennings; Bruce Reynolds, his brother-in-law John Daly, Jimmy White and a friend of his called Alf Thomas and Ronnie Biggs. Harry Booth had opted out—partly because he had started making large amounts of legitimate money, and partly because he doubted that the Train Robbery would ever come off. There followed the rest of the first firm: Gordon Goody, Charlie Wilson, Roy James and Jim Hussey. From the second firm there was Roger Cordrey, Bob Welch, Tommy Wisbey and Frank Munroe. Old Stan was in for a drink, but a full whack was to go to Brian Field and another to the Ulsterman: after deducting the

£2 million for the Germans and the various drinks, the money would be split seventeen ways.

Buster thought the gang was too large—that there were several they could have done without—particularly Alf Thomas who had been introduced by Jimmy White as a big-time thief, but much later confessed that he had never come away with more than £1,500. Bruce and Gordon, on the other hand, wanted additional heavies to deal with any force they were likely to encounter. Bruce had suggested that they should dress up as soldiers and travel to the track in two Land Rovers and an Army lorry. This plan was not just an expression of his military fantasies: there was an army camp near Bicester, so the sight of a small convoy in the middle of the night would not arouse undue suspicions; and if, by any chance, they were stopped by a police patrol they could overpower them, pretending that it was part of some manoeuvre.

Once this scheme had been adopted, everyone entered into it with enthusiasm. Charlie and Roy bought uniforms, badges and berets from army surplus stores: they were of course the uniforms of the Parachute Regiment with the motto "Who dares, wins". They bought the square coloured stickers which decorate and identify army vehicles, and had special number plates made up with the military placing of numbers and letters. When it came to distributing the uniforms Bruce had the crown of a major with John as his lieutenant. He also decided that for the sake of security they should call each other by numbers—Bruce as number one, John as number two, and so on down the line—but this idea was never adopted by the others; indeed Roger never intended to wear a uniform. They bought dark-blue overalls, to wear on the track itself so that any passing train would take them for railway workers; and Bruce and John bought white overalls so that the first to arrive at the farm should be mistaken for decorators.

Both Roger and Bruce independently purchased the same Hitachi VHF radios to tune into the Buckinghamshire police. Bruce bought a pair of Zeiss binoculars and Bob Welch a pair of handcuffs for the train driver: he told the shop-assistant that they were for amateur dramatics.

It was left to Jimmy White to get hold of the vehicles. With Bruce he stole a light-blue Land Rover from Oxendon Street near Leicester Square and handed it over to Gordon who had it painted khaki. He bought a second Land Rover for £195 which was already painted dark green; and he paid a further £300 for an Austin army lorry which he found in Edgware. Roy had the idea of buying a second lorry which they could take to the bridge and then drive away afterwards in the wrong direction and abandon it, perhaps with some empty mail bags, but his plan was never adopted.

They anticipated an aerial search after the robbery and so all the vehicles had to be under cover; but because they were limited by garage space this meant they could only take the lorry and two Land Rovers to the farm. To transport the money from the farm after the hubbub had died down they decided upon a horse-box which would be large enough to carry several million pounds yet seem unobtrusive in a rural setting. Charlie was sent out to buy one, and he handed it over to his friend Joey Gray who was to drive it up to the farm on the Sunday after the raid—the day agreed upon for their final departure.

It would be loaded there with everyone's money and driven by an overland route to a boat belonging to a friend of Gordon's which was to be moored on the Thames south of Oxford at Long Wittenham; from there Gordon, and the German whom Karl was to send to see to his interests, would journey down the Thames through London. Those who either did not trust the Germans or did not want their money in Switzerland, would send it on to London with Joey Gray in the horse-box. Brian Field would collect his own whack from the farm, and that due to the Ulsterman.

Once their transport had been decided, there was the question of supplies—the food, plates and cutlery they would need to live at the farm from the Wednesday to the Sunday—and perhaps even longer if the "scream" had not died down. Once again this was left to the ex-paratrooper Jimmy White. With Frank Munroe he went out to buy a gross of eggs, two dozen tins of baked beans, tins of tomatoes, ten pounds of bacon, three dozen loaves of bread. They bought fifteen sets of knives, forks, and spoons, cups, saucers, plates, large cans of beer, salt, pepper, butter, twenty-four pounds of tea, a crate of Carnation milk, a catering tin of instant coffee and thirty pounds of sugar. Charlie provided a box of fruit and a sack of potatoes from his father-in-law's green-grocer's shop; and at the last moment Bruce added a tin of red peppers and a Monopoly set. Jimmy White and Alf drove the supplies down to the farm.

As the date planned for the robbery drew nearer, there was a mass of last-minute preparation. Each one knew the role he was to play at the bridge. Bruce was to go up the track towards Linslade with a walkie-talkie radio to warn the others when the train approached. John Daly was at the amber signal; Roger and Roy at the red signal on the gantry. Roy was also responsible for cutting the telephone wires to the farms near the bridge; and with Bill and Jimmy White for the uncoupling of the coach. They would remain on the east side of the track with Alf Thomas and Bob Welch in reserve. On the other side, waiting for the fireman and ready to storm the driver in his cab, were the heavies—Gordon, Charlie, Tommy, Frank and Jim Hussey. Next to them would be the old train driver, Stan, with Ronnie Biggs minding him. Between the two groups, as a kind of coordinating NCO, was Buster.

They also worked hard at the route they would take from the farm to the bridge and back again. Using their Ordnance Survey maps, Bruce, Gordon, Buster and Roy marked out the small country lanes which would take them the twenty-seven miles across the vale of Aylesbury without using any major road or passing through any large-sized town. Their route led from the bridge through the villages of Wingrave, Aston Abbots, Cublington, Whitchurch, Oving, Pitchcott, Uppoer Winchendon and Chilton—and having worked it out they drove to Buckinghamshire in Bruce's Lotus Cortina and Roy's second car, a Mini Cooper, and went back and forth through the sumptuous summer English countryside, past heavy hedges, laden trees, deep-green grass, corn almost ready to be cut, bankers in their Old Rectories and stockbrokers' daughters on their ponies.

Sometimes they would race one another along these country lanes—such was their gaiety and optimism—but no one ever beat Roy. For now he was a professional racing driver as well as a professional thief. He had been drawn into go-kart racing by a friend, a mechanic called Bobby Pelham, and had graduated to the British karting team. On Boxing Day of 1962 he had gone to a Formula 3 race at Brand's Hatch and became convinced that he could win. With part of his whack from the Airport Robbery, he bought a Brabham Formula Junior racing-car, and entered three races. In the first, at Eltham Park, he led the field until he crashed. Roy was not injured but the car was a write-off. He got hold of another Brabham in time for the second race at Goodwood. There he was warned not to drive so dangerously, but

Otto Skorzeny, after his rescue of Mussolini in 1943

The First Firm, 1963

Buster Edwards' passport photographs; *left* before the robbery, and *right* after plastic surgery

Gordon Goody

Above: Bruce and Franny
Reynolds on their wedding day
Right: Roy James at the
Hotel Martinez in Cannes

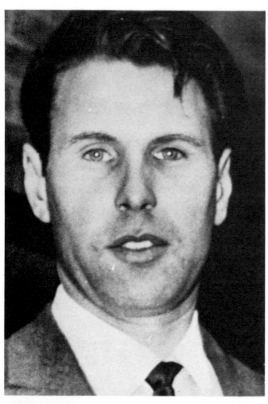

Charlie Wilson
Jim Hussey

The Second Firm, 1963

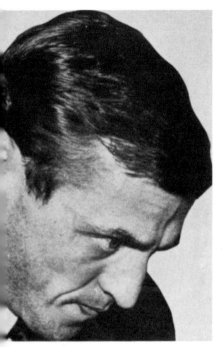

ob Welch
oger Cordrey
ommy Wisbey

Ronnie Biggs

Charmian Biggs

John Wheater

idegow Bridge on 8 August 1963

herslade Farm on 13 August 1963

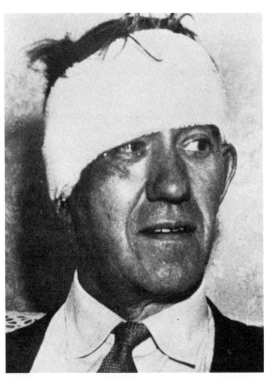

Jack Mills, photographed three days after the robbery

Bill Boal

once again he forced his way to the front of the field, and once again he crashed. The car was repaired and at Aintree he won.

It was the start of a meteoric success. His competitors were drivers such as Jack Brabham, Denny Holme and Jackie Stewart; and yet of the nineteen races which followed, seventeen were won by Roy James. He broke lap records and had contract offers from Shell, Esso and Jack Brabham. By the summer of 1963 he was poised for a career which might have taken him to the World Championship: he had the skill and the determination. He would soon have the money.

Although the plan was that everyone's whack should leave the farm in the horse-box, Roy had his especially converted 3.8 Jaguar in reserve. Others had made contingency plans. Bruce had prepared a friend of his called Mary Manson to be ready to come up to Tring with a furniture van. She was older than he was—small and dark with a husband and two children—and had first met Bruce and John when her brother, a thief, had asked her to lodge them. Since those early days she had become their most reliable auxiliary—acting as a front and running errands just as Derek Glass did for Buster. She did not do it for any substantial material reward, but was mesmerised by Bruce's unusual personality and addicted to the excitement of his dangerous life.

Roger had taken even more extensive precautions. Having been pulled in by the police after his most recent robbery on the Brighton Line, he now imagined that they would suspect him of any theft from a train. His plan was to go directly home from the track, trusting to Tommy, Frank and Bob to bring his whack to London. There a bank manager of his acquaintance who had previously laundered his stolen money, through three separate accounts, was told to expect a substantial sum.

When the others realised what Roger meant to do, they refused to allow it. Bruce in particular insisted that if one went, others would follow and each would then be in a position to betray the hide-out. Roger was told by Buster that he had to return to the farm and wait with them until the Sunday after the robbery, and he appeared to concur: secretly, however, he made other plans. He prepared a bicycle to take to the farm, and went to Oxford where he arranged to rent a room for the night of Tuesday August 6th.

The rest made no plans. They assumed that the more energetic members of the gang who had seen to every detail of the robbery itself would also take care of the getaway. Certainly when it was asked what would happen to the farm, they were told that Brian Field would make sure that it was cleaned up afterwards. Indeed Brian told Gordon that Mark, the silver-haired man who had first introduced them to the Ulsterman, had undertaken to perform that duty; and that a drink for Mark would have to come out of the takings.

On 31 July, Gordon and Buster had their last meeting with the Ulsterman. It was in Hyde Park, and the three men sauntered along the baked ground, watching the Londoners sprawled on the grass in their shirt sleeves. They reached the café by the Serpentine, and because it was so hot they sat down at a table to have a drink. The Ulsterman took off his jacket and hung it over the back of his chair.

Although they still did not know who he was, or how he came by the information, both Gordon and Buster had grown to like this quiet, self-effacing middle-aged man. They respected him too for the accuracy of his information, and for never promising what he could not deliver. Everything he had told them had proved correct; nothing had been wishful thinking. All that remained now was to fix a time and a place to hand over his share of the money. They agreed to meet him in a week's time at Brian Field's house near Pangbourne.

It was hot. Buster ordered three more glasses of lemonade. The Ulsterman stood to go into the café and find the lavatory. He had only been gone a few moments when Gordon noticed his jacket hanging on the chair. He glanced at Buster: their eyes met. Quickly Gordon leant forward and started to go through the pockets of the Ulsterman's jacket. There might always come a time in the future when it would be better to know who he was.

The pockets were empty. There was nothing in any of them. Gordon sat back. Then suddenly something occurred to him: he leant forward again, and took hold of the inside pocket, in the lining of the jacket. He twisted the lining out and there, on a white label sewn into the lining, was the name of the tailor and beneath it the name and address of the tailor's customer—the Ulsterman. Gordon memorised it, and sat back.

He said nothing to Buster, but Gordon deduced from the name that the Ulsterman was a Protestant, and from the address that he was a farmer. As he came back from the café, however, Gordon's features betrayed no sign of what he now knew.

The three men finished their second drinks, and then the time came to leave. Buster and Gordon thanked the Ulsterman and the Ulsterman wished them luck. Then he added, with his particular smile, "and by the way, if you do well on this one, I've got an even bigger job for you afterwards".

5. The Great Train Robbery

On Friday 2 August, five days before the robbery was due to take place, Gordon Goody flew to Belfast with his mother and a friend. They stayed in Lisburn with his uncle and Gordon went to some lengths to make his presence noticed: he faked a fight in a pub, and had the publican call the police, but this strategem failed because they could not be bothered to come out.

On Saturday 3 August, Roger Cordrey went to the house of some acquaintances in Oxford to ask if he could rent a room on the following Tuesday. They had no room, but they promised to find him somewhere, so he returned to Brighton to find that his wife had left him. For some months they had been getting on badly together, largely because he spent so much time away from home; and while feeling neglected, she had been befriended by another man. Now she had gone, leaving the youngest child with an old lady next door.

Roger was depressed by his wife's flight—the more so because he felt himself to blame—and it destroyed any pleasure he might have taken in the final preparation of his equipment. He went up to London on the morning of Monday 5 August, stayed with his mother in Hampton Court, and went to bed early.

He was woken at eleven by the telephone. The old lady in Brighton who was looking after his son had had a heart attack and Roger was told that someone must fetch the child. He got dressed, telephoned some friends to see if they knew where his wife could be, but was unable to trace her. He had no alternative but to drive down to Brighton in his car, fetch his son and drive him back to London. By the time he got back to Hampton Court early in the morning, Roger was totally exhausted.

The same day Roy had driven out to London Airport in his Mini Cooper with Jim Hussey to meet the German sent by Karl to look after his interests. They were equipped with a photograph and picked him out as he came through passport control—a tall, well-dressed man with fair hair and a crocodile brief-case who gave his name as Sigi. He said little as they drove back into London to stay with Jim in his parents' flat.

On the morning of Tuesday 6 August, the whole gang prepared to move. Bruce and John despatched their wives and children to stay with Jimmy White's wife in their caravan in Winchelsea and then set off in the old Land Rover to pick up Ronnie Biggs and old Stan who had told their wives that they were going on a tree-felling job in Wiltshire. They reached Leatherslade Farm in time for lunch, and since the stores were already there they lit the stove and cooked themselves something to eat. Afterwards they changed into white overalls, and while Ronnie and John stayed in the house, Bruce went into the garden to see where they could dig a pit to bury the mail bags. Old Stan sat on a deck-chair taking the sun.

From the fields behind the farm, a man appeared who introduced himself to Bruce as Mr Wyatt, a neighbouring farmer, and said that he would like to continue the arrangement whereby he had rented a field from the previous owners, the Rixons. Bruce said the he was not the owner, but only the decorator.

"Who is the owner, then?" asked Mr Wyatt.

"Mr Fielding from Aylesbury," said Bruce.

Mr Wyatt departed, and a little later Jimmy White and his friend Alf Thomas arrived with the lorry. They backed it into the shed and then took the Land Rover to return to London. There they crossed the Thames and picked up Frank Munroe, Tommy Wisbey and Bob Welch who all piled into the back with their sleeping bags and drove on to fetch Roger at Hampton Court. He appeared looking exhausted, with a kit bag and three empty suitcases for his money. He also wheeled out a bicycle: there were complaints from the others, but Roger insisted on taking his bike and they could hardly leave without him.

Half-way to Leatherslade Farm, they stopped for petrol and while the tank was being filled, a little boy wrote down their registration number in his notebook which caused some anxiety because Jimmy White had given the stolen Land Rover the same number as the one they had bought; since the police could check numbers against makes, it seemed sensible to use the legitimate registration.

When they reached the entrance to the track leading up to the farm, Alf leapt out to open the gate: it was now late in the afternoon and they could hear the sound of the milking machinery in the cow-shed. They drove up to the farm to find that Roy, dressed like a local farmer in old tweeds and a cloth cap, had already arrived in the other Land Rover with Charlie, Buster, Bill, Jim Hussey and the strange German in a smart suit.

Jimmy White now began to skin and cook a rabbit they had run over on the road. The others started blowing up their air-mattresses and laying claim to corners of the four bedrooms, one of which was reserved for Sigi whom Jim had been told to keep out of the way. Bruce came up to explain to him that while they were at the track, he was to remain at the farm; and if for any reason they did not return, he was to change into a pair of *Lederhosen* which Bruce had brought to the farm, and make his escape as a tourist on Roger's bike.

While Sigi remained in an upstairs room, the other stranger, old Stan, shuffled around from room to room, sucking his pipe and smiling. None of the thieves apart from Bruce, Buster and Ronnie Biggs had ever seen him before, and the sight of his beaming, gullible face confirmed their worst fears. Quite clearly he had little idea of what was going on, and if anything went wrong and he fell into the hands of the police he could identify every one of them. They all tried to avoid him, and every time he entered one room, they would sneak out of it with averted faces. Occasionally he would corner one of them and say, "What's your name, son?" "Joe Bloggs," would come the answer, or "Elvis Presley". Later Bruce told Ronnie that Stan had to be kept out of the way, so Ronnie took him up to a bedroom and left him there. When the rabbit was ready, Ronnie took a plate up to him: the others ate it downstairs. When Jimmy White handed a plate to Tommy Wisbey, he noticed that he was not wearing gloves.

"Put your gloves on, Tom," he said.

"Oh yeah," said Tommy, reaching into his pocket for them.

Only one member of the gang was missing—Gordon. By Wednesday morning he had still not arrived. No one was particularly anxious, but Bruce was always irritated by Gordon's independent ways, and became increasingly angry as the day wore on. The others were growing nervous in anticipation of the night's work, and Buster handed out pep pills to those who wanted them. Some dozed on their air-mattresses; others played Monopoly, or made sure that their uniforms fitted them, and checked their equipment—their masks, gloves, coshes and pick-axe handles. Buster had the same type of pipe-spring cosh as he had used on the Airport Robbery. Jim Hussey's was a length of lead piping with a leather strap; Charlie's a length of copper cable. Some of them had prepared balaclava helmets to disguise their faces; others had stocking masks; and one had a black hood with holes cut out for his eyes. They all had gloves. Buster's were leather with string backs; Roy's were made of wool; Jim Hussey's of black velvet.

Old Stan, of course, had neither cosh nor mask though since he was to drive the train Ronnie had made sure he had gloves. Nor did he wear a soldier's uniform. Roger too remained in a scruffy old jacket and trousers which he had carefully searched for anything which might identify him. He had a spare set of clothes in a suitcase upstairs. He was bored, depressed and very tired. He had hardly slept on his air-mattress the night before and was still worrying about his wife. Moreover Buster and Bruce had told him that morning that he could only leave the farm with the rest of them on the Sunday after the robbery. They had put it gently, but he knew they meant what they said. Late in the afternoon he felt so exhausted that he was afraid he might doze off on the job, so he took a sleeping pill and went upstairs.

They stayed in the farmhouse for fear of being seen. Jimmy White was allowed out with Ronnie Biggs to change the plates of the lorry and the Land Rovers from civilian to military numbers and stick on the square, regimental emblems. Then, as it started to get dark, they saw a Jaguar stop at the foot of the lane. Out stepped Gordon Goody.

He had flown back from Belfast the day before under the name of McGonegal. His friend had driven him to the airport in a hired car, promising to return with his mother a week later as Mr and Mrs Goody. Gordon had taken a bus from Heathrow Airport to Reading where he had been met by Brian Field and driven to the Fields' small, comfortable house in a quiet lane on Whitchurch Hill outside Pangbourne.

He stayed there for the night. The next day, Brian Field went to his office, but Gordon stayed behind. Everything he would need he had with him—his Spanish truncheon, his balaclava mask, his

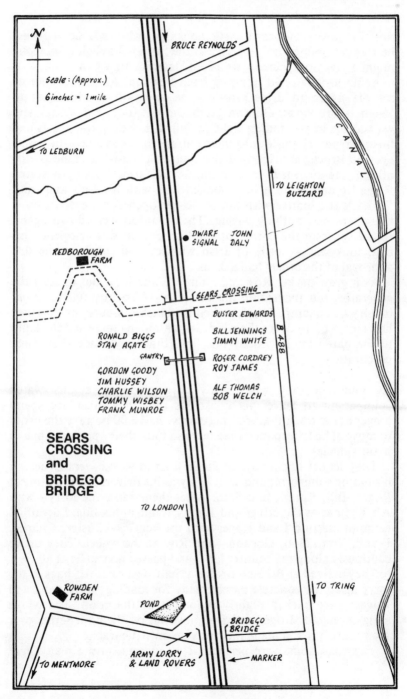

N

scale : (Approx.)
6 inches = 1 mile

TO LEDBURN

BRUCE REYNOLDS

CANAL

TO LEIGHTON BUZZARD

DWARF SIGNAL   JOHN DALY

REDBOROUGH FARM

SEARS CROSSING

BUSTER EDWARDS

RONALD BIGGS
STAN AGATE
GANTRY

GORDON GOODY
JIM HUSSEY
CHARLIE WILSON
TOMMY WISBEY
FRANK MUNROE

BILL JENNINGS
JIMMY WHITE

ROGER CORDREY
ROY JAMES

ALF THOMAS
BOB WELCH

B 488

**SEARS
CROSSING
and
BRIDEGO
BRIDGE**

TO LONDON

ROWDEN FARM

POND

TO TRING

BRIDEGO BRIDGE

TO MENTMORE

ARMY LORRY
& LAND ROVERS

MARKER

fine silk gloves. He was a meticulous thief who took no chances: he was determined not to arrive at the farm in daylight. Someone might arrive unexpectedly who could later identify him.

At seven Brian had returned from London. Almost at once he set off again to drive Gordon the twenty-five odd miles to Leatherslade Farm. Gordon got out at the foot of the track and walked up in the fading light to join his colleagues. He found them already changed into their uniforms. He avoided the angry eyes of Bruce, and ignored the muttered oaths of some of the others. He prowled around the small farmhouse, and seeing Roger comatose on a lilo, nudged him with his foot and said, "What's the matter with him?" Roger opened his eyes to show that there was nothing wrong. Then Gordon went down again, found space in the corner of the kitchen, sat down, opened his bag, took out a bottle of Irish whiskey and much to the dis-approval of the others had a drink.

As it grew darker Roy and Jimmy White went out to start the generator, but they could not get it to go, so Roy fetched a car battery and a lamp. They checked the black-out curtains that they had nailed up to cover the windows, and then connected the lamp to the batteries. It was by this light that they made their final preparations.

By midnight they were ready. Bruce looked at his watch —impatient to leave, yet conscious that they must not spend longer at the track than was necessary. At 12.30 he gave the order to move. The fifteen men filed out and took their appointed places in the vehicles.

They set off in convoy. In the first Land Rover went Bruce, in his major's uniform, and John Daly as his driver. Behind him sat Roger, Bill, Ronnie and Stan. After them came the lorry—with Alf Thomas as the driver and Jimmy White at his side. Last of all came the second Land Rover with the heavies—Buster, Charlie, Frank, Tom, Bob, Gordon—and Roy at the wheel. They drove cautiously along the country lanes and passed no traffic at all.

They arrived at Bridego Bridge at half-past one. Alf backed the lorry up to the concrete block, ready for loading, while the Land Rovers were parked slightly beyond it by the pond. The whole gang except for Roger and Stan now put on the boiler-suits over their uniforms and made their way up onto the track.

The conditions were perfect. It was warm, and already light

enough to see up the track to the gantry. Bruce and Ronnie unrolled the marker—a piece of white cloth suspended between two metal poles—and stuck it into the ground where the engine was to stop. Meanwhile the others broke into the workman's hut and took out two pick-axes and an enormous crow-bar to use against the HVP coach. Then they all started walking up towards the gantry. Roy cut the telephone wires from the two boxes on either side of the four-track railway. When that was done he set off down the embankment into the fields with Bruce to cut the telephone wires leading to the nearest farmhouses. He shinned up telegraph poles and managed to cut them all except one which might have fallen onto the roof of a farmhouse and awakened its owners.

They returned to the gantry. While the others waited on the embankment, Roger, Bruce and John walked back to Bridego Bridge, picked up a Land Rover and drove round on the road to the point nearest to the dwarf signal. They walked across the field, found the signal and opened it up. Roger wired up the amber light with leads from the batteries to crocodile clips onto the bulb. It was fitted with a switch, and he explained to John that, when Bruce gave the word over the walkie-talkie, he had only to cover the green light with the glove and turn the switch.

They left John at the dwarf signal and walked back to the Land Rover. Bruce drove Roger back to the small bridge half way between the two signals which carried a farm track over the line from the road to Redborough Farm: then he drove off again to take up his position further up the line, from which he was to warn them of the train's approach.

Back at the gantry the heavies were in position on the western side of the track with Ronnie and Stan a little further down the line. They were silent: occasionally a train would hurtle past and they would duck out of sight on the embankment. Then suddenly Gordon heard the sound of footsteps and out of the obscurity came the trudging figure of a tramp. Gordon gripped his cosh, took it from his pocket, and drew down his balaclava mask: with one leap he was onto the man, his brawny arm gripped around his neck. He raised his cosh and was about to smash it down on the old tramp's head, when he heard Roger's choking voice say, "Stop larking about, you stupid idiot". He released him. "Jesus," he said, "I thought you were the enemy."

Roger went on to the gantry where Roy and Buster were waiting for him. Roy had the walkie-talkie and was in touch with Bruce: everything was "sweet". Now Roger climbed the gantry while Roy came after him carrying his equipment. They climbed along the narrow monkey-walk and Roger went down behind the signal. He opened it up and Roy handed down the batteries, the glove and the wires with crocodile clips and switch.

In the distance they heard the sound of an old steam engine, and as it grew nearer Roger told Roy to get down off the gantry. He himself hid behind the signal: and as the train puffed past him underneath, Roger was enveloped in a cloud of filthy smoke. When it had passed he found himself covered in smuts.

The steam engine which pulled a goods train came to a halt a few yards up the track. As it happened it had stopped just where Ronnie and Stan were hiding on the embankment. Next to them were Frank and Bob Welch. The driver and the fireman of the train were so near that they could hear their voices. The thieves were still and quiet; then, to his horror, Bob Welch saw Stan put his pipe in his mouth and take out a box of matches. He was just about to light up when Bob leaned across and with one hand grabbed the pipe and matches. A moment later the train set off again.

When the goods train had gone, Roy returned to the gantry to help Roger. He shone a torch into the signal and Roger connected up the four six-volt batteries and attached the leads to the red bulb. He then waited by the switch. Roy spoke to Bruce over the walkie-talkie to make sure it was working: they had prepared a system of morse signalling with the torches which they would use if either of the two sets of walkie-talkies broke down, but Bruce's voice came over loud and clear. Roy reported that they were ready. It was ten to three. Now they waited.

One train passed going north, then another going north, then another going south. In between the night was quite silent. At the bend in the track, Bruce could see the lights of Linslade. His eyes were fixed on the signal point in the distance waiting for the moving line of tiny lights from the windows of the sorting coaches. He was in a trance of anticipation. Back at the gantry the others too were silent—waiting with their own thoughts, their own pulse, their own excitement. John, at the dwarf signal, was alone and more nervous of failing in the job he had been given. Only the two older men had feelings quite different to the others. Old Stan was terrified; and Roger on the gantry was still bored, tired and depressed.

It came to three o'clock. One minute passed; then another. Then Bruce's voice came over the walkie-talkie. "It's coming down, chaps. This is the real thing."

On the gantry Roger put his glove over the green light and switched on the bulb behind the red. At the dwarf signal, John covered the green light; and then, afraid that the glove might be insufficient, he unscrewed the bulb before turning on the lamp behind the amber lense.

Roy climbed down off the gantry. "It's coming," he told the others: then he walked back the length of the locomotive and two coaches to where Bill and Buster were waiting for him. Jimmy White had crossed the track to join Ronnie and Stan next to the heavies; Alf and Bob Welch were waiting in reserve near the gantry.

They saw the train: with the muted roar of its diesel it was slowly drawing up to the gantry—lamps shining from the front of the engine, and pin-pricks of light from the small windows of the Post Office coaches. At the signal it came to a stop—the huge throbbing locomotive monstrous in the silence of the night. On the right-hand side the five masked men crouched behind the telephone box, waiting for the fireman to come from the engine to contact the signal box. They waited, but nothing happened.

Further back down the track Roy and Bill darted under the coupling between the second and third coaches, waiting for a signal to start. Buster went forward to see what had happened at the cab, and as he did so he saw the fireman, David Whitby, returning from the telephone on the left-hand side of the track.

"What's up, mate?" he asked Buster.

Buster beckoned.

Whitby crossed the two tracks which separated them. When he reached him Buster grabbed him, dragged him to the edge of the embankment and flung him down to where Alf and Bob were waiting.

"Hold him," said Buster.

Bob grabbed him by the legs, then leaped on him, gripping him around the neck with one arm and threatening him with a cosh in the other. "If you make a noise, son, you're fucking dead," he said.

"All right, mate," said Whitby. "I'm on your side."

"Good boy," said Bob. Then: "Where are you from?"

"Crewe," said Whitby.

"Well, when this is over, we'll send you some money."

Buster had no sooner disposed of Whitby than he ran towards the engine, shouting to the others on the other side of the track. He was about to cross over in front of the engine to tell them what had happened, when he saw the engine driver at the open door of the cab. Afraid that the driver would realise what was happening and start the train, Buster took out his cosh and ran to the steps. The door to the cab was ten feet above him, and as he climbed the rungs of the steel ladder the driver, Mills, started to kick at his hands. While hanging on with one hand, Buster hit at his legs with the cosh in the other. He made no headway until simultaneously Jim Hussey appeared behind him and with one push with his massive palm lifted Buster up into the cab. while Gordon, coming in from the other side, grabbed Mills from behind. As Gordon pinned his arms to his body Buster hit Mills twice over the head with the cosh. The blows opened his scalp and immediately blood poured over his face. Mills gave up the fight.

He was flung back into the driver's seat and left in the charge of Charlie who started to wipe away the blood with a rag. Buster climbed down out of the cab again to tell Roy and Bill to uncouple, while Gordon crept down the narrow passage which ran alongside the diesel engine to open the back cabin for the others.

Roy and Bill uncoupled in a few seconds. They unscrewed the vacuum pipe and hastily screwed on the cap to the loose end coming from the second coach. The steam pipe and the concertina-like covering between the coaches they left to break apart when the train was moved.

Now everyone climbed on board. Roger came down from the gantry, tripping at the bottom and cutting his leg on the metal frame. Roy, as he came out from under the coaches, was almost hit by another train which hurtled past: and the same train almost caught Frank who was hanging from the handles on the side of the engine. Jim, Tommy, Buster, Frank and Alf got into the back cab while Gordon, Roy and Roger climbed in at the front. Then the signal was given for old Stan to be brought on board. He came—followed by Ronnie Biggs just as Whitby was brought in on the other side. Mills was now lifted from the driver's seat and handcuffed to Whitby. They were dragged towards the corridor which connected the two cabs, and as this happened Stan saw the pale, blood-stained face of his fellow driver. He immediately started to tremble, and in this shaken state was pushed toward the driver's seat. With his pipe still in his mouth he sat at the controls. He put his foot on the driver's safety device and turned the handles to release the brakes and move the train; but while the engine roared behind them, it did not move.

"Move it," Gordon shouted at him.

Still trembling, Stan muttered inaudibly.

"Come on now, move it," Gordon shouted again.

"The vacuum," mumbled Stan. "I can't get the vacuum."

Gordon would not wait. He grabbed Stan by the shoulders and lifted him out of the seat. "Get out of it," he said. And then turned to Bob Welch. "Get the other driver," he said. He went with Bob to the corridor. The handcuffs were unlocked and Mills, still white in the face and covered in blood but conscious, was thrust back into the driver's seat.

"Move this train," said Gordon, "or you'll get some more stick."

"All right," said Mills, "I'll do it."

He sat at the controls: again the engine roared but the train stayed still.

"Move this fucking train," said Gordon in his growling, menacing voice.

"Come on, old girl, come on," said Mills.

"Get on with it," said Gordon.

"Hang on," he said. "We've got to wait for the vacuum . . ." As he spoke, the train started to move forward. The steam pipe and the concertina covering between the coaches were torn apart and slowly the engine with the front two coaches moved down the line.

Charlie was now beside Mills, identifiable to the others because of the bright blue eyes behind the balaclava mask. "Don't worry, mate," he said to him. "No one's going to hurt you now."

Gordon had gone to the cabin door and was hanging from it looking for the marker. He saw it and shouted to Mills to stop. The train stopped, but still short of the marker. "On," Gordon shouted. The train lurched forward. "O.K. stop," shouted Gordon. The train stopped, still short of the marker. "On again," he said.

"Well, make up your minds," said Mills.

The third time it stopped, they were exactly at the marker and there by the bridge were John and Bruce.

"Well done, chaps," said Bruce, "well done."

Now the moment came for the coach. Mills and Whitby were handcuffed together again and taken by Alf to lie face down on the embankment. "You can smoke if you like," Alf said to them.

Whitby took out a cigarette and offered one to Mills. Mills refused but Alf asked for one and as they were lighting up Whitby noticed the army lorry and a Land Rover by the bridge below. Then Alf told them that it was over they would both get a few quid. "But keep your mouths shut," he said. "There are some right bastards here."

Bruce told Ronnie to take Stan back to the Land Rover; and then, with the supernumeraries out of the way, the gang started their assault on the coach. While someone shouted "get the guns", to frighten the sorters, Buster picked up an axe and went to the rear of the coach where steam was pouring out of the broken tube. With Gordon behind him, he started to hack at the wood around the lock. Meanwhile Charlie was lifted by Frank to the level of the window, which he started to break with his cosh. Further down the coach Tommy Wisbey had gone beserk with the enormous crow-bar smashing the windows, but Charlie's cosh was more effective and he was first into the coach, followed almost immediately by Frank.

The first thing he saw was a group of men piling sacks of mail against the door. Charlie ran at them with his cosh raised: they ran past him back down the coach where Frank whipped them across the shoulders and told them all to lie face down. There was no resistance: they did as they were told, and as they did so the door burst open and Buster was in followed by Gordon. They ran to the other end to ensure that the sorters were subdued, then back to the cage by the door where the Ulsterman had told them the money would be. Bill now took the axe from Buster and with a single blow smashed the padlock. Gordon pulled open the door, dragged out a sack and cut it open with his sheath-knife. He took out an HVP and cut it open: it was packed tight with bundles of money.

"This is it," he said.

Immediately the others who had climbed into the coach behind Buster, Gordon and Bill, now jumped down again onto the track. Buster pulled the first bags from the cage and threw them down onto the track: the others formed a chain down the embankment ending with Jim Hussey on the concrete block and Bob Welch on the lorry.

The bags were heavy. Roger, who was next in line to Roy, could hardly keep up with the others. Luckily he was standing at the top of the embankment so he had only to push them on and roll them down towards Jim Hussey. Even Roy, who was exceptionally fit, and giants like Charlie, Gordon and Jim, were quickly exhausted by the effort; yet they were all part of a machine—they could not stop. Only Ronnie Biggs and old Stan, sitting in the Land Rover and seeing the train and the men silhouetted against the dawn sky, were detached from what was happening and realised its enormity.

All at once Bruce shouted "that's enough", for though there were still six sacks left in the cage, their time was up. Buster jumped down off the train. Gordon went to fetch Alf, and together they brought the handcuffed driver and fireman back into the HVP coach, ordering them to lie down by the sorters. "Now don't move for half an hour or we'll be back," said Alf.

With that the whole gang went down to the lorry and the Land Rovers. They rode in the same vehicles as before, the heavies in the second Land Rover, except for Bob Welch who remained on the back of the lorry. As it turned onto the road, he saw in its headlights a bag which had been dropped at the bottom of the embankment, but it was too late to stop and pick it up. The convoy was on its way.

Bob sat back on the sacks of money. Shortly after they had started, Jimmy White climbed through to the back saying that the load was too far forward and had to be more evenly distributed. They moved the sacks, and Jimmy climbed back into the cab. The sky was now bright with the dawn: it was a magnificent sight to accompany the exhilaration they felt now that the job had come off. Bob started to recite Omar Khayyam to himself—

> Awake! for Morning in the Bowl of Night
> Has flung the Stone that puts the Stars to Flight
> And Lo! the Hunter of the East has caught
> The Sultan's Turret in a Noose of Light.

He had memorised a number of stanzas, but before he had reached the last he had fallen asleep.

It was now almost light, but as yet they had passed no traffic on the road. All they saw was a single airman, walking back to his camp. In the front Land Rover Roger held one of the VHF radios, tuned in to the frequency of the Buckinghamshire constabulary. No message of any kind came over the air, and as time went on he started to worry, thinking that perhaps the radio was faulty, or that he was tuned in to the wrong frequency. As they waited to turn into the road which led past the farm from Long Crendon to Oakley, two cars went by. They reached the track leading up to the farm, and just as they turned into it the radio came alive with a call to all cars. A train had been robbed near Linslade.

As a precaution Buster and Jim jumped out of the second Land Rover and hid in a ditch by the cow-shed at the foot of the track, to make sure they had not been followed. They were both nervous and exhausted. Jim looked at his hands and saw that the sweat had shrunk his black velvet gloves so that they now only covered half his hands. Suddenly Buster saw something flutter in the wind, and in his over-wrought state he imagined it to be a projectile which was following a bugging device hidden in one of the sacks. He panicked and ran up the quarter-mile to the farm with Jim behind him. As they reached the farm, the last sacks were being unloaded from the lorry. Buster ran in to warn the others that something was coming up the track, but Gordon was already at an upstairs window with binoculars and saw that there was nothing. Nor would he have cared in particular if there had been a police car coming up the track, so confident was he after what they had achieved. There was a stack of pick-axe handles by the door; they were strong enough to deal with anything which could now be sent against them.

Outside the farm Jim threw off the last two sacks and then closed the tailboard of the lorry. Alf backed it into the garage and covered its protruding bonnet with a tarpaulin. The Land Rovers were already parked out of sight, so when they closed the door of the farmhouse there was no way of knowing from either the air or the road that it was occupied.

They were all now totally exhausted. Roy went straight upstairs, fell onto his air mattress and went to sleep. John and Gordon remained by the bedroom window, John now with his binoculars, Gordon with the radio and his bottle of whisky. Every now and then a message would come through from the Buckinghamshire police as different units were told about the robbery. "You won't believe this," said one policeman, "but they've stolen a train." Then he turned the dial and there was suddenly was Tony Bennett singing "It's the good life", which seemed to them all so appropriate that they too started to sing "It's the good life"; for downstairs in the living-room Buster, Charlie, Tommy and Roger were unpacking the money; from one sack after another came bundles and bundles of bank-notes.

There were one hundred and twenty sacks. They were opened in the kitchen by Tommy and the HVPs thrown into the living-room where they were cut open by Buster and Charlie. Then Roger made piles of the money—five-pound notes on one side, one-pound notes and ten-shilling notes on the other, with a special pile for Scottish and Irish money. The five-pound notes were in packets of two-and-a-half thousand, the pounds in packets of five hundred and the ten-shilling notes in packets of two hundred and fifty pounds. While Roger was stacking it against the walls, old Stan came in with a cup of tea. He looked at the money and said to Roger, "I suppose you lot are used to this sort of thing."

When the bags were empty, Roger and Charlie counted the money. There was £1,200,000 in five-pound notes, and £1,300,000 in one-pound and ten-shilling notes, making a total of around £2,500,000. Although they had expected double the number of sacks, and double the amount of money, most of the gang were so staggered when they heard this sum and saw the wall of bank-notes reaching to the ceiling that they went quite mad. Charlie jumped up and down and pointed to a sack of money saying: "Look at that, Bobbikins. There's eighty grand in that pile," while some of the others took old pound notes and used them to light their cigarettes. Then they remembered the Germans.

Sigi had remained upstairs with Jim Hussey who had told him of their success; if £2,000,000 was handed over to him, as he expected, it would leave only £500,000 for the rest—whacks of less than £30,000. It was therefore quite evident to Bruce and Buster that the Germans would have to take less. The others hovered around waiting to see what was decided: eventually Bruce proposed that the Germans should take £1,000,000 which would leave whacks of around £90,000 for them.

There was some argument—especially from Frank Munroe and Bob Welch—but even £90,000 seemed to them all to be such an enormous sum of money that they could not put much force into their objections. Sigi was therefore called downstairs and told that since the robbery had raised half of what was expected, his firm would have to take half of what they were promised. Sigi said nothing; nor did his face express any feelings either of anger or disappointment. All he asked was that his share, because of its size, should be in five-pound notes.

This too caused some trouble after he had gone back to his room, but Bruce and Buster insisted that it was the least they could do for him: Roger and Charlie therefore counted out £1,000,000 in five-pound notes before laying out eighteen sacks—one for each of those present at the farm and one each for Brian Field and the Ulsterman. Only when Buster came back into the room and saw the eighteen sacks did he ask why there were so many.

"There's an extra one for Stan," said Roger.

"He's not on a whack," said Buster. "He's on a drink of twenty grand."

"Ronnie said he was on a whack."

Buster spoke to Bruce who removed the eighteenth sack—embarrassed that Biggs should have tried this on. Then they started to pull out the drinks that had previously been agreed: £20,000 for Stan; £12,000 for Lennie Field; and £10,000 for Joey Gray who was to bring up the horse-box. After these had been taken off the top, they started to fill the seventeen sacks—stopping when there was £90,000 in each and only a pile of Scottish and Irish money with some ten-shilling notes which no one seemed to want.

People were either called down to receive their share or it was taken up to them. Roy who had been sleeping was woken up by Charlie bringing him his £90,000 in two kit bags and a suitcase. Ronnie and Stan took theirs upstairs, and while they did so Bruce, who was still angry with Ronnie for trying to get a full whack for Stan, told Buster to go up and steal back ten thousand pounds.

"Leave off, Bruce," said Buster. "How can you do that?"

"Go on," he said, "He's a horrible bastard."

So while Bruce called Ronnie and Stan down again, Buster sneaked up and nicked ten thousand from Ronnie Biggs's mail bag. It was mostly in ten-shilling notes and was put aside to pay Brian Field's friend Mark who was to clean up the farm after they had gone.

Until that time came, there was nothing to do but wait.

6. Flight from the Farm

At Sears' Crossing the guard of the mail train waited for his train to resume its journey until he noticed from the gauge in his van that the vacuum had been released from the braking system. He then climbed down onto the track and walked up towards the engine to see what had gone wrong, only to find after the tenth coach that the train had disappeared. After he had recovered from his astonishment he ran to the telephone by the gantry but found that the wires were cut. He returned to his van and followed the safety procedures for such an eventuality by taking detonators and placing them on the rails a thousand yards behind the train.

He walked back to the front of the train and then on down the line in search of the missing engine and coaches. He found them at Bridego Bridge. He climbed onto the HVP coach where he found his fireman and driver, the latter with dried blood on his face, and the five Post Office sorters. Together they got out of the coach and waved down a train travelling south on the slow line. At Cheddington they telephoned Euston to give the news of the theft. The duty officer at Euston telephoned the Metropolitan Police at Scotland Yard who in turn telephoned the information room of the Buckinghamshire County Police in Aylesbury. It was now one and a half hours after the raid.

By five o'clock that morning the Assistant Chief Constable of the Buckinghamshire police was at the track, accompanied by the head of the Buckinghamshire CID, Malcolm Fewtrell, the son and the brother of policemen, who took charge of the case. He gathered together what clues there were—the blood-stained cloth, a railwayman's cap, the broken coupling—and appointed an exhibits officer to take charge of them. He then went to Cheddington Station and took statements from the eighty-odd men who had been on the train. No one—not even Mills, the driver, Whitby, the fireman, or the five sorters from the HVP coach—could tell him anything besides the sparse facts of what they had experienced. Nor was it clear at this stage just how much money had been in the stolen mail bags.

Detective Superintendent Fewtrell, an able and conscientious policeman, recognised at once that the investigation of a robbery of this size would be beyond the resources of a provincial police force. Later that morning, therefore, he advised his Chief Constable to "call in the Yard"—that is, to apply for assistance from the CID of the Metropolitan Police; and later that day he went to London to attend a meeting which had been called in the headquarters of the Post Office.

Present at that meeting were officials of the Post Office; Frank Cook, the senior Post Office investigator; and George Hatherill, deputy chief of the CID at Scotland Yard. Cook told them that as much as three and a half million pounds might have been stolen; while the police had to confess that as yet they could only guess at the identities of the criminals. All they knew was that about fifteen men had been involved, and that the fireman, Whitby, had noticed an army lorry parked by the bridge.

Commander Hatherill agreed to send down two detectives—Gerald McArthur, who was at the conference, and Jack Pritchard—which seemed to Fewtrell and the Buckinghamshire police somewhat meagre assistance for a major crime. They returned to Aylesbury, reaching police headquarters at eleven that night.

They started work with what they had got. The Criminal Records Office in London had come up with a list of men known by them to be capable of a robbery of this kind; but evidence had to be found to connect them with the crime itself. The three detectives tried to imagine what they would have done if they had been the thieves—whether they would have driven to London or Birmingham on the motorway; or whether they would have found somewhere to hide out. The next morning they resumed their conjecture and it was Pritchard who fastened on the fact that as the thieves had left the train they had told the men in the HVP coach not to move "for half an hour". This suggested that they were at that moment hiding out within half an hour's drive of

Bridego Bridge.

They decided to back this theory, and use all their resources of men and propaganda to search for a possible hiding-place within a radius of thirty miles from the scene of the crime. Every policeman from Buckinghamshire, and from neighbouring forces, was to be mobilised in the search of barges, houses and barns within the area; and through radio, television and the newspapers the public was asked to recall either the movement of army vehicles on the night of Wednesday 7 August, or unusual activities in remote dwellings.

At Leatherslade Farm the news came over the radio at mid-day on the Thursday that army vehicles were thought to have been used in the robbery of the train. It caused some dismay. The lorry and the Land Rovers could not now be used again: only Jimmy White, who had spent the morning with Alf making a false bottom in the lorry, and fixing civilian plates back on to the Land Rovers, would not give up hope and started to paint the cab of the lorry with yellow paint to imitate the markings of a brick company.

Roger awoke in the early afternoon. He went to the bathroom to wash the smuts from his face and the dried blood from his leg. He then changed into the jacket and trousers that he had brought with him, took £3,000 from his share of the money, and came downstairs into the living-room. He gave his old clothes to Ronnie Biggs who was burning incriminating evidence in the stove. He made himself a cup of tea and a boiled egg and then sat down to watch the others.

They were all edgy. It had once been thought wisest to wait at the farm until the Sunday, when Joey Gray would arrive with the horse-box; but now no one wanted to stick to that plan. The possibility that they were hiding in a farmhouse had been discussed on the radio, and it suddenly seemed absurd to sit on their money for three more days while the police searched for them. The fact that they could no longer use the vehicles that had brought them there provoked slight panic: they were trapped in the middle of nowhere. Only Roger, Buster, Bruce and Gordon had prepared contingency plans—Roger with his bike and the room in Oxford; Bruce with Mary Manson; and Gordon and Buster with Brian Field.

Sensing that the others would not stop him, Roger announced his decision to leave, and since no one objected, he wheeled out his bike and cycled off down the track toward the road. Soon after he had left, Bruce announced to the others that there was a change of plan. They would not wait until the Sunday but would leave on the following day—the Friday. Everyone was pleased with this decision, and they set to work to clean up the farm. They wiped down all the surfaces and burnt all the clothes and shoes that had been worn on the raid—either in the kitchen stove or on a bonfire which Jimmy White lit in the garden. They also tried to burn the mail bags on this bonfire, but the canvas seemed to be impregnated with a chemical which made a thick, black smoke. They returned instead to the hole Bruce had started to dig in the garden.

Old Stan, still nervous because of his failure to drive the train, saw them digging the hole and went trembling to Ronnie Biggs. "They're going to kill me," he said. "Look, they're digging a grave." Ronnie brought up Bruce to reassure him, and soon the whole gang was laughing at his fears.

The masks and some mail bags were thrown into the hole but it was not big enough for them all, so the rest of the mail bags were taken down to the cellar. Frank suggested setting fire to the farm as they left, but the idea was turned down because the fire would draw it to the attention of the police. They remained confident in the arrangements made through Brian Field to have the place cleaned up after they had gone: after all, it was Field who had arranged the purchase of the farm, and so it was in his interest that it should never be linked with the robbery.

Roger cycled slowly along the country lanes which led from Brill to Oxford. There was no sign of the police and he reached the city at eight in the evening. Although his wife's friends had said they would book a room for him, he did not want to turn up without any luggage on a bicycle. He therefore stopped at a commercial hotel and booked himself in for one night. He made telephone calls to Brian Field and Mary Manson on behalf of Gordon and Bruce, and then to the bank manager in London whom he used to pass stolen money into his bank account.

In a stuttering, trembling voice, his accomplice told Roger that he wanted nothing more to do with him. Somewhat shaken, Roger went out into the street and bought an evening paper which gave the reason why. Already their "tickle" was called the "biggest ever mail robbery". Thirty masked and armed thugs, according to the press, had got away with up to a million pounds. He was amused by the inaccuracy, but realised how much more difficult such a furore would make it for him. The police knew that he was part of a gang which stopped trains; and thinking that his talents were unique in the criminal world, he assumed that they would already be looking for him.

What he needed now was another accomplice—someone straight—who would help him hide the money. In his mind he reviewed a list of his friends—rejecting some because they were thieves themselves and might take the money, and others because they were too honest and would realise what he had done, until at last he settled on an old friend of his called Bill Boal.

Boal was perfect for his purpose. Originally from Durham, he had come to London at the age of sixteen and had trained as an engineer. He was short, stocky, strong, quarrelsome and eccentric. Although he was excellent at his work, he could never successfully work for others or have others work for him. He hated Trades Unions and whenever he was employed he would refuse to join one, even if the particular factory had a closed-shop.

He and Roger had met just after the war when they were both living in Kingston and played snooker together. Later Bill came to lodge with Roger and his mother in Hampton Court. At the end of 1948, Bill, quite independently of Roger, had had his first and only excursion into crime. He had bought some stolen clothes and re-sold them to a fence, together with a dress suit that Roger had given him. The fence was raided by the police, the clothes were traced back to Bill and both Bill and Roger were arrested. The charges against Roger were later dropped but Bill was tried and sentenced to eighteen months.

After that the two friends had lost touch with one another, but had met again at a dog track in the late 1950s and resumed their friendship. Bill by this time had married. His wife was a strong-minded London girl called Rene. They had three children, whom he loved very much. If they were ill, it was always Bill who cared for them; if they had to be taken to the dentist or to the hospital, it was their father who went with them. He was still prejudiced and eccentric, but also warm-hearted and gregarious. He was loved not just by his children but by his neighbours in Fulham.

Bill by now had his own engineering workshop in East Sheen and made a modest living tooling components for larger firms. He himself had gone straight since his spell in prison, but he knew that Roger mixed with criminals and this fascinated him. He had fantasies himself of big-time crime and half hoped that one day Roger would involve him. He also knew about Roger's passion for gambling; he would occasionally lend him money, and at the time of the train robbery was owed five hundred and fifty pounds.

It was the opportunity of getting this loan repaid that Roger used as a bait when he telephoned Bill from Oxford on the Thursday night. He told him that if he came to Oxford the next day, and helped him with some business, Roger would be in a position to repay the full amount. Bill Boal agreed to come.

Having arranged an accomplice, Roger now went round to see the friends of his wife who had promised to find him a room. They gave him a drink and told him that they had arranged accommodation with a Mrs Pope of 28 Edith Road. Roger said that he would go there the next day, and returned to his hotel for the night.

Brian Field's dark-blue Jaguar was seen coming up the track to Leatherslade Farm just as it was getting dark. With him came his wife Karin. He reported that though the whole country was in an uproar as a result of the robbery, there was no sign of the police in the vicinity of the farm. Bruce, Gordon and Buster took him aside and told him that they had decided to leave the farm the next day, but because they could not use the military vehicles, they needed his help. They asked him to take Roy to London that night, and return next day with two vans which Gordon and Buster could use to transport his share and the Ulsterman's to Brian's house near Pangbourne. Brian had never intended to be so closely involved with the robbery itself, but now, under pressure, he had no choice but to comply. Roy was given some money by Buster to buy the vans, and set off with the Fields, while the others settled down to eat a large omelette.

Later that night Roy returned to the farm with his Jaguar. Kit bags filled with half the Germans' million pounds were packed into the cavernous boot which Roy had specially prepared, and he set off again to make a dash back to Buster's empty flat in Twickenham (June had gone to stay with Derek Glass) where Sigi was to hide out until they could get him out of the country. He returned at three in the morning to fetch Sigi and the other £500,000. On the road back to London he drove so fast that the silent, inscrutable German trembled with terror, but he was delivered safely to Buster's flat where Roy helped him stack the kit bags in the kitchen and showed him where he could sleep.

Bruce and Buster had told him to stay with Sigi, but Roy was determined to put in an appearance at his garage in case any curious friends dropped by, and to telephone from there to Joey Gray to bring the horse-box to Leatherslade Farm. He therefore left the German to his own devices and drove on to Battersea.

Everyone rose early back at Leatherslade Farm on the Friday morning. Bruce and John set out at once on foot to hitch-hike to Tring. Later in the morning Roger returned in a Wolsey he had bought second-hand in Oxford. He had with him the morning paper in which they were front page news, but he told them that there was still no sign of any police in the area. Frank Munroe asked if he would take care of some of his whack; Jimmy White wanted a lift into Oxford and Roger agreed to do both. They drove first to his lodgings at 28 Edith Road, where Jimmy helped him carry the suitcases into the front room, and then out to Black Bourton to buy a Rover which had been advertised for sale in the morning paper. Roger then drove back to his lodgings in the Rover. Jimmy White returned to the farm in the Wolsey which he handed over to Alf who loaded it with his money and set off for London.

Bruce and John returned that evening with Mary Manson with her Ford Cortina and two Austin Healey sports cars. They found the rest of the gang impatient to leave: the news had come over the radio that the police were searching all isolated properties within a radius of thirty miles. The Fields had not turned up with the vans, nor Joey Gray with the horse-box, and Roy had not returned with his Jaguar.

Bruce took charge of his own staff: he gave the first Healey to Jimmy White who packed his money into the boot and set off for London. John and Stan piled into the Cortina, Ronnie Biggs and Bruce into the second Healey, and they all set off for Redhill. They reached Ronnie's flat late at night and found his anxious wife: for while he had been away his brother had died and she had asked the Wiltshire police to find him. They had searched every lumber camp in the county without tracing either Ronnie Biggs or Stan Agate.

The dipped headlights of three vehicles were spied from Leatherslade Farm soon after sunset. The first was Brian Field's

Jaguar, driven by his wife Karin; the second and third two vans driven by Brian and Mark — the silver-haired business man who had first introduced the Ulsterman and who had undertaken to clean up the farm. Gordon, Buster and Jim Hussey immediately started to load their money, along with the money for Brian, Lennie, Mark and the Ulsterman, into the back of one of the vans; Charlie and Bill, despairing of both Roy and Joey Gray, started to load their bags into the other. It was only then that the other three from the second firm — Tommy, Bob and Frank — realised that they were about to be left behind with no means of escape.

They too started to load their money into the vans and said that they were coming with the others to Brian Field's house at Whitchurch Hill. Brian Field went pale at the thought of these three unknown thugs coming to his respectable suburban home; quivering with anxiety and outrage, he told them it was quite impossible, that they would give them all away: but Gordon and Buster insisted that he take them along, and faced with this resolve of eight massive, determined and now anxious men, there was little that the plump, perspiring solicitor's clerk could do. He shrugged his shoulders and got into the Jaguar next to his pretty wife who was apparently more collected than he was.

The column pulled out at half-past eleven leaving Leatherslade Farm deserted. Gordon went in the first of the two vans and communicated with the others by walkie-talkie: the route he and Buster had chosen from the ordnance survey maps was even more obscure than that from the farm to the bridge. They avoided all main roads — at one time driving through a cornfield — and reached the Fields' house, "Kabri" (the name formed from the first syllables of their two names), an hour later. One of the vans was backed into the garage; the other parked on the drive in front of the house, while Brian left his Jaguar in the narrow lane outside. The money was unloaded into the garage and the ten men and one woman crammed into the small house. Gordon, who knew his way around, went upstairs to commandeer the spare bed while the others lay down to sleep on the sofa, the armchairs and the floor.

Throughout that day Roy had failed to reach Joey Gray to alert him to the change of plan. He was so eager to appear to be leading his normal life that he did not dare to leave the garage. When it closed he went to the flat of his mechanic, Bobby Pelham, and persuaded him to hide £500 of his money: then, before setting off back to the farm, he slumped onto a bed intending to sleep for half an hour before leaving.

He was so exhausted by now that he slept for five hours: when he awoke it was a quarter to eleven. He ran down to the Jaguar and drove fast to the farm, but there was no one waiting by the gate and no sign of life. He was afraid that the police might be waiting for him, but he also had to be sure that his friends were no longer there. With his lights switched off he drove slowly up the lane and approached the farm itself ready to storm through onto the track on the other side if the police had laid a trap; but when he reached the yard there was no one there. The lorry and the Land Rovers stood in the garages and shed, but his friends had gone. With no means of knowing where they were, Roy could do nothing but return to London and wait for a call.

Roger's old friend Bill Boal kept his appointment at Oxford's Public Library on Friday afternoon. Roger took him back to his lodgings at 28 Edith Road and showed Bill the suitcases, but refused to tell him what they contained. "I need to take them somewhere safe," he said, "and if you can think of a place, then I'll be in a position to pay you back that money."

Bill Boal racked his brains to think of anyone who might help them and eventually remembered a family in Bournemouth. It was too late to leave that day, so Bill prepared to spend the night in an upstairs bedroom. Roger asked him to take two of the suitcases with him, and as he staggered up the stairs with them Bill Boal asked: "What's inside them, Roger? Lead?"

Roger did not reply, but Bill must have suspected that it was something at least as valuable as lead; for later that evening he found himself alone in Roger's room on the ground floor and saw a pile of five-pound notes on the sideboard. Uncertain as to whether Roger would really repay his debt, Bill Boal decided to recover some of it there and then: he took thirty of the five-pound notes and put them in his pocket. The pile was not noticeably diminished.

The next morning they drove down to Bournemouth in Roger's Rover, leaving the suitcases in their lodgings. The journey of eighty miles took almost three hours, and it was an hour before Bill could find the street where his friends were supposed to live. While Roger remained in the car, he went to the door of the house and returned a few minutes later to say that they had moved away several years before.

Fed up with his friend, Roger decided that since they were there they had might as well find somewhere in Bournemouth to hide the money, so using Bill as a front he rented a holiday flat above a florist. As they drove out of Bournemouth Roger told Bill that he was to come up to Oxford next day with his wife and three children, and they would all drive down to Bournemouth with the suitcases. Bill agreed to the plan so Roger dropped him at Winchester station to take a train to London while Roger drove on to Oxford.

The incongruous household at "Kabri" rose early that Saturday morning. The first to leave were Tommy, Frank, Bob and Jim Hussey who were driven by Brian Field into Reading. There they paid out cash for a second-hand car and a van, bought some suitcases, and returned to "Kabri" for their money. As soon as it was loaded in the van, they set off in convoy for the south coast.

Charlie and Bill, meanwhile, were waiting for a call from Roy, while back in London Roy was waiting for them to call him. Eventually they made contact with one another through Brian Field, and Roy came to fetch them in his Mini Cooper. They returned later that day to fetch their money from "Kabri" and drove it to Charlie's stow in the East End. Bill went off with his entire whack but Roy left most of his with Charlie's, drawing out £20,000 for immediate expenses and for what he felt to be a debt of honour. He drove Charlie back to Clapham and then went on to Micky Ball's home in Fulham, where he delivered £12,500.

On the Saturday afternoon Derek Glass appeared at "Kabri" to fetch Buster with his own wife as well as June and their children in the car. June sat clutching her daughter Nicki in a permanent state of terror, while Buster, as jovial as ever, packed the suitcases containing his £90,000 into the boot of the car along with the ostentatious display of fishing-rods and plastic buckets which had been laid on by Derek Glass.

The two families returned to Derek Glass's house in Kingston upon Thames. It was from here that Buster telephoned Karl in Cologne to tell him that there had been a change of plan. Sigi and their money were in London, and the boat had been cancelled. Buster could hide Sigi but he had no means of getting him out of the country.

Karl sounded calm. He told Buster to call him again in two days' time. Buster now drove to St Margaret's Road where he found Sigi looking white and shaken. Buster told him that it would not be safe for him to remain where he was — the flat where they had planned the robbery — so he would move him to another place off the Old Kent Road until Karl had arranged his escape. Sigi was in no position to argue, and he even accepted that the £1,000,000 should be taken from him and hidden in Charlie's lock-up garage in the East End until the time came for his departure. These moves were made on the Saturday night.

Gordon was now the only Train Robber to remain with Brian and Karin Field, for he did not trust Brian and was determined not to depart until he had himself given the Ulsterman his share of the money. He spent Saturday evening watching television, switching from channel to channel to catch all the news about what was already being called "the most daring mail robbery of all time" or more simply "the Great Train Robbery". It was now known that £2,600,000 had been stolen, and much was being made of the battered driver Mills; but the police as yet seemed to have neither suspects nor clues.

On Sunday afternoon the Ulsterman arrived, driven by Mark in a small, grey Austin van which he parked by the garage. While Mark came into the house to see Brian Field, Gordon came out to the van and talked to the Ulsterman who told him that they had come through no road-blocks. The Ulsterman did not get out of the van until Mark came to load the money: then he opened the rear doors and lifted a false bottom from the floor of the van. Gordon untied the first kit bag and started to pass in bundles of bank-notes which the Ulsterman accepted with an impassive expression on his face. He did not ask how much was there or show any emotion whatsoever: he simply packed it tightly into the compartment under the floor of the van.

Gordon, however, was moved by the occasion: it made him happy to think that after so many meetings, over so many months, the whole thing had come off so well. The information had been superb and they in their turn had used it successfully with detailed planning and minimal force. It was almost the perfect crime.

When the money had been stowed away, the Ulsterman replaced the false floor on the van and Gordon shook hands with their informant for the last time. He thanked him, saying how happy they all had been at the outcome, and how without him the job could never have been done. Then the two men parted and Mark and the Ulsterman drove away.

It was only when the first firm were back in London and relieved of the claustrophobia they had felt at Leatherslade Farm, that they realised how dangerous it would be if the police found the farm in the state in which they had left it. They realised too that they were taking an enormous risk in trusting Mark, a man whom none of them knew, to clean it up after them.

On the Monday morning Charlie rang Brian Field at his office and asked him cryptically: "Has the dustman been?" Brian reassured him in his sycophantic voice that everything had been taken care of, but Charlie was not satisfied and rang around to arrange a meet with the others. This was not particularly easy: Buster could only be contacted through Derek Glass, and there was a complex code whereby if the meet was said to be at a certain underground station at a certain time, they would assemble an hour later outside a station one down the line.

The meet was called for five at Clapham North: so at six they came together outside Clapham Common underground station — Bruce, John, Buster, Charlie, Roy — the inner circle of the first firm with only Gordon and Jim Hussey absent. They discussed the farm. Roy and Charlie both insisted that they could not rely on Mark and Brian Field to clean it up. They must go back and make sure themselves that the job had been done; and if it had not, do it there and then. Roy was particularly anxious because he had not worn gloves, never envisaging that the police might find the farm: but even those who had been more careful were aware of how little was required by a good forensic scientist or fingerprint expert to link a man to a place. Buster, for example, had left a pair of trousers and a pair of shoes at the farm, together with two blankets from the house he had rented in St Margaret's Road.

They decided to call Brian Field to a meet the next morning outside Holland Park underground station. The same group was there, and as soon as they saw Brian Field their hearts fell into their stomachs. His usual manner of smooth confidence had deserted him; his plump face was white with anxiety. He told them at once that he could not now be sure that the farm had been cleared. Charlie leapt on him and might have killed the cringing clerk had he not been restrained by the others. Brian Field looked as if he expected no better. He repeated that he had been let down; that Mark had promised that he would see to the farm. He apologised to them all, but pointed out that if the police found the farm he would be the first to be arrested.

"If it happens," he said, "and I get pulled, I swear that I'll never say anything. I'll never make a statement. I'll never put any of you in it, and all I ask in return is that you look after my wife."

They all knew what had to be done: they had to return at once to Leatherslade Farm and remove from it anything that might be associated with the robbery. They arranged to meet that afternoon at Hanger Lane in West London: in the meantime they went home to change into more suitable clothes and try and round up some of the others to go with them.

Roy went first to Battersea for his Jaguar; he then picked up Charlie in Clapham and drove him to Whitechapel so that he could change his clothes in the garage. They set off back across London, and as they drove up Western Avenue towards Hanger Lane the news came over the radio that mail bags and military vehicles had been found in a farmhouse near Brill.

Roy turned to Charlie. "We're nicked," he said.

Bruce, John and Buster were waiting for them: they too had heard the news. There was little they could say in the street, so they drove out to Staines and stopped outside a small café which Roy liked because it reminded him of France. They sat there at a table together, discussing what could be done. Even now, Charlie would not admit defeat. He wanted to wait until dark and go to the farm and burn it down, but the others all knew that it was useless. Having found such a treasure trove of evidence, the police were unlikely to leave it undefended. All they could do now was either front it out and live as usual, or go on the run at once. Each one had to choose for himself and act alone. Realising how much more likely it now was that they would not remain free to enjoy the life that the money promised them, they felt utterly dejected; but they were saddened too because more certainly and more immediately they were to lose each other's companionship. As they left the café outside Staines station, they shook hands for what they knew might be the last time.

Part Two **Retribution**

7. Arrests

With nothing better to go on than the single clue — "don't move for half an hour" — Malcolm Fewtrell of Buckinghamshire CID and Gerald McArthur of Scotland Yard had mobilised all the forces at their disposal to search for a hide-out within thirty miles of Bridego Bridge. They realised that the thieves might have tuned in to their wave-lengths, and ordered radio silence: but they deliberately told the press about what they were doing in the hope that the gang might be panicked into a premature departure. They also wanted to recruit the public to help with the search — not just for a farm or a cottage but for the army lorry and Land Rover that the fireman Whitby had seen from the bridge.

There were other lines of investigation. Detective Chief Superintendent Elwell of the Hertfordshire police had suggested asking estate agents about any likely properties which had recently been bought or rented. It was a small force to investigate such a large crime, and already by the Sunday there was criticism that Scotland Yard had responded to the challenge by sending only two detectives. The *Sunday Express* quoted the complaints of anonymous police officers: "We have nothing against country police, but how can you compare them to the Flying Squad?" It also reported that the police were re-reading their dossiers on "three of the best organised robberies in the history of British crime" — a £250,000 mail van robbery in 1952, a £250,000 bullion theft in Finsbury; and "the £62,000 payroll snatch at London Airport last year".

Even before the week-end information came tumbling in both to Scotland Yard and to police headquarters in Aylesbury, while in London there were many unofficial enquiries. The intuition, experience and contacts of policemen had often proved more reliable than the computer at the Criminal Records Office. Detective Chief Superintendent Millen, the chief of the Flying Squad, was approached in a London Club by a barrister whose client, now in a provincial prison, would talk to the police in exchange for certain privileges if the police could ensure that it never leaked out.

Ernie Millen and George Hatherill, Commander of C Department, went to visit the informer in prison and coaxed him into giving out information: much of it was only rumour, but it seemed to confirm the theory that the mail train had been robbed by a London gang. It also prompted Hatherill to appoint another senior detective to lead the investigations in London.

Their choice was Tommy Butler, a dedicated, almost a fanatical, policeman who had risen quickly in the Metropolitan Police. He had been involved in the investigation of corrupt policemen in Brighton and such criminals as Jack Spot and Billy Hill. He had even been sent to Cyprus to try and find Colonel Grivas, the commander of Eoka. He was a small man, now aged fifty, with receding hair, dark eyebrows and a thin pointed nose like Mr Punch. He had never married and lived with his mother. He worked day and night to catch criminals and because of his experience in the Flying Squad — that autonomous elite of Scotland Yard detectives — he held in his head a list of thieves who would be capable of carrying out the Great Train Robbery.

While these London detectives were sifting through the slime of the London underworld, the country police were searching the outbuildings of Mentmore Park and a haystack near Cheddington. They went with tracker dogs to Rowden Farm and continued to dust down every corner of the diesel locomotive and the HVP coach for fingerprints; but there was nothing to be found. Then on Monday 12 August, the day Butler was appointed to head the London end of the investigation, a farm labourer called John Maris, who milked the cows in the shed at the foot of the lane, walked up to the field by the side of Leatherslade Farm to look at some of his cows. He knew that there were new owners and he now peered through the hedge to see if anyone was there.

He noticed first that the windows of the farmhouse had been blacked out by material, with only a corner turned back. He climbed through the hedge and once in the yard saw the lorry in the shed. It faced out towards the house, and though the bonnet had been daubed with yellow paint, it was recognisable as a five-ton army truck. He went to the garage door and saw that it was locked with a padlock. He walked round to the door of the farmhouse and found that that too was locked. Beside it on the ground there was a length of new rope.

Finding all this suspicious, John Maris went back on a tractor to his employer's house in Oakley. He rang the police and reported what he had seen and then returned to the cowshed to wait for them to arrive. He waited in vain. In Aylesbury they had more leads of this kind than they could cope with — up to 400 calls a day; but Maris was persistent and next morning he telephoned again. This time the message was relayed to the police station at Waddesdon, and Sergeant Blackman and Constable Wooley drove off to investigate. They found the lorry and, after they had broken into the garage, the two Land Rovers. They then went round to the front of the house, where they saw the ash of a bonfire and a half-dug hole.

They managed to open a window to the farmhouse and climb in. The first thing to strike them was the large amount of food stacked in the kitchen. They went upstairs and found sleeping-bags, blankets and some old clothes. They came down again and in the alcove under the stairs found a bag of potatoes and a crate of fruit. They pulled these back and saw the trapdoor leading to the cellar. Police Constable Wooley lifted it up: he went down the steps and found a heap of Post Office mail bags and the torn up paper wrappers bearing the markings of various banks. He picked up a bag and a wrapper and carried them up to his sergeant. They had found the hide-out.

While the constable remained at the farm, the sergeant went at once to telephone his superiors in Aylesbury. Malcolm Fewtrell was about to take Commander Hatherill to have lunch with his Chief Constable, but when the news came through that the farm had been found, they all set off towards Brill. As soon as they arrived Fewtrell and McArthur realised that this was certainly the hide-out they had been looking for: and furthermore, as Fewtrell said to his colleagues, "the whole place is one big clue".

Determined not to spoil the evidence (the fingerprints in the HVP coach had been jumbled with the tiny prints of curious children) Fewtrell immediately ordered a cordon of policemen to be placed round the farm, while Hatherill spoke to Scotland Yard and told the fingerprint experts to be prepared to come down the next day. Then Hatherill returned to Aylesbury and held an impromptu press conference to announce what they had found. Journalists were allowed a carefully supervised tour of Leatherslade Farm on the condition that they would keep away thereafter. A cordon was kept around the farm throughout the Tuesday night, and at dawn on Wednesday the experts arrived — Detective Superintendent Maurice Ray and his team from Scotland Yard's Fingerprint Department. They started work at once.

The day after the farm was found, Buster telephoned Karl to say that the sooner they could move Sigi the better. Karl had already made arrangements, and asked Buster to deliver Sigi and the money to St Katharine's wharf by Tower Bridge at mid-day on Thursday.

Buster's own money was with friends, but the Germans' £1,000,000 was in Charlie's stow in the East End. He drove down to Clapham to pick up Charlie, and as the two men drove east they discussed their chances of escaping detection and arrest. Buster's were better than Charlie's because he was not a "known associate" of either firm; Charlie, on the other hand, was linked with Roy who had not been wearing gloves at the farm and so was sure to have left prints. "It looks as if I'll have to go on the run," said Charlie. "Me, who's never been further than Southend."

"Remember the Germans," said Buster. "They promised to help."

"Yeah, but will they? Getting their own man out is one thing. Getting us out is another, unless we keep back some of their dough as insurance."

"That'd be naughty," said Buster. "Really naughty."

"But they'd have to help us, wouldn't they?"

By the time they reached Charlie's garage the idea of holding back some of the Germans' money had grown on them both and they counted out and crated only £500,000. The other £500,000 the split and kept half each for safe-keeping. They left the crate there to be collected on the Thursday and drove south to the Old Kent Road where Buster told Sigi that he was going out on Thursday, but with only half his money. Sigi seemed so pleased with the first news that he hardly noticed the second, and when Buster assured him that they would "bring it over later", he accepted it as a safe and sensible solution.

On the Thursday morning Roy and Charlie picked up the crate containing the £500,000 in a Ford Transit van while Buster fetched Sigi in his car. They met up near Tower Bridge where Sigi was transferred to the van. At mid-day they were parked outside the tall wooden gates of St Katharine's wharf when a docker came out, took the keys of the van from Roy and drove it through the gates: the van was returned ten minutes later but it was the last they saw of both Sigi and the £500,000. When Buster telephoned Karl two days later, he was told that both had reached their destination. Karl too appeared to accept that it was "safer" to split the £1,000,000. Buster told him that he would hold half of the remaining £500,000 and Charlie Wilson the other half; and that both consignments would be delivered when things had quietened down.

On the previous Sunday, August 11, Bill Boal had arrived in Oxford by train as he had promised with his wife Rene and their three children. Roger had met them at the station and driven them to 28 Edith Road where he paid for his room, and returned the keys to his landlady while Bill Boal loaded the heavy suitcases into the Rover.

They drove to Bournemouth — to all outward appearances a family on holiday together. Rene Boal was irritated with her husband for insisting on taking her to the seaside when she had not felt well that evening, and with Roger for making them come to Oxford when he could surely have fetched them from London. When they reached Bournemouth that afternoon, Rene and the children were dropped on the beach while Roger and Bill drove on to the flat above the florist's shop to unload the suitcases.

Bill now asked Roger for the money he owed him so that he could go back to London with his family. Roger gave him £200 but said that if he wanted the rest he would have to stay with him in Bournemouth. Since £200 of his debt was still outstanding, Bill Boal agreed and the two eccentric codgers returned to the beach for Rene and the children. He persuaded them that they must return to London without him, for only then would Roger pay the money he was owed. Rene was the dominant partner in the marriage and would not have allowed her husband to stay if she had not known that he was overdrawn at the bank by £650, so she herded her children into Roger's car and was driven to the station. Before she got on the train, Roger handed her a small, square parcel and asked her to deliver it to his sister Maisie in Hampton Court.

With Rene and the children out of the way, Roger and Bill returned to the flat. Roger's chief fear now was that the money would be stolen: since the flat they were in had no front door of its own he felt insecure, and so he decided that they would put the money in the boots of two second-hand cars — his money in one and Frank's in another — and hide them in rented garages. The next morning they both went to inspect a Ford Anglia, and while Roger stood in the background Bill Boal paid a deposit of £73.14s. with money that Roger had given him. They spent the rest of Monday looking for a flat or a house they could buy for cash, and only collected the Anglia on the Tuesday morning. They continued to study the notice-boards outside estate agents' offices until Roger saw in the evening paper that the police had found Leatherslade Farm.

Roger was confident that he had always worn gloves at the farm, and had left no other incriminating evidence, so the news did not alarm him. He continued with his plan to hide the money, and on Wednesday morning took Bill to buy an Austin van at the Northbourne Service Station. They then put some of the money in the Rover and locked it in a garage they had rented the day before, and using the Anglia as a runabout they started to look for a second garage where they could hide the van. Bill saw a card in a newsagent's window which advertised a lock-up garage and made an appointment to see the owner. She was a policeman's widow called Mrs Clark, and she was immediately suspicious of Bill Boal who boasted that he was going to start a business in Wimbourne where he could earn more than £5 an hour, and with no hesitation paid three months' rent in advance from a bundle of bank-notes.

Mrs Clark gave Bill the garage key, but no sooner had he left than she telephoned the police. Twenty minutes later Bill and Roger returned with the van in which they had loaded the rest of the money. Since Bill could not drive, Roger backed it into the garage while Bill came into Mrs Clark's kitchen just as there was a knock on the front door. Mrs Clark left the kitchen and opened the door to two plain-clothes detectives.

Roger had left the garage, and was walking away from the house, when he noticed the two men at the door talking to Mrs Clark. Bill too had seen them and slipped out of the back door to join Roger.

"Let's get out of here," said Roger.

The van was already locked in the garage, so Roger started walking back down the street, but Bill returned to the kitchen of Mrs Clark's house. "Are your friends still here?" he asked. "They looked like policemen."

The two detectives, meanwhile, had noticed Roger walking away and had followed him in their car. They stopped alongside him, leaped out and pounced on him, saying that they had seen him come out of a house whose owners were away and asking him to go with them to the station.

Roger tried to bluff them. "How do I know that you're police officers?" he asked. "Show me some identification."

This irritated the two detectives and they tried to bundle him into their car. Roger struggled to stop them and screamed for help on the off-chance that some passer-by might intervene and enable him to escape. Everyone ignored him except Bill Boal. He saw the scuffle but instead of running away he came up to the two detectives and asked what was going on.

Just at that moment another police car arrived, summoned by a neighbour who had seen the struggle. Roger and Bill were both handcuffed and taken to Bournemouth police station, Bill protesting all the while that he had never seen Roger before and did not know who he was. Roger doubted that he would get away with his denial, since they both had a key to the same flat, but to help his friend he asked to go to the lavatory as soon as they reached the station and there stuck the key up his back-side.

Sure enough, when he returned to the charge-room, he was searched and then taken down to a cell while Bill Boal was questioned. The police as yet had no evidence that either of these two men had committed any crime, but Bill Boal's behaviour made them suspicious. He admitted that he had bought the Austin van but would not explain why, but then as the police continued to question him he suddenly lost control and screamed that he was an honest, well-known business man and would not be interrogated in this way.

As Bill went down to his cell Roger was brought up and questioned in his turn. He was asked where he had got the £160 they had found on him; but realising they were thrashing around for a specific lead he said nothing, and they sent him back to his cell. There he waited for the inevitable and the inevitable happened. A detective sergeant returned to the garage belonging to the policeman's widow with the keys that he had taken from Roger and Bill. There he unlocked the suitcase that was in the van and found £56,000. He rushed back to the police station and went into Roger's cell, saying, "Where the hell did you get all that money?"

Roger acted the cretin, hoping that he could somehow bluff his way out of it, but was stymied by not knowing what story Bill had told. In order to put the police in a better mood, he told them about the Rover in the first garage, realising that since Bill had written the address on a label and tied it to the key, they would find the money anyway.

It was now two in the morning, but in spite of the hour Detective Sergeant Davies went to the garage and found six suitcases which, when the money was counted, were found to contain £78,982. At three in the morning he went to the flat above the florist where he found a further £5,910. The total recovered was now almost £141,000 and it was clear that it must be from the Train Robbery.

Fewtrell, McArthur and Pritchard arrived from Aylesbury in time for breakfast. At ten that morning they started to question Bill Boal. Bill began to cry, admitting now that he was "in trouble up to his neck". He insisted that he did not know that "the money was from the railway job". "Look, Guv'nor," he said to McArthur, "Let me tell you everything I know. You can put it down in writing and I'll sign it." He was cautioned and made an exotic statement about how Roger had forced him to stay in Bournemouth by threatening to cut his throat. He said there had been another man in touch with Roger, and that as they drove around the town they were followed by this confederate. He ended his statement by saying "I didn't take part in the robbery of the railway. I had nothing to do with it. Roger may have but I didn't."

Roger was questioned next. McArthur and Pritchard read out a series of questions similar to those put to him by the Bournemouth police, but now as before Roger said nothing. He was taken out. "Well, we tried to treat you the fair way," said one of the policemen. "Now we'll have to try other methods." As they took him down to his cell, Pritchard turned to McArthur and said, "I don't suppose you want to watch this, do you sir?"

Roger was terrified. He had heard that criminals were sometimes beaten up by the police, and he thought this was now about to happen to him: but instead he was just pushed into the cell and the heavy door shut behind him.

A little later he heard a scream and thought it was Bill Boal. He shouted out but no one replied. After that there was a long silence, and Roger decided that there was no further point in keeping the key hidden in his rectum, but when he tried to retrieve it, it had disappeared. He was so alarmed by this that he shouted for the police. It was Fewtrell who came to see him. Roger told him what had happened and a police doctor came with forceps to recover the key.

Later that day the two prisoners were taken to Aylesbury and they spent the night in the police cells. The next day they were brought before the magistrate's court where they saw Rene Boal, and Roger's sister and brother-in-law, Maisie and Alfred Pilgrim, all charged with receiving. They all looked totally shocked, and when Bill saw his wife he completely lost his reserve. He asked after his children, and seeing him so distressed Rene could not bring herself to berate him for his fatal friendship with Roger Cordrey.

On the morning of Friday 16 August, a man called John Ahern was riding to work on his motor-cycle with a fellow clerk, a Mrs Nina Hargreaves, on the pillion when they decided to take a stroll in the woods near Dorking. About twenty yards from the road they saw a brief-case, a hold-all and a camel-skin bag. The brief-case was enveloped in cellophane bags: he drew them back, unbuckled the case and opened it to discover bundles of one-pound notes.

They immediately set off to summon the police, and by nine o'clock a Detective Inspector of the Surrey police had arrived and taken in charge not just the three bags but a suitcase filled with money which he found about thirty yards further into the wood. All this luggage was taken back to Dorking police station and found to contain £100,900. There was also in the bottom of the camel-skin bag, half-hidden by the lining, a receipt dated February 1963 for 358 German marks and 40 pfennigs made out by the Café Pension Restaurant Sonnenbichl, Hindelang, Prov. Allgaen in favour of Herr and Frau Field.

The Surrey police delivered the four bags together with the money and the receipt to Fewtrell and McArthur in Aylesbury who knew by now that Brian Field was the clerk at James and

Wheater, the firm of solicitors who had acted in the purchase of Leatherslade Farm. Fewtrell immediately contacted the German police through Interpol, and within forty-eight hours they had reported back that Brian and Karin Field had indeed stayed at the Pension Sonnenbichl in February of that year.

They also knew that Field had acted for a variety of criminals, including Gordon Goody who was already one of their principal suspects, but it was not until towards the end of August that Fewtrell took out a search warrant for "Kabri" and arrived there early one morning wth Detective Sergeant Pritchard and other officers.

Brian Field met them at the door in his dressing-gown. To all outward appearances he had neither the nervous mannerisms of a man who was afraid of arrest, nor the dejected demeanour of someone whose whack — or a large part of it — had been dumped in panic by the relative who was hiding it. He did not even ask to see Fewtrell's warrant, and while Karin made coffee for their visitors he answered quite calmly all the questions they asked him about Lennie Field and Leatherslade Farm. He explained how the firm had defended Alexander Field and had been left in charge of his affairs while he served his sentence. Lennie Field had come in one day and asked them to arrange the purchase of Leatherslade Farm: Brian had assumed that it was as an investment of his brother's money. He had gone on one occasion to visit the farm with Lennie Field, but the conveyancing had all been done by his employer, John Wheater.

When asked about visits abroad he told them that he often went abroad for both business and pleasure. He had been on holiday with his wife in southern Germany earlier that year. Fewtrell and Pritchard asked him about the holiday as if moving from their professional interrogation into more general conversation. Was it expensive? What were the hotels like?

Brian Field fell into their trap. He described enthusiastically the little pension where they had stayed in Hindelang; and when Fewtrell told him that his daughter was thinking of going to Germany, Brian actually wrote out the name and address of the Pension Sonnenbichl. This satisfied Fewtrell and Pritchard; although they found no incriminating evidence in the house itself, at least they now had the provable link between Brian Field and the bags in Dorking Wood. They were not however ready to arrest him, and raised no objection to a trip to Gibraltar which he had planned for the next day.

There was a final, unforeseen discovery. The Surrey police, in making enquiries about people who had recently come to stay in the neighbourhood of Dorking Woods, had been led to a caravan on the Clovelly caravan site at Box Hill, which was only four miles from where the money had been found. The owners were not there, but the panelling on the wall of the caravan had recently been removed and replaced. The police prised off the thin wood and discovered bundles of bank-notes packed into the wall which when counted came to £30,440. The caravan was immediately taken to police headquarters where fingerprints were found matching those on the record of Jimmy White.

Maurice Ray had also identified fingerprints at Leatherslade Farm. Charlie Wilson's prints had been found on a drum of Saxa Salt and the cellophane wrapping of a Johnson's first-aid kit. Bruce Reynolds's had been found on the Monopoly board. The police now knew some of the men they were looking for, and had only to decide how best to find them.

There were two schools of thought. George Hatherill, who was Commander D Department, and Ernie Millen who was Detective Chief Superintendent in charge of the Flying Squad, both wanted to publish photographs of the wanted men and their wives. Tommy Butler, on the other hand, wanted to keep his cards to his chest and wait for his own men to find the suspects in the pubs and clubs of South London.

In this he was backed by a detective inspector who led one of the eight teams which made up the Flying Squad — Frank Williams — the same man who as a local Kennington detective had been sent to investigate Buster's phoney smash-up of the Walk-In Club.

Williams was a tough, grim-faced, balding man who in the course of his experience in South London had developed a particular philosophy of police-work which was not always approved by his superiors. He thought that every good CID officer should get to know the habits, haunts and associates of criminals by mixing with the criminals themselves. In his judgement this was the only way for the police to obtain good information. Since the incident of the Walk-In Club, for example, he had got to know a friend of Buster's called Bernie Carton, and frequently had a drink in the pub he now ran in Clapham.

Butler, though he conceded that Williams was the best-informed officer in South London, was also aware of the dangers of bribery and blackmail which arose from such close contact with their adversaries. He preferred the law to be black and white, and disliked the kind of compromises and negotiations which went with Williams's philosophy. Nevertheless, on the particular issue at hand — whether to publish the photographs of the wanted men or not — he sided with Williams; but to no avail. The senior officers had their way. Mary Manson's name had already been printed in the papers as "Cockney Mary", who together with a man called "Pug" had bought an Austin Healey at the Chequered Flag garage in Chiswick. Now, on 22 August, the names, descriptions and photographs of Bruce Reynolds, Charlie Wilson and Jimmy White were released to the press and the manhunt started.

Charlie Wilson was picked up at his house in Clapham a few hours before his name appeared in the papers. The others behaved just as Butler had feared and went into hiding. Only Bruce's friend, Mary Manson, gave herself up to the police and was charged with receiving the £820 she had paid for the Austin Healey. For a time she was in danger of being implicated in the robbery itself, because the police were convinced that a woman had been at the farm, and samples were taken of her pubic hair to compare them with those found in one of the sleeping bags; but there was insufficient evidence for the more serious charge and after six weeks she was released on bail.

Gordon Goody was the next to be arrested. Upon leaving "Kabri" he had gone to a friend's house in Barnes, where he buried his money under concrete and Marley tiles in the back passage. Here he also burned a pile of clothes and shoes he had worn at the farm.

When he got back to his mother's house in Putney he discovered that his well-planned alibi had gone wrong. On 6 August, the day he had flown from Belfast to London under the name of McGonegal, his mother had quarrelled with her brother-in-law because his daughter — her niece — who was going out with a respectable young man, had refused to back up her cousin's alibi. Therefore Gordon's mother and his friend had flown back to London on the 7th as Mr and Mrs Goody.

With his alibi blown, Gordon knew that he could not stay in Putney. The connection between the train robbery and the airport robbery had already been mentioned in the press, so it was only a matter of time before the police came for him. He therefore fled to Blackfriars where he had a bolt-hole above the Windmill pub which was run by a friend called Charles Alexander. He had stayed there during his trial at the Old Bailey, and he kept in the wardrobe of his room a selection of clothes and shoes. He remained there in hiding with his small, intrepid girlfriend, Pat, carrying messages back and forth between Putney and Blackfriars.

The discovery of Leatherslade Farm on the Tuesday did not frighten Gordon because he knew how careful he had been to wear gloves all the time he was there, and to make sure that everything he had not taken away with him had been burned by Jimmy White. He was more worried when Pat told him that the Flying Squad had been to his mother's house on Friday the 16th and had forced their way in without a warrant. Afraid that the Flying Squad could be just as unscrupulous as he was himself, and might well plant evidence against him, Gordon thought he would appeal to the more ordinary and honest detectives who had brought the case against him for the Airport Robbery, and so with a certain audacity he wrote a letter to Detective Superintendent Oxborne of Ealing CID.

"Dear Sir," he wrote. "No doubt you will be surprised to hear from me after my double trial at the Old Bailey for the London Airport Robbery. At the time of writing I am not living at my home address because it seems that I am a suspect in the recent train robbery. Two Flying Squad officers recently visited my home address whilst I was out and made a search of the premises, and honestly, Mr Oxborne, I am very worried that they connect me with this crime.

"The reason I write to you now is because you always treated me in a straightforward manner during the Airport case. I will never forget how fair and just yourself and Mr Field were towards me. That case took nearly eight months to finish and every penny I had, and to become a suspect in this last big robbery is more than I can stand. So my intentions are to keep out of harm's way until the people concerned in the Train Robbery are found.

"To some people this letter would seem like a sign of guilt but all I am interested in is keeping my freedom. Hoping these few lines find you and Mr Field in the best of health. Gordon Goody."

He posted this letter on Wednesday 21 August and the next day — in spite of what he had said about keeping out of harm's way — he borrowed Charles Alexander's Sunbeam Rapier and drove up to Leicester to visit another of his girlfriends, a Midlands beauty queen called Maggie Perkins. He met her at the Grand Hotel on the same afternoon as the photographs of Charlie, Bruce and Jimmy White were printed on the front page of the evening papers. Gordon was too intent on his beauty queen to notice, but the florist in the foyer thought he was Bruce Reynolds and telephoned the Leicester police.

While Gordon was dining with Maggie Perkins, the Metropolitan police were checking up on his identity, which he had given as Charles Alexander of the Windmill pub. They telephoned through to their Leicester colleagues that Charles Alexander was behind the bar of the Windmill. After Maggie Perkins had departed, Gordon went to bed; at two in the morning two detectives burst into his bedroom, dragged him off to the police station, and accused him of using a false name. They also searched him and found among other things his address book and a five-pound note which Maggie Perkins had lent to Gordon to pay his bill. Such notes were rarer in those days than they are now, and the Train Robbery was still in the front of their minds, so they checked its number against a list of stolen notes, whereupon Gordon said: "I've got no worries about that one"; then, "Look here, guv., my name's Gordon Goody and I live at 6 Commondale, Putney."

While the officer in charge noted this down, Gordon picked up his address book and quickly blacked out the telephone number of Jimmy White whose picture he had seen displayed on the notice board of the police station. An officer tried to stop him, but Gordon said that it was only the number of his girlfriend in Leicester whom he wanted to save from publicity.

When Scotland Yard were asked if they had any interest in a Gordon Goody they immediately dispatched two Flying Squad officers who took him to Aylesbury. There he was questioned by Butler and held overnight, but the next morning to his astonishment was told he was free to go: indeed Tommy Butler and his assistant, Vibart, drove him from Buckinghamshire to the corner of Commondale in Putney.

Although delighted by this extraordinary piece of luck, Gordon realised at once that it might look strange to some of the others.

On 4 September Ronnie Biggs was arrested, which was particularly alarming because Biggs had never worked with either firm before. Gordon became afraid that Charlie, who was held in Bedford Jail, would suspect that he had bought his freedom by naming names and might send some of his heavy friends to deal with him. He therefore drove down to Bedford with Pat Wilson and went in to visit Charlie under the name of Joey Gray. He asked Charlie not to draw any wrong conclusions because Charlie was in prison while he was free.

"Fuck off out of it," said Charlie. "What are you talking about?"

"I only want to reassure you, mate," said Gordon, "Because if I was you, the same thoughts would have gone through my head."

"Don't be fucking ridiculous," said Charlie. "I ain't worried about any of our firm. But that old man, Stan, you'd better do something about him, 'cause if he ever falls into Butler's hands, he'll shop us all."

Gordon returned to London and met with Buster under the Sunbury clock-tower to discuss the old train driver. They remembered that Ronnie Biggs's alibi was to have been that he and Stan had been cutting down trees in Wiltshire, which would lead the police straight to him. The thought of this amiable old man under interrogation by Tommy Butler made their blood run cold. He would tell everything and identify every one of those who had been at the farm. There was only one course of action left open to them: they must find him and kill him to silence him for ever.

They set off for Redhill in Buster's car, for Buster had once been with Bruce when they had dropped Stan off at his home. He hoped to remember where it was, but when they reached Redhill he became completely confused and drove around for several hours without recognising the street where Stan Agate lived. When it grew dark they gave up and returned to London.

Although it was natural for the Train Robbers to think they had been betrayed, it was largely the methodical work of Chief Superintendent Maurice Ray and his team of fingerprint experts which had put the police on their trail. Ronnie Biggs, for example, though he had been seen by the local police on 24 August because he was known to be a friend of Bruce's, was arrested a fortnight later because his prints had been found on a Pyrex plate, a bottle of tomato ketchup and the Monopoly board.

By the same process Roy James and John Daly were identified as two of the gang; Roy's picture appeared in the papers as a wanted man on 24 August, under the erroneous nick-name of the Weasel, and John Daly's soon after. Jim Hussey was pulled in for questioning on the morning of 7 September, probably because of his association with some of the others, and so confident was he that he had never removed his gloves that he denied any knowledge of Leatherslade Farm and allowed the police to take a print of his palm. He had forgotten that his sweat had shrunk his velvet gloves, and the print taken matched exactly a palm print on the tail-board of the five-ton lorry.

Tommy Wisbey was questioned on 10 September and then released. He was not particularly worried because the police were pulling in almost every known thief, and when Frank Williams told Rene that they wanted to question him again, he came back from Spain where he was on holiday and presented himself at Scotland Yard. He too let Butler take a palm print which matched one on the bath-rail at Leatherslade Farm. At one stage a police officer came up and said, "Do you want to do some business, Tom?"

"I wasn't on it, mate."

"Well, think it over, and if you decide that we could make things easier for you, send someone round with a parcel."

"How can I? I wasn't on it. I'm skint."

Later, he was arrested and taken to Aylesbury.

Some weeks after the Train Robbery there was an internal re-organisation of Scotland Yard. Ernie Millen was promoted to be Deputy Commander and Tommy Butler took over his job as head of the Flying Squad. He now had all the reins of power in his hands and he used them in a determined, almost obsessive, drive to discover and arrest the remainder of the gang.

The combination of names, fingerprints and known associates had by now given him an accurate idea of who had been involved. Bruce's friend, Harry Booth, had been taken in with Mary Manson but was released because he could prove that he had been in Switzerland on the night of 7 August. Frank Munroe was pulled in for routine questioning but was released like Gordon for want of evidence. With some of the others Butler was waiting and watching — hoping that when the time came to arrest them they would be caught with some of the money — for though £141,000 had been recovered in Bournemouth and £101,000 in Dorking Wood, Charlie, Ronnie and Jim Hussey had brought nothing at all: £2¼ million was still missing.

Butler had not ignored Brian Field and the camel-skin bag. The day after the farm was found, Brian's employer, John Wheater, had telephoned the police, offering his assistance. He told them he had bought the farm for Lennie Field, the brother of a client, and gave his address as 150 Earl's Court Road. Since the police could not find Lennie there, they returned the next day, when Wheater mentioned that Lennie Field's brother, Harry Field, had lived at 262 Green Lane, London N.16. On 9 September detectives had found Lennie Field at that address and he was brought in for questioning. He admitted knowing Brian Field and John Wheater but denied knowing anything about Leatherslade Farm. Butler accused him of buying the farm, and visiting it with Brian Field in July, whereupon Lennie said: "You're making a mistake. It must have been somebody who looks like me. Did Brian say it was me?"

"Whether he did or not," said Butler, "I think it was you acting on behalf of those who were going to rob the train."

"I'm not going to say any more," said Lennie, "until you get Mr Wheater here. I want a solicitor."

Wheater arrived later in the day, and when confronted with his client, Lennie Field, he turned to Butler in confusion. "This puts me in a very awkward position," he said. "Under the circumstances, do you think I ought to act for him?"

"That's a matter for you," said Butler. "He's asked for you to come here."

"Very well," said Wheater.

"I never purchased any farm, did I, Mr Wheater?" said Lennie. "You know I didn't."

Wheater, who had been sitting, now stood and turned pale — realising for the first time that his cunning clerk had put all the blame onto Lennie Field. He loosened his tie and collar, stared at Lennie, and said: "I'm confused. I'm confused. I'm not sure now. I thought he was the man at first, but now I'm not so certain." He turned to Butler. "Can I see you alone?" he asked.

Lennie Field was taken out of the room.

"This puts me in a very embarrassing position," Wheater said again. "I'm not at all sure now that he is the man who entered into negotiations respecting the farm. I only saw him twice and, although he's remarkably like the man, I really cannot say. There is a startling resemblance; in fact he is the spitting image of the man who paid the deposit.''

"But you said he came regularly to your office," said Inspector Bradbury.

"I only saw him twice at my office."

"So the position is," said Butler, "that this man, according to you, is not the man who entered into negotiations to buy Leatherslade Farm?''

"I'm not at all sure that he is the man," said Wheater.

Both John Wheater and Lennie Field were now allowed to leave, but on September 14 Lennie was arrested at 262 Green Lanes, taken to Cannon Row police station and charged by Tommy Butler. The following day Tommy Butler went with two other Flying Squad detectives and a woman police officer to "Kabri" where they introduced themselves to Brian Field as police officers concerned with the Train Robbery.

"Yes, I know about the case," said Brian Field. "I've already made a statement about it.''

"We have reason to believe that you were involved," said Butler. "You will be arrested and charged with it.''

"I didn't take part in the robbery," said Brian Field. "You're making a mistake. I know that the firm and myself were involved in the business with the farm with Lennie Field, but that's not robbery.''

Butler and his men searched the house and found nothing except Brian Field's wallet, containing £110. Afterwards they set off for New Scotland Yard where Butler repeated his caution and said that he wanted to clear up some further points.

"By all means," said Brian, his quick brain already racing ahead. "But tell me: will this case go to the Old Bailey, or to the Buckinghamshire Assize Court?''

"I can't answer that," said Butler.

On 17 September it was John Wheater's turn. Tommy Butler with his team of detectives arrived at his house at Ottways Lane, Ashtead, Surrey, early in the morning. They told him that they had a warrant for his arrest for conspiring to rob a mail train, and also for being an accessory after the fact.

"This is a mistake, you know," said Wheater. "This will ruin me." And seeing that Butler's men were about to begin their search, he said: "Don't think I'm being rude, but I would like to search you people first. I don't want anything put on me."

Butler laughed. "Surely you don't mean that? You must have been listening to too many fairy stories from your clients."

Wheater blushed. "Yes, probably I have. I'm sorry. I shouldn't have said it."

The detectives searched the house and took away with them various notebooks and papers, including the telephone directory. Wheater was taken to New Scotland Yard, and from there to Aylesbury where he was charged with robbery, and with being an accessory after the fact to robbery.

By the middle of September the police operation had already been remarkably successful. They had five of the principal thieves in custody — Roger Cordrey, Charlie Wilson, Ronnie Biggs, Jim Hussey and Tommy Wisbey: they had a call out for five more — Bruce Reynolds, John Daly, Buster Edwards, Roy James, Jimmy White: and they suspected, but had no evidence against, another four — Frank Munroe, Bob Welch, Gordon Goody and Alf Thomas. Of the gang which robbed the train, only Bill Jennings had escaped their notice entirely; nor could they know about Brian Field's friend Mark, or the Ulsterman.

Although both Butler and Fewtrell were puzzled as to why the driver, Mills, had first been taken from his seat in the diesel and then brought back to drive the train, they did not realize that there had been another driver; nor had they investigated Biggs's original alibi about chopping down trees in Wiltshire because Biggs, knowing that Charmian had asked the Wiltshire police to find him, had never used it. They could certainly have used old Stan, for however many names might be handed up to them from informers in the criminal underworld, and however likely it was that if one man was on the job another would have been with him, they could not be certain in their own minds — nor could they hope to prove a case in court — unless there was actual proof. They would have assumed, for instance, that if Bruce was on the job, Harry Booth would have been with him — but in this instance it had been shown that he was not.

The proof until now had come either from the contradictory and incriminating behaviour of suspects such as Roger Cordrey or John Wheater — or from fingerprints found at the farm by Detective Superintendent Maurice Ray; but there was another expert who had come to Leatherslade Farm three days later after its discovery — a slim, jovial man called Dr Ian Holden. He was not a policeman but a civilian employee of the Metropolitan Police Laboratory at New Scotland Yard. His area of expert knowledge was less precise than Maurice Ray's and on the first afternoon at the farm he had merely walked around looking at various objects, and keeping out of the way of the fingerprint men.

There was little at first which appeared to be of much use to him. The mail-bags, the food, the rolls of lavatory paper, were all of of an impersonal nature. Outside the farm there was the rope, the pick-axe handles by the door, the lorry and Land Rovers — one painted khaki over its original blue — which had little value as forensic evidence. He also noticed the pots of paint which Bruce and John had brought with them to carry conviction as decorators; and the single pot of yellow paint which Jimmy White had used to paint the bonnet of the lorry, some of it covered with gravel.

On 19 August the lorry and the two Land Rovers had been driven away from Leatherslade Farm to Aylesbury police station. Dr Holden later went to examine the vehicles more thoroughly; and in doing so he found, on the pedals of the Land Rover, traces of yellow paint — presumably the same paint which had been daubed on the bonnet of the lorry and spilt on the gravel around it.

Then came the arrest of suspects. On 15 August, Detective Sergeant Hensley had been to Bill Boal's house at 23 Burnsthwaite Road in Fulham where had not only taken possession of the money Bill Boal had given to his wife, but various articles and objects which were turned up by his search of the house — two sacks, a peaked cap, and a jacket with a knuckleduster in its pocket, all found in a cupboard under the stairs. These were all handed to the liaison officer at New Scotland Yard and locked away.

On 23 August Dr Holden had himself gone to the Windmill pub in Blackfriars and taken from Gordon Goody's room a suit; his wallet (containing £3.10s.); some well-washed denims; a spare pair of trousers; and some brown suede Tru-form shoes, size ten, with a criss-cross pattern on the rubber soles which he thought might match footprints found at the farm.

On 26 August in his laboratory Dr Holden started a minute examination of the objects he had so far recovered. He started with those taken from 23 Burnsthwaite Road. The two sacks, the peaked cap, the jacket and the knuckleduster — none of these objects could be linked with the farm or with Bridego Bridge. The jacket, however, had a hole in the pocket through which a small collection of little brass knobs — clock-winding keys and things of that sort — had fallen into the lining. One of these in particular attracted his attention — a small brass knob with grooves and ridges in the metal handle. In itself it was not interesting — something which had been made to wind up or alter a clock — but in the grooves of the handle there was a substance which aroused Dr Holden's curiosity. It was yellow; and when he had scraped out a tiny particle of the substance and examined it, he saw as he had suspected that it was yellow paint. Remembering the open tin of yellow paint that he had seen at the farm, Dr Holden made a note to compare the two.

Later that day and on the following morning Dr Holden turned his attention to the articles belonging to Gordon Goody which he himself removed from the Windmill pub the week before. The suit, the trousers, the denims — none showed up anything of any interest. Even the criss-cross pattern on the soles of the suede shoes did not match his photograph of the footprint at the farm. But as he scraped the mud off the soles of the shoes, he noticed something which did alert him — small stains of yellow which could certainly have been made by paint. He scraped off a sample to examine it. Besides the yellow paint there were stains made by a khaki paint similar to the khaki paint on the Land Rover.

On 29 August Dr Holden received from Fewtrell's exhibits' officer the tin of yellow paint which the constable had himself retrieved from the "Museum" which the Rixons, who were still the owners, had made at Leatherslade Farm and planned to open to the public for a five-shilling entrance fee. He made spectrographic analyses of the paint from the tin and the paint from Gordon Goody's suede shoes and compared the two: they were similar but not identical. He next analysed the khaki paint from the shoes and the khaki paint from the Land Rover: they were identical. On September 4 the lorry was brought to New Scotland Yard, and on September 6 Dr Holden took samples of yellow paint from the cab. He found that the yellow paint from the cab was identical to the yellow paint from the tin but only similar to the yellow paint on the shoes. On 19 September he went back to Aylesbury and examined the two Land Rovers. He took a sample of khaki paint from the larger Land Rover, and samples of yellow paint from the pedals. His spectrographic analyses showed that both paints were identical to the two paints found on the shoes, but from the pattern of the paint on the shoes and the paint on the Land Rover pedals, he could not say that the shoes had put the paint onto the pedals.

There was a piece of the puzzle missing. Why was the yellow paint on the shoes and the pedals different from the paint in the tin? On 28 September Dr Holden returned to Leatherslade Farm and found what he was looking for: in the gravel covering the spilt paint there were fine mineral materials which, when added to the paint from the pot, made it identical to the paint on the shoes and the pedals.

He now felt that he had proved a link between the shoes, and the wearer of the shoes, and Leatherslade Farm. Of course both paints were of a common variety; but to have both paints on the same shoes made for impossible odds against a coincidence.

He had not forgotten the little brass knob from Bill Boal's jacket. He made a spectrographic analysis of the paint scraped from the grooves in the handle and compared it with that of the yellow paint from the tin at Leatherslade Farm. After allowing for dirt in the grooves and dust in the lining of the jacket, they were identical.

Dr Holden left no stone unturned. He had after all been at his job for seventeen years and knew that not only had he to satisfy himself and Chief Superintendent Tommy Butler, but that in time he would have to satisfy a jury. It was an axiom of his that there is a world of difference between a witness who is an expert and expert witness. His job was to be both.

He went down to Sheen, to Bill Boal's workshop: and then to Fulham — to 23 Burnsthwaite Road — where Bill Boal had lived with his wife and three children. In both places Dr Holden looked around for yellow paint. In Fulham he collected one sample from a window frame: he even took some from the outside of the house next door. None of these matched the paint from the little brass knob.

Dr Holden's discoveries were vital to the police. Without the paint on what came to be called the "knurled knob" there was nothing to link Bill Boal to Leatherslade Farm, and thus little to prove a case of either robbery or conspiracy to rob against Boal. At most he could only have been convicted of receiving stolen property and of being an accessory after the fact.

In the case of Gordon Goody, the discovery of the two distinct paints on the soles of his shoes was little short of a miracle. Here was a man who was known to work with Bruce Reynolds and Charlie Wilson, had walked out of two trials for the Airport Robbery, had humiliated the forensic experts by exposing their failure to notice the forged link in the chain, and had boasted in advance that he was about to take part in something big. The police had already discovered his botched alibi in Northern Ireland, which led them to suppose that the robbery had been postponed for twenty-four hours. They had also recorded his use of a false name in Leicester, but until that moment they had no concrete proof that he had been to Leatherslade Farm.

On 3 October Gordon was told to report to Putney police station. He went there with a sense of foreboding because he knew that the police had taken some of his things from the Windmill, and thought they might use them to concoct evidence against him.

At two in the afternoon Tommy Butler swept into the police station surrounded by an entourage of Flying Squad detectives. In his hands he carried a loose, brown paper parcel. He went to Gordon, opened the paper and showed him the brown suede shoes.

"Are these your shoes?" he asked him.

"Yeah," said Gordon. "They look like mine."

"Have you ever lent them to anyone?"

"Of course not."

"All right, then. You're nicked."

"What for?"

"Robbing the train."

As if to equal Dr Holden, Detective Superintendent Maurice Ray now came up with his most spectacular piece of fingerprint evidence. On one of the cans of beer he found a fragment of a fingerprint, made through a pin-sized hole in a glove, which he matched with the prints on file of Bob Welch.

When Bob Welch had returned from Pevensey Bay, which he, Tommy and Frank had used as a base from which to hide their money, he had telephoned his wife, Pat, from a call box near to his home to ask if everything was all right.

"Yes, fine," she had said.

"I'll be back in about ten minutes."

"Good," she said. Then she added: "Oh Bob, can you bring

some of that ointment? Bruno's feet are bad again."

This reference to their dog's feet was a pre-arranged message to warn him that the police were in the house. Bob drove slowly past the bottom of his street and saw three Flying Squad cars parked by his house. He sped off to a friend in South London who had contacts in Scotland Yard to find out why they should suspect him, and was told that he had nothing to worry about — that they were pulling in everyone. The next day Bob, like Tommy, reported to Scotland Yard, where he was questioned by a junior officer and then released.

Several weeks later, on 26 September, he was telephoned by this same friend and told to go at twelve to a side-street by the Thomas à Becket pub in the Old Kent Road. Bob was immediately suspicious, but said he would be there: he reached the spot by eleven to see if there was any sign of a police trap but it was deserted. He got out of his car and walked down the wooden fence which lined one side of the road, knocking a slat loose every ten or fifteen yards so that if he had to run for it there would be a way out.

At twelve an unmarked police car drew up in the side-street and Bob's friend approached him with a plain-clothes policeman.

"Have you had a holiday?" asked the policeman.

"No," said Bob. "I can't afford it."

"Well, get yourself a few quid and have a holiday."

"Where shall I go?"

"I don't give a fuck where you go. Just go and have a holiday and don't come back till I fucking tell you to."

Bob left that day for the West Country. He stayed on a farm near Beaford in North Devon, hoping that the anonymous countryside would lend him anonymity; but he lived like a successful gambler and was visited by his friends including Frank Munroe, who told him that the police were still looking for him in London. This led Bob to decide to go abroad: he tried to get hold of Buster through Derek Glass, to see if he could get help from the Germans, but eventually Frank obtained a passport by making a false application, and a date was fixed for his departure.

Before he left, Bob went back to London. He thought it possible that he would never return, and wanted to see the city where he had spent his life just once before he parted — not just the streets and buildings, but family and friends. But someone had grassed on him, and as he came out of his brother's betting shop near London Bridge station, the Flying Squad were waiting for him. He was taken to Scotland Yard, questioned by Butler, and after his finger and palm prints had been taken he was locked in a cell for the night.

Early next morning he was awoken by Butler who came into his cell followed by another officer. "Had a nice sleep, Bob?" he asked. "Had a cup of tea?"

"I'm all right," said Bob.

"Well, son, you're nicked," said Butler.

"You're fucking joking," said Bob.

"No, I'm not. I'm deadly serious. You're nicked."

While Butler went out to prepare a charge sheet, another Flying Squad officer offered Bob a cup of tea and whispered in a quiet voice: "Bob, this is a twenty-year lot."

"Don't talk to me about a twenty-year lot," said Bob. "I don't fucking want to know."

"Can you put up seventy grand?" the officer asked.

"Don't talk to me about any grands," said Bob.

"You and Tom should put up seventy grand apiece," said the officer. "It'd make things easier for you."

"Tommy hasn't got seven bob, let alone seventy grand," said Bob.

At that moment Butler returned and Bob Welch was charged with robbery and conspiracy to rob the mail train.

John Daly had put himself in the hands of a fellow-thief called Godfrey Green who had sent his money and child to Cornwall and hidden John and his wife Barbara in a basement flat in Eaton Square. They became in effect his prisoners, for they relied upon Green to pass messages to Bruce and deliver provisions. John grew a beard and went on a diet of fish and salad to change his appearance. Barbara, who was pregnant, grew fat as he grew thin: she was nervous by disposition and suffered increasingly from the restrictions and from the separation from her child.

On the morning of 3 December, as John was sitting in his pyjamas and dressing-gown, half a dozen policemen led by Butler and Williams burst into the flat. Almost certainly John had been betrayed by Godfrey Green — afraid that now Mary Manson had been released on bail he would lose control of John's money; but John was wily enough to say nothing to the police and refuse to allow his palm prints to be taken. He was taken off to Aylesbury while Butler rang Mary Manson to ask her to take care of Barbara Daly. The shock of the arrest seemed to have affected her mind: she had become silent and withdrawn — the first of the civilian casualties on the Robbers' side.

A week after John's arrest, the police received an anonymous telephone call from a woman to say that Roy James was at 14 Ryder's Terrace in St John's Wood. He had been in hiding for three months, for as soon as he had seen that Charlie was wanted, he knew that the police would be after him. He had run to his flat, collected together anything of an incriminating nature such as books about trains or the boiler-suits he had used to disguise himself as a railway worker — and had had them burnt by a friend who worked at the enormous coke-fired power-station in Battersea.

He was harboured first by a bookmaker in Putney and for the six weeks which followed Roy only left his house for essential business. His most immediate concern was his money which was being hidden by a big-time gangster who was a friend of Charlie's. With Charlie in prison, Roy was afraid that this man would steal his whack, and it was only by threatening to bring in his own heavy friends that Roy got it back — less £7,000 for "expenses".

His next concern was Bobby Pelham who had been frightened by the Flying Squad into surrendering the £500 hidden in his house and making a statement which implicated Roy. The word went out that Pelham was a grass, and a day or two later someone tampered with the brakes of his car. It was only because Pelham was a mechanic that he recognised the fault in time.

Roy had other problems. The bookmaker in whose house he was staying gambled himself and was usually out of the house until three or four in the morning: Roy therefore found himself alone for most of the day and night with his young wife, and as the weeks passed it became increasingly obvious to Roy that she wanted him to take advantage of this enforced intimacy. She was an attractive girl, around Roy's age, but it went against the grain to sleep with the wife of a man who was taking a considerable risk in harbouring him. Finally, one night, after Roy had gone to bed, she came into his room. "I've had enough of this," she said, climbing into the bed beside him.

Roy shrank away from her.

"Don't you like me?" she asked.

"Of course I like you," he said, "and if only you'd got in touch with me before all this happened, I'd have taken you out."

"No you wouldn't," she said.

"Well we can't do anything now."

"Why not?"

"Don't you see? It wouldn't be right."

"He wouldn't know."

"All the same, I can't do it."

He eventually persuaded her to leave his bed, but from that night onwards the atmosphere in the house changed for the worse. She was rude to him, even in her husband's presence, and Roy began to fear that like Potiphar's wife she wanted her husband to think that Roy had made a pass at her. He decided to move. A house was found for him by a friend at 14 Ryder's Terrace and he moved there at the beginning of October.

At first he hardly went out at all. He read books and listened to the gramophone. Later, after he had grown a beard, he would go out at night wearing a beret like a Frenchman to walk in Regent's Park; but though comfortable and relatively safe, the life irked him and he decided that when the right time came he would give himself up; for if he was on the run for the rest of his life, he would never be able to return to motor-racing or his mother — the two things that mattered most to him. He calculated, however, that if he waited until after the trial of those already arrested, he would have a better chance of acquittal or if convicted of a shorter sentence.

On the night of 3 December, when the police came for him, he sat reading in his pyjamas behind the drawn curtains of his living-room in the mews house. Suddenly there was a heavy knocking on the door. He went to the window, drew back a corner of the curtain and looked down at the street below. A woman stood holding a parcel, but Roy knew by instinct that there was something wrong and rushed to his bedroom to put a pair of trousers and a jersey over his pyjamas. He picked up a leather bag containing what money he had kept with him — about £12,000 of changed-up bank-notes — and climbed out of the skylight, just as two Flying Squad detectives broke open the windows of the balcony.

Roy ran along the roof of the terraced mews houses. Below him there was pandemonium. Forty police officers with arc lights had surrounded the house to catch this one small thief who seemed for a moment to have slipped through their fingers. One police officer got onto the roof in front of him, but Roy dodged him and came to the thirty foot drop at the end of the terrace. He threw down his bag and jumped, but no sooner had he hit the ground than he found himself face to face with a detective. He tried to dodge him but he slipped on the wet grass and was caught.

"That's nothing to do with me," he said, pointing to the bag on the ground beside him.

He was dragged into a police car and placed between two giants of the Flying Squad. Tommy Butler got into the front seat and turned to face him.

"You're Roy James, aren't you?" he said.

"That's right."

"Why did you climb onto the roof instead of opening the door?"

"Open the door? I should think so — just to get myself nicked."

"We're taking you to Aylesbury now," said Butler, "where you'll be charged with the robbery of the train."

"Well, that's it then," said Roy. "I suppose I'm lucky I didn't break my neck."

On the same day as Tommy Butler was planning the raid on Ryder's Terrace, Detective Chief Inspector Bradbury took another anonymous call. He was told that £50,000 of the money stolen from the train would be left in a telephone box in Great Dover Street, Newington, in South London. He passed the message on to Detective Inspector Frank Williams who, more than anyone else, understood what it implied. For weeks now Williams had been negotiating some sort of deal with Buster Edwards and Alf Thomas. Buster, whose prints had been found on some paper wrappers at the farm, had been promised that if he gave himself up with a large part of the stolen money, the police would guarantee strict fairness according to the evidence they had. The deal with Alf was more complicated. No evidence against him had been found at the farm, and he was not known to work with either of the two firms involved, but some identifiable bank-notes had been traced to some of his friends who had been pulled in and charged with receiving.

This seemed to suggest that Alf was part of the gang, but unlike Gordon Alf was a minor thief and was assumed quite rightly to have played a minor role; Butler, who was generally meticulous upon questions of evidence, was prepared to let him go. He had by then found most of the thieves, but as his deputy Frank Williams pointed out to him he had recovered little of the money. Alf was therefore pulled in, and by a mixture of threats of charges against him, and more serious charges against his friends, the deal was done. Alf was released; and shortly afterwards Butler and Williams found two sacks as promised in the telephone box in Great Dover Street. Butler was still sceptical, but when they got back to Scotland Yard and cut open the sacks they saw that they were indeed filled with bank-notes.

Williams was jubilant: Butler less so. He reported to his superior, Commander Hatherill, that £50,000 of the stolen money had been recovered, but could not say why. Hatherill in his turn announced this to the press the next morning while the bags of money were driven up to Aylesbury and taken into custody by Detective Superintendent Fewtrell. Fewtrell had read about the find in the evening newspaper, and wondered how his colleagues in London could know that the sum recovered the day before was exactly £50,000. He himself had had to bring in specially trained bank clerks who took several days to count the money found in Bournemouth and in Dorking Woods. He was more surprised still when he later saw the money because it was damp and musty as if it had been buried, and the notes were all stuck together. The bank inspectors were brought in to peel them apart, and when the money was finally counted there was only £47,245.

8. The Trial

By the end of the year, nine of the sixteen men who had been at Bridego Bridge were in custody and awaited trial; two — Alf and Frank — had been pulled in and then released; two — Bill and Stan — had been overlooked by the police altogether; and three — Buster, Bruce and Jimmy White — were still on the run.

With no prospect of an early arrest of these last three, the authorities decided to proceed with the trial of the others. It was to be, inevitably, a show trial. The robbery itself, through its audacity and the amount of money stolen, had fascinated the public both in Britain and abroad. The effort by the police to catch the criminals has also been exceptional; 120 officers had worked on the case; 1,700 exhibits had been prepared for presentation in court; 2,350 written statements had been taken from witnesses.

The crime had been committed in Buckinghamshire, and so the proper place for the trial was in the county town of Aylesbury. The Assize Court, however, was too small for such a major case. It would have been possible to have taken the case to the Old Bailey in London, and Brian Field hoped that it would be because he knew from experience what could be done with a London jury; but doubtless for the same reasons it was decided that the trial should be held in Aylesbury where the chamber of the recently built rural district council was converted into a court.

Because it was a show trial — and because most of the accused had plenty of money — many of the best barristers in England were retained. Brian Field retained Lewis Hawser, whom he had promised to hire for Bob Welch. Charlie Wilson had hoped to be defended by Jeremy Hutchinson, another barrister with a high reputation among thieves, but in the event he was not available and John Mathew was retained. In all there were nine Queen's Counsel — each with his junior — arraigned for the defence against two Queen's Counsel — Arthur James and Neil MacDermot — and their juniors for the prosecution.

There were ten charges. The first, against all thirteen of the accused, was of conspiracy to rob the mail. The second count, which was against all except John Wheater, was of armed robbery of 120 mail bags from Frank Dewhurst, the senior Post Office official on the HVP coach. The third, fourth and fifth were charges of receiving against Bill Boal; the sixth, seventh and eighth were parallel receiving charges against Roger Cordrey. The ninth was a receiving charge against Brian Field and the tenth was a charge against John Wheater of obstruction of justice.

All the accused pleaded not guilty to all the charges except for Roger. He decided that, since he had been caught red-handed with the money, it was pointless to deny that he had received it: and since it was proved that he had rented a room in Oxford — which was near to Leatherslade Farm — at the time of the robbery, it was equally futile to deny that he was part of the conspiracy. In return for these pleas of guilty, which the prosecution accepted, the charge of robbery itself was left on the file and Roger was removed from the dock.

The trial of the remaining twelve opened before Mr Justice Edmund Davies on 20 January 1964. The court was packed with people — lawyers, policemen, journalists, relatives and curious members of the public. The proceedings started with the junior counsel for Brian Field objecting to the first juror. Karin Field had been approached by a man who had said he could get at one or two of them, and it was the hope perhaps of Brian Field that this would be enough to have the trial moved to London. Chief Superintendent Butler was called to report on his investigation into this incident, after which Judge Edmund Davies rejected the challenge and the jury of twelve men was duly sworn in.

Arthur James, QC, opened for the prosecution. His thesis was quite simple. Leatherslade Farm where, among other things, mail bags and blank wrappers had been found, had been used as the base for the thieves who had robbed the train. The fingerprints of Charlie Wilson, Ronnie Biggs, Bob Welch, Tommy Wisbey, Jim Hussey, John Daly and Roy James had all been found at the farm; yet when first approached by the police, they had all denied that they had ever been there.

Brian Field, Lennie Field and John Wheater were connected with the farm through its purchase; Gordon Goody through the traces of yellow and khaki paint which had been found on his shoes and matched exactly the yellow paint used to paint one of the Land Rovers: and Bill Boal through the yellow paint which had been found in the grooves of the small "knurled knob". Bill Boal had also been found with Roger Cordrey in possession of a large sum of the stolen money, which gave rise to the alternative charges of receiving. Brian Field too was charged with receiving because of the money which had been found in his camel-skin bag.

In strictly legal terms, the case was not as strong as it seemed. There was no evidence at all to connect any of the accused with the scene of the crime itself — Bridego Bridge or Sears Crossing — and the fingerprints of Jim Hussey, Bob Welch, Ronnie Biggs, Roy James and John Daly which had been found at the farm were all on movable objects — Jim Hussey's on the tailboard of the lorry; Bob Welch's on a can of Pipkin beer; Ronnie Biggs's on a plate, a bottle of tomato ketchup and the Monopoly box; Roy James's on a plate and a magazine. Even Tommy Wisbey's and Charlie Wilson's prints, which were on fixed objects — Tommy's on the bath-rail and Charlie's on a window-sill — could possibly have been made at some other time.

The paint too was an unknown quantity because what one expert can establish another can refute: and when it came to the "minor conspiracy" involving Brian Field, Lennie Field and John Wheater, it may have been clear that one of them must have been involved in the conspiracy, but it was not clear which it was. Certainly the prosecution could have used Stan Agate, the red-faced old man whom Mr Wyatt — the neighbouring farmer — had seen sitting on a deck-chair at Leatherslade Farm the day before the robbery. It would have been useful too if one of the accused had turned Queen's evidence — but even with the prospect of up to twenty years in prison, not one of them bore witness against any of the others. The two firms, which had once so mistrusted one another, were loyal in adversity.

They were also optimistic, and their advisers fed their optimism as more and more money was paid out for their defence. Yet as they hired the best brains to act on their behalf, they did nothing whatsoever to act the part of innocent men. They were dressed in expensive suits and had — with the exception of Lennie Field and John Wheater — insouciant expressions on their faces. They were ignorant of the rural mentality; and just as they had not realised the curiosity that would be shown by a cowman in the new owners of Leatherslade Farm, so they miscalculated now the impression that would be made on a country jury by working people with no apparent profession wearing well-cut clothes. This, of course, was the hope of the prosecution: that the whole of their case would be greater than the sum of its parts.

One of the first witnesses to be called was the driver of the mail train, Jack Mills. He hobbled into court, still apparently weak from the assault of five months before. He gave his evidence in a quiet, shaky voice; and whether or not he was a "right fucking actor", as Charlie Wilson whispered to Bob Welch, his appearance had its effect upon both judge and jury. He was followed by other witnesses who described the raid on the train, including Frank Dewhurst and some of the Post Office workers from the HVP coach.

On the fifth day the prosecution opened its case against Bill Boal. The police officers from Bournemouth were called to describe how they had arrested him and dragged off his clothes at the police station. Bill Boal, when he gave evidence, insisted that he had been beaten up, and he denied certain statements which were ascribed to him such as "Fair enough, it came from the train job". Roger Cordrey was brought to the court to give evidence, but at the last moment was advised against it. It was thought that if he went on the stand to say that Bill Boal was innocent, he would inevitably be asked who was guilty: and if he refused to say, it would not only destroy the effect of his evidence in favour of Bill Boal, but quite possibly spoil the good impression made by the plea of guilty entered on his own behalf.

On the thirteenth day of the trial Dr Ian Holden gave his evidence, which was of great importance because the yellow and khaki paint was the only link between two of the accused and the farm. It was of even greater complexity, deriving as it did from a spectographic analysis of the various samples.

However, Dr Holden not only presented his scientific findings to the court; he also expressed an opinion that "the khaki paint (on the shoes) is entirely consistent with having come from the same source as the paint used to paint the Land Rover, and the yellow paint with the mineral material would be entirely consistent with having come either from the garage or from the pedals of the Land Rover".

"Again, from your experience in these matters," asked Neil MacDermot, QC, "do you think it is possible that these correspondences are consistent with the paints coming from different sources?"

"In theory I think it would be possible," said Dr Holden, "but in practice I should think it would be very highly improbable."

"As an expert experienced in the examination of such exhibits, are you able to express an opinion yourself as to the source of the paint on the shoes?" asked MacDermot.

"From my examination of the samples," said Dr Holden, "I would be satisfied without any doubt that those paints had come from the same sources as the paint used to paint the Land Rover or that on the floor of the garage."

They moved on to the knurled knob found in Bill Boal's jacket. Here Dr Holden was almost as emphatic. He described how he had been to Boal's home and workshop in search of a yellow paint which might explain away the paint on the knob; he had taken flakes of yellow paint from the back window; had even taken samples of yellow paint from the house next door. All had been examined on the spectrograph; and "did you," asked MacDermot, "find any correspondence between the paint on the brass knob and the samples of paint which you had taken from Boal's premises and the house next door?"

"No, there was no correspondence."

"Again, Dr Holden, are you able to express any opinion from your experience in these matters as to the source of the paint on the brass knob?"

"This would be consistent with having come from the yellow paint in the squashed tin or the clean paint spread on the floor at the garage."

"To what extent at all could you be satisfied that they came from the same source?"

"I would say this was highly probable, but there would be just the possibility that it could come from another tin of the same batch of paint or one very, very similar."

Thus the expert forensic scientist, who was also an expert witness, pronounced on the one "shred" of evidence which connected Bill Boal with Leatherslade Farm; and the jury, who were to be reminded by the Judge of Mr Justice Devlin's adage that "proof beyond a reasonable doubt does not mean proof beyond a feverish or haunting doubt . . .", were left to draw their own conclusions.

It was not, of course, that the inference to be drawn from his evidence was not attacked, first by Mr Sime, QC, for Bill Boal, and then by Mr Sebag Shaw, QC, for Gordon Goody. Under cross-examination by Mr Sime Dr Holden told the court that there was no trace of yellow paint in the lining of the jacket itself. Sebag Shaw was more aggressive in his cross-examination — drawing from Dr Holden the admission that three weeks passed between finding the paint on the soles of the shoes and taking samples from the pedals of the Land Rover; and it was nine days after that — on 28 September — that he had found corresponding paint on the floor of the garage. He implied, but did not say outright, that someone had planted the paint.

"Is that suggested, Mr Shaw?" asked the Judge.

"My Lord, I am not desirous of making any suggestions. I was exploring the situation so far as one could. It is for the jury to make what they think is a right deduction from it all. I am content merely to look at the facts . . ."

In re-examination, MacDermot asked Dr Holden to express in mathematical terms the combined probabilities of finding two different paints on the soles of one pair of shoes which were identical to two different paints in one place.

"Well, it is, of course, very difficult to assess in numbers," said Dr Holden, "But if one took it that there were one thousand different colours of paint — and one particular firm advertises that number of different colours — the possibility of getting that one particular colour of paint on one's shoes would be 1,000 to 1, and the possibility of picking the right two would be 1,000 times 1,000 which is a million to one. . . . That is why I said it was highly improbable you would get it from anywhere else."

"How confident do you feel of that expression of opinion?"

"Well, if I had to go out and find another pair of shoes with both those paints on, even if my life depended on it, I do not think I would even bother to try. I do not think I could find them."

On Thursday 6 February, the fourteenth day of the trial, came the first sensation. Mr Sabin, a junior counsel for the prosecution, was examining Detective Inspector Morris of the Surrey Constabulary who had gone to see Ronnie Biggs on 24 August to ask him about Bruce Reynolds.

"Did you ask him if he knew any of the men wanted for the Train Robbery in Buckinghamshire?" he asked.

"I did," the Inspector replied.

"What did he say?"

"He said: 'I knew Reynolds some years ago. I met him when we did time together'."

The examination proceeded, followed by the cross-examination by Biggs's counsel, Wilfrid Fordham. But when Inspector Morris had left the court, the jury were instructed to leave too; and Mr Fordham asked the Judge what should be done in view of this improper admission before the jury that Biggs had previously been in prison.

"Mr Fordham," said Mr Justice Davies. "That the Inspector who, of necessity, must be a man of great experience in his duties, should have so far forgotten his duties as to bring in a phrase of that kind quite gratuitously is grossly improper and cannot be too strongly condemned."

After a short recess, in which Fordham conferred with Ronnie Biggs, he asked the Judge to discharge Biggs without a verdict and order a retrial. Mr Justice Davies had no alternative but to grant the application and Ronnie Biggs left the court to wait in Aylesbury jail for a new trial.

The prosecution closed its case on the seventeenth day of the trial — Tuesday 11 February. There then followed the legal submissions by defence counsel, in the absence of the jury, that there was no case to answer. It was, more or less, a ritual because it was rare that the highly qualified staff of the Director of Public Prosecutions went to the expense of bringing a case to court if there was insufficient evidence to send it before a jury. But it offered an opportunity for the highly trained barristers to match wits. Some of the submissions were quite short, and like that of Mr W. Raeburn, QC, the counsel for John Daly, "disarmingly simple. It is that the evidence against John Daly cannot amount to proof on either of the counts upon which he is charged. . . . The evidence . . . falls into two categories . . . the finding of his fingerprints on a set of Monopoly and the other is that he . . . went underground when the hue and cry had been raised.

"As regards the first count, my submission is that there is only a tenuous connection . . . the fingerprints are found not on anything remotely connected with the crime, but upon a toy which was introduced into the farm; nobody knows by whom, nobody knows to whom it belonged and it is not at all a matter of inference that the fingerprints came upon the particular parts of that toy at any time subsequent to its having come to the farm.

"The rest of the evidence . . . is, at the highest, mere suspicion. It is consistent with a man who realises that people with whom he has associated are being sought by the police . . . and while no doubt, being wise after the event, one can see that it would have been very much better in such circumstances for him to have voluntarily assisted the police in their enquiries, that is a very long way from saying that it amounts to any sort of proof . . . that he was a party to a conspiracy."

The submissions were completed by Thursday 13 February, and Mr Justice Davies withdrew to consider them. In court on Friday 14 February he announced that he had overruled all the submissions except for Mr Raeburn's. "I propose to uphold the submission in relation to Mr Daly," he said, "in respect to both counts, and when the jury are returned they will be directed to acquit him."

The jury duly returned and upon the direction of the Judge acquitted John Daly. An application by Wilfrid Fordham for his costs to be paid out of public funds was abruptly refused. John Daly was then discharged, and the man Bruce had always chosen as his partner because he was lucky left the dock a free man.

On Friday 14 February, the twentieth day of the trial, the defence began. Bob Welch, Tommy Wisbey and Jim Hussey had combined to invent an elaborate story to explain both their prints at the farm and their subsequent denial that they had ever been there. It ran as follows: on Saturday 10 August, Bob and Tommy had driven over to see Jim; Jim had come out into the street to tell them that he could not go out for a drink because he was looking after his sick mother. Just at that moment another friend of Jim's called Ronnie Dark drove up in a lorry. He had arranged to meet Jim that evening and now came to tell him that he would be late for the appointment because he had to drive the lorry loaded with fruit and vegetables down to the country for a Mr Stanley Webb whom he had met in the Bali Hai restaurant.

Jim told Ronnie Dark that he would like to have come with him but had to stay with his mother; on the other hand these two friends of his — Tommy and Bob — would go with him and drive him back. Tommy and Bob agreed, but before they set off Jim said he wanted an apple. He went to the back of the lorry, untied the tarpaulin and looked for an apple. This was how his palm print came to be on the tailboard.

Ronnie Dark set off driving the lorry, followed by Bob Welch and Tommy Wisbey in the car. They drove down the A40 for twenty or thirty miles and stopped just beyond High Wycombe at the Lantern Café. There they were met by Stanley Webb in a Land Rover who led them along various country lanes until they came to a farm. Here they unloaded the bags of potatoes, boxes of oranges and some cans of beer. Ronnie Dark and Tommy Wisbey then went up to the bathroom to wash their hands. While they were there Stanley Webb came in thereby forcing Tommy to lean over the bath to keep his balance. This was how his print came onto the bath rail.

They left in Tommy Wisbey's car and were led back onto the A40 by Stanley Webb, and when a few days later they read about the discovery of Leatherslade Farm, it never occurred to them that it was the same farm as that to which they had delivered the fruit and vegetables.

There was a further important point about Ronnie Dark. August 7 was his birthday, and he had had a small birthday party in his flat lasting from half-past eight at night to half-past one in the morning of August 8. Jim Hussey had been there — indeed Ronnie Dark had fetched him from his flat and had taken him home again. The only misfortune was that he could not remember Ronnie Dark's address, had now lost touch with him and so could not produce him in court.

Luckily his solicitor, Ellis Lincoln (the brother of Ashe Lincoln, QC, counsel for Bob Welch), did not give up hope. He inserted an advertisement in the *Daily Telegraph* and the *Evening Standard* asking for Ronnie Dark to step forward; and on the twenty-third day of the trial he was produced with a theatrical flourish as the star witness for the defence of these three men.

Unfortunately, although he corroborated their story in every detail, and even produced his sister to corroborate his corroboration, he was a small, frightened Cockney with a long criminal record. He was not the kind of witness to impress a country jury, and the story as he recounted it sounded blatantly untrue. So too did the story of a taxi driver, who came forward to swear that at 10.30 on the night of 7 August he had driven Roy James from his flat in Nell Gwyn House to the Bagatelle Club; had picked him up again at 2.30 in the morning and taken him back to the flat, gone up for a cup of tea and stayed talking until four o'clock.

On Thursday 20 February, the twenty-fourth day of the trial, Mr Sebag Shaw, QC, opened his defence of Gordon Goody. He explained that Gordon had used the name McGonegal to return from Ireland because he had been smuggling watches. After the Train Robbery he had gone to ground in the Windmill in Blackfriars because he was being pestered by reporters who were following up the connection made between the Airport Robbery — for which Gordon had stood trial — and the robbery of the train. For the same reason he had used the name Alexander for his trip to Leicester where the hotel receptionist had mistaken him for Bruce. "Do you not think that is the most extraordinary coincidence?" asked Mr Sebag Shaw. "I do not know what Dr Holden would have put the odds on that one at. He would have said a billion to one. He was not asked about that, but that is what happened."

It was dangerous for Gordon to use this line of defence — admitting to his own bad character — and the prosecution made the most of it by implying that he was lucky to have been acquitted for the Airport Robbery: but the nub of the case against Goody was the paint, and to refute the evidence of Dr Holden Mr Sebag Shaw produced his own experts, who were just as technically qualified as Holden, but could not match him as a witness.

Pat Cooper courageously came onto the stand and lied with the sincerity that only love can inspire; but in cross-examination she was led through Gordon's telephone book which had the numbers of several of his fellow accused. This proved nothing at all, but clearly had its effect upon the jury.

The trial moved into March. Popular interest had waned. Distinguished Counsel came and went — leaving their brief to their juniors on those days when nothing spectacular was expected. There were occasional dinners given for Mr Justice Davies by the Midland Circuit: and the Judge had a cocktail party for the Bar. Colds and influenza flew around the court-room, attacking even the Judge on his dais and leaving only the defendants immune.

The Train Robbers' wives and girlfriends made regular journeys to Aylesbury to visit their men-folk in prison, bringing them clean clothes and the delicacies that were allowed to prisoners on trial. Some of them were irritated by Charmian Biggs, who they thought spent too much money on her clothes; but the women were held together by Mary Manson who until John Daly's release had been in charge of his wife Barbara — still in a state of nervous shock — his children, and Bruce's son, Nick.

What the husbands feared most of all was that other thieves would think that their wives had access to the money from the robbery; and in the course of the trial Charmian Biggs was approached by a man who said that with five thousand pounds he could bribe some of the jurors to bring in a verdict of not guilty. Charmian reported this to Ronnie Biggs in Aylesbury Jail, and he in his turn told the others. They all knew that it was an attempt at extortion — because if anything could be done with the jury it would have been done by their friends. They knew too that, if this first attempt succeeded, then all the wives would be easy prey for the predators of the criminal world.

Charlie took charge. He sent word out to his friends that an example must be made of this man. Charmian was instructed to tell him to go to an address in Clapham where a woman would hand over the money. When he arrived, Charlie's friends were waiting with a mallet and nine-inch nails. As he sat in the living-room waiting for the money, they grabbed him and dragged him out of the house — intending to nail him onto a tree on Clapham Common through his arms and knees.

When the man realised what was going to happen to him, his terror gave him a moment of superhuman strength with which he broke away from his captors. He sped down the street, with Charlie's friends after him. He ran into a shop, screaming, "help me, help me, Charlie Wilson's henchmen are after me". The henchmen caught up with him in the room behind the shop. There was now too much commotion to take him out into the street, so they set on him there and then, and only when some of his bones were broken did they feel that the lesson was properly taught. They left him bleeding and unconscious; and from that time on no one tried to get money from any of the Train Robbers' wives.

Back in the more civilised atmosphere of the Rural District Council chambers at Aylesbury the trial meandered on through the "minor conspiracy" involving Brian Field, Lennie Field and John Wheater. Brian Field was first in the witness box and he blamed Lennie Field. "First of all, I believe, Leonard Field had either a newspaper advertisement or it might even, I believe, have been the particulars . . . it certainly was some form of printed paper which referred to Leatherslade Farm. . . . He merely said it was a property in which I think he said he was either interested in purchasing or wanted to go and see. . . . Of course, as you know, conveyancing was not my line and it was then I said, 'You had better see Mr Wheater'."

"Was there any mention by Leonard Field," asked Lewis Hawser, "about this property, as to why he wanted it or what he wanted it for, at that stage?"

"I got the impression, from what he said, that it was not for himself. He was not buying it to live in or anything like that; but it was merely a business transaction either for resale or something like that. . ."

When it came to Lennie's turn in the witness stand he blamed Wheater, "I was in the office when Mr Wheater came in. I think I was just about ready to go. I do not know the actual words that were said, but. . .he asked me if I would be interested in investing five thousand pounds for a thousand pounds' profit." He admitted that he had been down to see the farm with Brian Field, but insisted that having seen it he lost interest in the deal, and that his name had been used in the conveyancing without his knowledge. His evidence — even under the formidable cross-examination of Lewis Hawser — was so convincing that by the end of the day Chief Superintendent Fewtrell noted down that in all the thirty days of the trial Lennie Field was the best witness yet.

There followed a week-end's respite, and on the Monday morning Lennie Field returned to the witness box. He stood up and said to the Judge: "My Lord, there are certain matters that I would like to state that I lied upon in this court. I fully understand the implications of them and the position in which they put me. I never learned what Leatherslade Farm was used for on the 14 August. I learned on the 9 August. On the 9 August I saw Mr Brian Field. I was told what Leatherslade Farm had been used for."

"By whom?" asked Mr Justice Davies.

"Mr Brian Field."

"What did he tell you?"

"He told me Leatherslade Farm had been bought in my name, what it had been used for and that I could get a substantial sum of money. . . . I asked him there and then what would happen if anything come about with the police like the place was found or anything of that nature. I was then given an assurance that all I would have to do in that event would be just to stay away from the office and that he and Mr Wheater would take care of everything and I would not be involved. I lied about the meeting that Mr Wheater was there. Mr Wheater was not present on any occasion. Mr Wheater was not present at any time during that week. Mr Wheater made no agreement whatsoever with me."

This change of evidence caused a sensation in the court: it also destroyed Lennie Field's credibility. This new version of events was much nearer to the truth than any of the others, yet when it came to the turn of John Wheater to go on the witness stand, he also appeared to blame Lennie. "My recollection of the matter is that Brian Field brought Leonard Field into my office and said that Leonard Field wished to purchase a property and would I deal with it. Then he left and Leonard Field sat down and produced the particulars of sale, the one that has been exhibited." John Wheater, an ex-army officer with the accent and demeanour of a man who had been to a public school, and with character witnesses of the highest order, was intrinsically more believable than Lennie Field — the self-confessed perjurer and brother of a horse-doper and bank robber. Though Wheater — or rather his counsel — had to explain away his incongruous behaviour before Butler, it was plausible to put it down to incompetence rather than criminal dishonesty.

On Tuesday 10 March Mr Sime, QC, for Bill Boal, started the first of the closing speeches for the defence; on Saturday 14 March, Mr G. R. Stanwick delivered the last. On the following Monday the Judge, Mr Justice Edmund Davies, began the summing-up of a case which had been one of the longest and most complex in legal history. His responsibility was not only to clarify the issues for the jury, but to conceal any prejudices he might himself have formed. "When this case began eight weeks ago today," he told the jury, "I took the course which, in my long experience in the law, was unprecedented, of making some remarks to you jurors before the trial proper began. One of the things I then said, and now repeat, is that your function and mine in this trial are wholly dissimilar. I am the judge of the law. . . but all issues of fact are yours and yours alone to determine. . . You will avoid. . .any assumption of guilt made against any accused person simply because he was accused. It is quite unnecessary to tell British jurors that. . . . The Crown accuse, the Crown must prove. . .at no stage in relation to any of these accused men, in regard to any single issue, is there any sort of duty to disprove anything cast upon them. We have that, I hope, quite clearly in our minds and, indeed, it is second nature to every citizen of this great country.''

After a discourse on the nature of the charges, and on certain general principles of evidence, he turned to the case of Bill Boal, referring briefly to the knurled knob — the only evidence which linked him to Leatherslade Farm. ''Can any reliability be placed upon the yellow paint which Dr Holden says he found on the knob? Mr Sime says, 'No, it is a yellow herring', as he put it. The Crown say that is not right. The Crown do not invite you to regard the paint evidence in Mr Boal's case as anything like as strong as the paint evidence in which they have adduced in the case of Mr Goody; but they say to you. . .that that yellow paint on the knob is part of the Crown case in relation to Mr Boal which you gentlemen have to consider.''

He did not suggest — because it had not been suggested by Bill Boal's counsel — that the paint had been planted on the knurled knob. When he came to deal with the paint on Gordon Goody's shoes, however, he faced the issue squarely. ''Let us consider before we go on to the scientific evidence what the necessary implications of this ugly issue are. We will not shirk from it. If we think there is room for doubt as to the propriety of a policeman's action, well that is that. . . . There can be misguided people amongst police and detective forces as there can be in law, in industry, anywhere. If we think that there has been a policeman here who has been so evil-minded as to do a bit of planting of evidence then we will give effect to that suspicion, but we will not lead ourselves to the manifest and outrageous injustice of jumping to conclusions. We will examine the full implications of the evidence before we come to so ugly a conclusion or give room to so ugly a suspicion.

''Let us remind ourselves of the necessary implications of this ugly issue. . . . Dr Holden is of necessity in this deception, if deception there was, for this reason. The only basis of comparison between the spectra in relation to the khaki paint are the spectra supplied by Dr Holden, nothing else. It accordingly, of necessity you might think, follows that if there had been villainous misconduct of the kind here suggested, Dr Holden must have been a party to it. How does that strike you? How does that strike you, having seen him and heard him . . .?

"There is one other matter, of course, which you will not lose sight of, will you? If a person, a policeman, detective, scientific officer, like Dr Holden. . .is going to be a party to a plot such as is inevitably suggested to have been concocted and perpetrated in this case, you would have thought possibly that such evil-minded a person or persons would take care, would he not, would they not, to see that there could be no possible room for doubt that the paint alleged to be found in various places at Leatherslade Farm . . . and the paint alleged to have been found on Mr Goody's shoes was indubitably the same; no point in perpetrating the plot otherwise, is there? Yet according to the defence, that is not the case. The yellow paint could have come from the same source, yes; but the whole basis of the defence scientific evidence is the khaki paints on the shoes and khaki spectra produced by Dr Holden are not the same. What then becomes of the suggested plot that there was planting of khaki paint on the shoes in order to link them up with Leatherslade Farm? These plotters, if plotters there be, have not, if the scientific evidence for the defence be right, succeeded in taking the most elementary precautions, have they? They have applied different paints to the one and to the other, although the very object of the exercise must be to plant identical paints.

"Gentlemen, if there ever was an issue of fact for a jury, which has nothing to do with the judge, it is that issue. It is an issue which I gladly pass to you without the slightest indication I hope of how my mind works in relation to it."

It took Mr Justice Edmund Davies six working days to deliver his summing-up. At 3.36 p.m. on Monday 23 March the jury retired to consider their verdicts. They were reached at 8.15 p.m. on Wednesday 25 and the court was convened at half-past ten the next morning for the verdicts to be delivered. The Judge ordered the court to be closed so that no one could enter or leave; only each prisoner was to be taken from the dock as his case was dealt with.

"Members of the jury," asked the assistant clerk of Assize, "are you agreed upon your verdict?"

"We are," replied the Foreman of the jury.

All the accused, except for John Wheater, were found guilty of conspiracy to rob the mail. All, with the exception of Brian Field, Lennie Field and John Wheater who was not charged with it, were found guilty of robbing with violence Frank Dewhurst of 120 mail bags. Because Bill Boal had been found guilty of robbery, the jury was discharged from delivering a verdict on the receiving charges against him; Brian Field, who had been acquitted of robbery, was also acquitted of receiving but was found guilty of obstructing the course of justice. So, too, were Leonard Field and John Wheater.

The prisoners left the dock. Mr Justice Edmund Davies announced that sentence would not be passed on them until Biggs's case had been heard. In the meantime he discharged the jury. "You and I have been sitting in this court for so long that, to quote another judge on another occasion, 'Life will never seem quite the same without you'. On behalf of the county, and indeed the whole country, I thank you."

The prisoners were taken back to the hospital wing of Aylesbury Jail to wait for Ronnie Biggs's trial before being sentenced by the judge. Most of them had been resigned to conviction; only Bill Boal and Lennie Field, who were both innocent of the major charges, remained indignant; and Jim Hussey was disappointed because, after John Daly, he was thought to have had the best chances of acquittal.

They were left now to speculate upon what sentences they would receive for their crime. The optimists thought fifteen years; the pessimists thought twenty, or even twenty-five. Gordon in particular understood that a case which had caused such sensation, and a trial which had lasted so long, could not end with the whimper of modest punishment. An example would be made of them all. For that reason he decided that it would be best not to wait and see. Charlie came to the same conclusion, and the two of them planned to escape while the going was good. Roy decided that he did not want to join them; nor did Roger, Brian Field or John Wheater. But Jimmy, Tommy and Bob Welch thought that they would go and so did Lennie Field and Bill Boal, who said that once away he would travel overland to Australia.

The chief reason for escaping before they were sentenced was that the hospital wing of Aylesbury Jail was less secure than a proper prison. Except for Bill, Brian and John Wheater, they all slept in cells which could only be unlocked from the outside, but at night there was only one prison officer in the corridor outside the cells, and another sleeping in the room above. During the day Gordon was given the job of cleaning these prison officers' quarters and he discovered that it was possible to get into the loft from a cupboard in one of their rooms. Once in the loft they would be able to pass under the roof to the end of the building, remove some tiles and climb down into the street.

They decided upon a date, and Charlie sent out word to his friends so that they would be waiting with cars. Gordon meanwhile had files, key-blanks and money sent in. During the day he would watch the keys hanging from the warder's chain, and in his cell at night file away that part which he had memorised. After a week his key was ready. He tried it during the day and it fitted: the problem was how to use it at night when it was locked from the outside. He tried stretching his long arm through the hole through which the warders kept watch on the prisoners at night, but he could not do it.

The lock on the door to the large, empty dormitory where Roger, Bill and Brian Field spent the night was much simpler than the locks to the cells. Gordon therefore had a chisel sent in and Bill Boal said he would cut out the lock, and creep along the corridor to release Gordon. Gordon would then tie up the warder, unlock the other door, tie up the warder in the room above and escape under the roof with anyone who wanted to go.

The night arrived: all was prepared. Gordon and Charlie waited in their cells fully dressed, for Bill Boal to come and release them; but in the dormitory Bill Boal had changed his mind. He had suddenly decided that he did not want to go — that the injustice of his conviction would be recognised sooner or later, and that if he went overland to Australia he might never see his wife and children again. Having made this decision, he certainly did not want to irritate the judge by helping the others to escape. Nor, for the same reasons, were either Roger or Brian Field prepared to leave the dormitory. Gordon and Charlie waited in vain; so too did Charlie's friends who arrived in Aylesbury with two cars.

Morning came. The "heavies" from the cells were furious with Roger and Bill; and more furious still when the prison officers went straight to the crevices beneath the sinks in the wash-rooms where Gordon had hidden the keys. Someone had grassed: Bill Boal was suspected, and Brian Field; but they were all just as angry with Roger who they felt, as one of the gang, should have risked a longer sentence to help them get away.

The trial of Ronnie Biggs opened on Wednesday 8 April 1964, and only lasted five days. He too had a far-fetched story to explain why his fingerprints had been found at the farm, and the second jury proved as sceptical as the first and found him guilty. Those charged with receiving had better luck. Roger's sister and her husband were acquitted; so too was Rene Boal. Bobby Pelham, Roy's mechanic who had hidden his money, pleaded guilty to receiving £545 and was given a conditional discharge.

On Wednesday 15 April all the convicted prisoners were brought not to the Rural District Council Chambers but to the old Assize Court to be sentenced. This was a much more sombre building, with dark panelling and the enormous royal coat of arms above the Judge's throne: after the contemporary atmosphere of the Council Chambers, the scene now seemed to have changed back to the more savage past.

Mr Justice Edmund Davies, wearing the wig and robes of his office, was flanked by the Sheriff of the County, also dressed in ceremonial attire. The barristers too wore robes and wigs, and the policemen their uniforms; of the principal players only the prisoners wore the clothes of the twentieth century and they now waited for their cue in the cells below.

"Put up Roger John Cordrey," said Mr Justice Davies.

Roger was brought up the stairs from the cells and stood in the dock.

"Roger John Cordrey," said the Judge. "You are the first to be sentenced out of certainly eleven greedy men whom hope of gain allured. You and your co-accused have been convicted of complicity, in one way or another, in a crime which in its impudence and enormity is the first of its kind in this country. I propose to do all within my power to ensure it will also be the last of its kind; for your outrageous conduct constitutes an intolerable menace to the well-being of society.

"Let us clear out of the way any romantic notions of dare-devilry. This is nothing less than a sordid crime of violence inspired by vast greed. The motive of greed is obvious. As to violence, anybody who has seen that nerve-shattered engine driver can have no doubt of the terrifying effect on law-abiding citizens of a concerted assault by masked and armed robbers in lonely darkness. To deal with this case leniently would be a positively evil thing. When grave crime is committed it calls for grave punishment, not for the purpose of mere retribution but so that others similarly tempted shall be brought to the sharp realisation that crime does not pay and that the crime is most certainly not worth even the most alluring candle. As the higher the price the greater the temptation, potential criminals who may be dazzled by the enormity of the price must be taught that the punishment they risk will be proportionately greater.

"I therefore find myself faced with the unenviable duty of pronouncing grave sentences. You, Cordrey, and the other accused, vary widely in intelligence, strength of personality, in antecedent history, in age and in many other ways. Some convicted of this indictment have absolutely clean characters up to the present. Some have previous convictions of a comparatively minor character and others have previous convictions of gravity which could now lead to sentences of corrective training or even of preventive detention.

"To some the degradation to which you have all now sunk will bring consequences vastly more cruel than to others. I have anxiously sought to bear in mind everything that has been urged on behalf of all the accused by your learned Counsel, to whom I am so greatly indebted, but whatever the past of a particular accused and whatever his position, all else pales into insignificance in the light of his present offences.

"Furthermore, the evidence, or rather the lack of it, renders it impossible to determine exactly what part was played by each of the eleven accused convicted of the larger conspiracy, or the eight convicted of the actual robbery.

"I therefore propose, after mature deliberation, to treat you all in the same manner with two exceptions.

"You, Cordrey, are the first of the exceptions. On your own confession you stand convicted of the first count of conspiracy to rob the mail and on counts 3, 4 and 5 of receiving in all nearly £141,000 of stolen money, but when arrested you immediately gave information to the police which enabled them to put their hands on nearly £80,000, and the remainder was eventually recovered. Furthermore, at the outset of this trial you confessed your guilt and I feel I should give recognition of that fact in determining your sentence. I do this because it is greatly in the public interest that the guilty should confess their guilt. This massive trial is the best demonstration of the truth of that proposition.

"In respect of the four counts you must go to prison for concurrent terms of twenty years."

After these last words there was a moment of silence in the court, and then a gasp; journalists and barristers alike were aghast at the length of this sentence after a plea of guilty; it gave them above all a forewarning of the sentences which would follow.

Roger was taken down, but not to the cells where the others were waiting. Bill Boal was brought up next, wth no knowledge of the sentence that Roger had received. This odd man stood blinking through his thick-lensed spectacles at the pale face of the Welsh judge.

"William Gerald Boal," said Mr Justice Davies, "you who are substantially the oldest of the accused have been convicted of conspiracy to rob the mail and of armed robbery itself. You have expressed no repentance for your wrong-doing, indeed, you continue to assert your innocence; but you beg for mercy. I propose to extend to you some measure of mercy and I do it on two grounds. Firstly, on account of your age, you being a man of fifty, and secondly because, having seen and heard you, I cannot believe that you were one of the originators of the conspiracy or that you played a very dynamic part in it or in the robbery itself. Detective Superintendent Fewtrell has confirmed me in that view of you which I had already formed, but your participation in any degree nevertheless remains a matter of extreme gravity. In the light of these considerations, the concurrent sentences you will serve are, upon the first count, twenty-one years and upon the second count, twenty-four years."

Bill Boal was taken down and Charlie Wilson brought up into the dock. Here there were no mitigating circumstances. "No one had said less than you throughout this long trial," said the Judge. "Indeed, I doubt if you have spoken half a dozen words. Certainly no word of repentance has been expressed by you. . . . If you or any of the other accused still to be dealt with had assisted justice that would have told strongly in your favour, but you have not. The consequence of this outrageous crime is that the vast booty of something like £2,500,000 still remains almost entirely unrecovered. It would be an affront to the public weal that any of you should be at liberty in anything like the near future to enjoy any of those ill-gotten gains.

"Accordingly, it is in no spirit of mere retribution that I propose to secure that such an opportunity will be denied all of you for an extremely long time. . . . On the first count you will go to prison for twenty-five years and on the second count you will be sentenced to thirty years."

Charlie Wilson was taken down: he was followed by Ronnie Biggs, Tommy Wisbey, Bob Welch, Jim Hussey, Roy James and Gordon Goody — all of whom received the same concurrent sentences of twenty-five years for conspiracy and thirty years for armed robbery. Then came Brian Field who received twenty-five years for conspiracy and five years for obstruction of justice.

Lennie Field, who followed Brian Field, was called "a dangerous man. Not only have you perjured yourself repeatedly in this trial to save your own skin but on your own showing at one stage you perjured yourself in an endeavour to ruin the accused, Brian Field." Like Brian Field, Lennie was sentenced to twenty-five years for conspiracy and five years for obstructing justice. John Wheater came last into the dock. "Whether or not all the facts, if known," said the Judge, "would speak in your favour or to your prejudice I have no means of telling and must not speculate, but I am disposed to accept the view that you allowed yourself to be overborne in some manner by your more masterful and able managing clerk. . . . Bearing in mind all relevant considerations I have come to the conclusion that you must go to prison for three years and you will be sentenced accordingly."

The reactions of the prisoners to their sentences were varied — but in a sense they were less stunned than the public. Bob Welch, who more than any of the others loathed the pomp and ceremony of the Assize, had bowed to the judge and said "Thank you, sir," as a gesture of irony and contempt. When Lennie Field was sentenced his mother had cried out from the gallery and he had shouted: "Don't worry, Mother. I'm still young." There were no other cries from the gallery: the Train Robbers themselves had told their women-folk that they should not come.

Down in the cells the warders, and the doctor who was there in case he was needed, all seemed as shaken as the robbers themselves. Lennie Field had collapsed with shock: Bill Boal sat with his face hidden in his hands. Only Charlie kept on joking. "How did you get on Bob?" he asked as Bob Welch came back to the cells.

"Twelve years," said Bob.

"Oh, terrific," said Charlie. "I got nine."

When Brian Field had come down, with tears in his eyes, Charlie had asked him what his sentence had been. "Twenty-five years," said Brian.

"Twenty-five?" said Charlie. "He made a fucking mistake. You must be joking. Bob here got twelve and I got fucking nine."

A warder came up to them. "What a wicked old man," he said. "But don't worry, boys. You won't do that bird."

As each was whisked off to a different prison, and they lost one another's company, despair was their predominant emotion. Even with full remission, they would not be free for twenty years. By the time they were released their wives would be old women; their children grown men. To Bill Boal and Lennie Field who were both innocent of the crime for which they had been condemned, the injustice was insufferable; but even for the professionals, who were guilty, the long sentences seemed disproportionate to their crime. Although ready themselves to break the rules of the game, they became sincerely aggrieved if the other side cheated — as they now felt it had cheated by sentencing them to thirty years.

They looked for ulterior motives to explain away the judge's ferocity; he was acting, perhaps, for the Cabinet seeking to take out on decent thieves their humiliation over the Profumo affair. Most of them assumed that because the sentences appeared to them to be so patently unjust — and because there was considerable public protest at the severity of their punishment — their sentences would be reduced on appeal. Others, like Charlie, were less sanguine.

The appeals were heard in the summer of 1964. Once again the best counsel were hired to argue before the Court of Criminal Appeal — but in the case of the principal conspirators their pleas fell on deaf ears. Mr Justice Fenton Atkinson described the robbery as an act of organised banditry, directed at a vital public service. It was an act of warfare against the community, touching new depths of lawlessness for which the type of sentence normally imposed for armed robbery was inadequate. The appeals were dismissed. The thirty-year sentences were to stand.

On Monday 13 July, however, the appeals of both Brian and Lennie Field against the conspiracy convictions were allowed. The

Court would not have been surprised, said Mr Justice Fenton Atkinson, if Brian Field had been convicted of conspiracy to rob, receiving, or even — possibly — of robbery. But the jury acquitted him of taking part in the robbery and also of receiving stolen money. They could only have done so on the basis that they were not satisfied that he was ever in possession of the bags containing money and had thus rejected the most essential element in the prosecution case. The jury must have accepted the possibility that someone else used the bags, filled them with money and left them in the woods. Once Brian Field was dissociated from possession of any of the stolen money, as he had been by verdict of the jury, was there any solid foundation for drawing the inference that he was guilty of conspiracy to rob? The court was satisfied that the few remaining facts were not sufficient to enable the jury, properly directed, to draw the inference of guilt against Brian Field on that count. His sentence of twenty-five years was quashed and only the five years for obstruction of justice allowed to stand.

The next day the Court of Appeal dealt with the cases of Roger Cordrey and Bill Boal. "The case is an exceptional one," said Mr Justice Fenton Atkinson. The jury had a difficult task and there was a possibility that the case of one particular accused might have become obscured by the totality of the weight of evidence against the others. Boal must have played a less dynamic part in the affair than the others whose appeals had already been considered. His physique and temperament did not fit him for a part in the actual robbery.

The Court came to the conclusion that a miscarriage of justice might well result if Boal's conviction on the robbery charge was allowed to stand. Accordingly the conviction was quashed and a verdict of receiving substituted for which the sentence would be fourteen years. The same was done for Roger Cordrey. Roger Cordrey's guilt, said Mr Justice Widgery, could fairly be likened to an extremely grave case of receiving where, in the absence of special considerations, the maximum would normally be fourteen years imprisonment. His sentence, too, was therefore reduced to fourteen years.

9. Escape

Bruce Reynolds heard the news of the thirty-year sentences in a mews house off the Gloucester Road in West London were, with the shaven head and moustache of a Prussian *junker*, he was living the life of a self-indulgent recluse. He was shaken but not put off his stride, for the severe punishment only dramatised further the "crime of the century" which Bruce in his fantasy had devised and commanded. His sympathy for the others was limited by his selfishness: he saw crime as a game of chance in which they had lost and he had won.

Nor did he seem concerned that his glory radiated to such a small audience — his wife Franny and his friend Harry Booth — for it was to satisfy himself that he defied authority. Although he came from a similar background to the other Train Robbers, he had not like them become a thief through the tribal traditions of South London, or even the bovine inertia whereby young thugs grow up to be old ones: he was neither as cunning as Buster nor as imaginative as Bob Welch, but he had a creative intelligence which outclassed them all. His temperament was that of an artist — romantic, impulsive and continuously frustrated when life could not be ordered as it might be in a novel or on a canvas. His most persistent fantasy was that of "the youngest major in the British Army", yet when he had been conscripted into the Army he had deserted on the second day.

Franny was but an adjunct to his ego whom he had swept up when she was almost a child. Before his last prison sentence he had lived with her elder sister, who while he was away had had an affair with Mary Manson's brother. Bruce was so angry that he arranged to be stabbed to get himself in the prison hospital —

intending to escape from there and take his revenge. The plan failed, but Mary Manson's brother — a diabetic — was later found dead from an overdose of insulin, either murdered by Bruce's friends or driven by his fear to suicide.

After the funeral the girl was despatched to Canada; and when Bruce was released he was met by Franny, her younger sister, with whom he had corresponded over the years of his sentence. They flew to Jersey. She was less pretty than her two sisters (the second, Barbara, had married John Daly), but she was just sixteen which satisfied Bruce's penchant for adolescent girls; and because she came from a home background even more wretched than his own she seemed to understand his frustrated and rebellious character. Her passive personality suited his active posturing: she followed wherever he went and went along with anything he suggested.

To remain with him in hiding she had sent her baby son first to Bruce's father in Dagenham, then to Mary Manson. They had stayed for a while in Thornton Heath until Harry Booth's Jaguar was stolen from outside the door as he delivered a case of Dom Perignon champagne. Harry, who was watched by the police, reported the theft from Chelsea but the thief was caught and insisted that he had stolen the car from Thornton Heath. Bruce and Franny therefore moved to a flat near Croydon until the sale had gone through of the mews house near Hyde Park which Bruce was buying through a friend.

It was in Croydon that they heard of John and Barbara's arrest. The news depressed them both and they decided to get drunk. When they were on their second bottle, Franny felt a cold draught blowing down the stairs: she went up to their bedroom to find the window open and the room rifled by a thief. Because Bruce kept his money in a brief-case downstairs, she was unconcerned; but when she went to the window to shut it she saw that the thief had left a ladder leaning against the wall. It was noticed too by a passing police-car, and as she came down the stairs there was a knock on the front door. She opened it to see two uniformed policemen standing on the step who asked her if she had been robbed.

"Yes," said Franny, "but it's all right. Nothing's been taken."

"Would you mind if we came in and had a look?" asked the first policeman.

Franny turned pale. "Well I'd rather not," she said. "You see I'm on my own. . ."

"We won't hurt you," said the policeman, "but we'd better take a look, if you don't mind."

There was nothing Franny could do. She stepped back: they walked into the house, down the corridor and into the living-room. There they saw Bruce Reynolds, standing completely naked.

"You see," said Franny, looking confused, "my husband's away and . . ."

"Of course," said the embarrassed policeman. "I'm sorry to have disturbed you." He took out his notebook to cover his confusion. "If you could just give me your name, sir. It's only a formality."

"Bert Smith," said Bruce.

"And your address?"

Bruce gave them a fictional address in Battersea, and after a quick look in the bedroom where the thief had broken in, the two officers departed.

As soon as they had left, Bruce put on his clothes, picked up his brief-case and fled to the mews house. Franny followed the next day. The two policemen checked the address in Battersea, found it to be false and noticing the photograph on the wall of the police station they realised too late that they had been face to face with one of the Great Train Robbers.

In Albert Mews Bruce and Franny were relatively safe. Harry Booth acted as their go-between with Mary Manson, who was looking after their baby, Nick, and John Daly who had been acquitted at Aylesbury. Though fortunate to be free, John's luck had run out in other ways: Green, the man to whom he had entrusted his money, had disappeared. John pursued him with necessary discretion, discovered that Green had changed his name to Hugget, and shortly afterwards read in a newspaper a notice from a Brighton solicitor asking anyone to come forward who had a claim on the estate of Hugget. John verified that this Hugget was the same man as Green and went to the funeral to make sure he was dead; but he could hardly step forward to claim his money. He had lost it all, and started to suffer a subtler punishment than that visited on his friends in prison. The police watched him so closely that no other thief would work with him; and his wife was ill. Worst of all, no one would believe that he had lost all his money.

By the summer of 1964, when the Appeal Courts had heard and dismissed the appeals of their friends, both Bruce and Buster made up their minds to go abroad. Buster came to see Bruce in Albert Mews and told him that if he decided to go abroad he would see if the Germans would live up to their promise of help. Bruce, without the advantage of £250,000 of the Germans' money, decided to use his own contacts: he had already arranged to fly from Elstree Airport to Ostend in a private plane and to have his money transferred to a bank account in Switzerland. He also had an acquaintance who claimed to have contacts among highly placed politicians in Mexico who would help him to settle if he chose to go there. Buster, who had imagined he would make for Australia because Australians spoke English, asked if he too, if he went abroad, could take advantage of these influential people, and the two thieves agreed to meet in Mexico City.

In August 1964 Bruce was ready to go. Harry Booth did a dummy run in the private plane to make sure that the route was safe: Bruce followed the next day with a false passport in the name of Keith Clemens Miller. Harry met him at Ostend and they drove together to Bruce's much-loved South of France where they hired a villa and waited for Franny to join them.

Her flight was more complicated because she wanted to take her son Nick with her. He had spent the past eleven months with Mary Manson and would hardly know her, so once Bruce had left the country Franny walked into Scotland Yard and gave herself up to Tommy Butler. He questioned her about Bruce and then let her go.

Franny was reunited with her son, and went with him and Mary Manson on holiday in Ireland. Certain that everywhere they went they were shadowed by police, they made no contact with Bruce, and upon their return to England Franny and Nick went to stay with John and Barbara Daly in Sutton. She remained there quietly while a passport was obtained for her in the name of Angela Green. In October she slipped out of the country with her son by Harwich and the Hook of Holland. A week later they were with Bruce in the South of France and a month after that the whole family flew to Mexico City.

In the same month that Bruce left the country, Charlie Wilson was abducted from prison. He had been sent to Winson Green near

Birmingham after his conviction at Aylesbury, and of all the train gang he seemed the most resigned to his thirty-year sentence. He did not bother to go up to London to hear his appeal, but despite this exemplary behaviour he was kept under close supervision with a light burning night and day in his special, high-security cell which had previously lodged the Russians' spy, Gordon Lonsdale.

When Charlie left his cell to work he was escorted by a warder; when he returned to his cell he was searched; and at night his clothes were removed to the end of his corridor. In spite of these restrictions, however, Charlie started to plan his escape. He brought some sugar back from the canteen and scattered it outside his cell so that at night, when the prison was silent, he could hear a faint scrunch every fifteen minutes as the warder came to look at him through the spy-hole in the door. He noted that at week-ends the older prison officers were replaced by younger, more vigorous "screws". He also managed to smuggle in some of the black grease used in the workshop to water-proof the mail bag straps, with which he blackened the bulb in his cell to lessen the light.

Three different groups of his "heavy" friends were waiting to help in his escape in return for the many favours he had done them in the past; but it was none of the three who came in to fetch him on the night of August 12. He lay asleep, wearing only a vest, under the dim light of the grease-coated bulb when at a quarter past three in the morning he was suddenly awakened by the rattling of his cell door. He thought at first it was the warder, but when the door opened three strange men came in.

"You're coming out," the first said to him.

"No I ain't," said Charlie, unwilling to leave with these unknown men; whereupon the third man drew a revolver and the first clipped Charlie's wrists into handcuffs. He made no further resistance but followed them out of his cell, down the corridor, past the unconscious trussed-up figure of a warder, out of C wing, and into the centre of the prison. From there they entered A wing, passed into the bathhouse, down the stairs and out into the grounds of the prison. It was a moonlit night, so they kept to the shadows of the buildings as they made for the twenty-foot prison walls — Charlie still naked except for his vest. There were no patrols of any kind, and when they reached the walls they climbed up a rope ladder, dropped it down the other side into a builder's yard, crossed another wall onto the towpath of a canal and drove away in two cars which were waiting on the road.

In a quarter of an hour they reached a flat on the outskirts of Birmingham, and once they were safely lodged behind a locked door, the manner of Charlie's abductors became more friendly. They put away the gun, unlocked the handcuffs and gave him some clothes. Two of them were Londoners but the third, the leader of the group, was a German who introduced himself as Klaus.

Charlie thanked him for what he had done but it was not, as Klaus explained, a favour. "We want our money." he said, "the £250,000." At first Charlie stalled, denying any knowledge of a quarter of a million pounds: but since only the Germans could know that he held it, he realised that Klaus must be their emissary and so agreed that once they were back in London he would hand it over. They remained in Birmingham for two days. Charlie telephoned to the friend in London who was hiding his money to prepare the Germans' share and arrange for a place to stay. His three captors came and went from the flat, bringing the daily papers which told of the national furore caused by his escape, and of the manhunt going on around them.

On the third day after his escape the four drove down the M1 to London and delivered Charlie and Klaus to a flat in Knightsbridge. Over the next few days the £250,000 was delivered in manageable consignments. When it was all assembled Klaus prepared to leave. He asked Charlie if he wanted their organisation to arrange his escape abroad, but Charlie declined his offer of help, preferring to make his own plans.

After Klaus's departure, Charlie remained for some months in the flat in Knightsbridge. He was cared for by a man who was not known to the police as one of his associates — coming rather from the Richardson gang. While waiting for the hue to die down Charlie grew a beard, but it gradually became apparent to him that the authorities felt so humiliated by his escape that they would never give up their search. As long as it continued Charlie could not see his wife and family, and so at the end of 1964 he decided to go abroad. He obtained a passport under the name of Ronald Alloway, and in March 1965 he crossed the Channel on an ordinary ferry from Dover to Calais, disguised as a schoolteacher on a hitch-hiking holiday. The first car to pick him up was driven by one of his friends. They went straight to the South of France where in June Charlie was reunited with his wife and youngest daughter.

A month later, Ronnie Biggs escaped from Wandsworth. It was arranged by a fellow convict, Paul Seabourne, who after his release in June 1965 was provided with £10,000 by Charmian. With some of the money he bought a red pantechnicon, cut away the roof and built inside a scaffolding tower which could be raised to reach the top of the prison wall. He obtained a rope ladder, an axe, and shotguns; and for £2,500 apiece he hired two of the chaps to help him with the escape.

Inside the prison Ronnie Biggs and a friend called Eric Flower arranged for £500 to be paid to two other convicts who would mind them on the day, which was fixed for Thursday 8 July and communicated to Seabourne by their visiting wives. At five minutes past three in the afternoon the pantechnicon stopped by the prison wall with two stolen cars nearby. Seabourne and one of his men raised the tower, jumped onto the top of the wall, and while one held a shotgun the other threw down the rope ladder. Biggs and Flower, on exercise down below, ran to the wall; two warders ran after them but were jostled by the two convicts, who had been paid to do so. In a few minutes Biggs and Flower were over the wall and away in the two stolen cars into the side streets of London.

Biggs's escape, following less than a year after Charlie's, was even more humiliating for the Home Office. While Ronnie and Eric Flower hid out in Dulwich, 150 police armed with rifles, revolvers and tear gas raided a deserted country house near Cranleigh in Surrey; and one hundred policemen, together with a Navy helicopter, surrounded Upton House near Poole in Dorset, the English home of Prince Carol of Roumania. An anonymous caller had seen Ronnie Biggs hiding in the grounds.

Six weeks after his escape, Ronnie moved from Dulwich to Bognor Regis where Charmian was able to visit him. In October 1965 he was smuggled out of the country to France, where in the Clinique Victor Masse in Paris his face was changed by plastic surgery. Two months later, on 29 December 1965, he flew from Orly Airport to Australia under the name of Terence Furminger and six months after that, when he had settled in Adelaide, he was joined by his wife and children.

The Germans who had kidnapped Charlie from Winson Green

prison had no means of finding Buster, whose hide-out was only known to Derek Glass. Though he still held £250,000 of their money, Buster was reluctant to go abroad unless he had to. He and June had hardly been out of the country before — indeed they both felt ill at ease if they strayed too far from the Elephant and Castle — and were happy for the time being in Wraysbury. It was a pleasant suburb of London, almost lost beyond the gravel pits, sewage works and reservoirs which lie south of London Airport, and hidden by the loops of the Thames. They had found an old-fashioned, red-brick house with leaded windows and a tiled roof, set back from a private road, screened by a copper beech tree, with a garden going down to the river.

June, disguised by a blonde wig from the Nicolette Wig Factory, had posed as the grass widow of a naval officer when she rented it, and had moved in with Nicky and a friend whose husband was in prison. Buster was smuggled in late one night, and to the outside world the women appeared to live alone with the child. There was an elaborate jumbling of identities: Nicky was called Katie and was taught to treat June's friend as her mother. June was Pauline and Buster Jack. The little girl picked it up like a new game, and on one occasion in a Post Office pointed to a "wanted" poster of her parents saying, "look, there's Pauline and Jack".

The life which followed should have been hell for them all. Buster could rarely leave the house, and when a man came to read the meter or clean the windows, he had to hide in a wardrobe. He went on a rigid diet to change his appearance by losing weight, eating only every other day, and then just steak or fish. He drank no alcohol, and as a result he lost four stone in three months.

To keep himself amused he taught himself to sew, to knit and to paint. He did oil paintings of the garden from inside the house; and when the light faded he would listen to the radio, watch television or work on a two thousand-piece jig-saw puzzle. He would sometimes go out into the garden and fish in the river; and when Derek Glass came with his family they would all go for trips in a cabin cruiser which they had bought and kept moored at the bottom of the garden.

For Buster and June these months together turned out to be among the happiest they had ever spent with one another. They were imprisoned together for twenty-four hours a day, yet they were always laughing at the absurd constrictions of this way of life. It was as if they were re-living the early years of their marriage when they had crouched behind the sofa to hide from the milkman, and dodged the rent-collector when they saw him in the street. Now, of course, they had £340,000 hidden in a trunk in the attic, but it was more or less useless to them. In their extremity, they found themselves free.

It would not last forever, and soon after Buster first discovered that the police were after him, he took steps to find out what evidence they had against him. He had friends who had contacts in the Flying Squad, and for a "monkey" (£500) he was told that his fingerprints had been found on one of the paper wrappers at the farm.

At first Buster thought that he had been framed — because he was sure he had kept his gloves on all the time he had been at the farm; but the contact in Scotland Yard insisted that the prints were genuine — and Buster later remembered that right at the end, when he had torn open an envelope of bank-notes to give some money to Roy James to buy the vans, he had indeed not been wearing his gloves.

He now sent a message through his intermediary, X., to ask "if anything could be done". Word came back that if he gave himself up, together with £50,000, the police would say that he had only been brought in to clean up the farm after the robbers had left — a charge which would probably result in a five-year sentence. Buster haggled. He said that £50,000 was too much — that he had not got that amount of money, and that since the police could not guarantee a five-year sentence he could see little advantage in giving himself up. The bargaining worked. They would settle, he was told, for £40,000–£35,000 to be recovered and £5,000 for "a drink". To this Buster agreed, and a date was fixed for handing over the money.

In the middle of these delicate negotiations, Buster was almost caught anyway. Before the robbery he had ordered some tailor-made suits from Harrods in Knightsbridge; now, having lost several stone, he sent Derek Glass to enquire whether they could be altered to his new measurements. The cutter, who had recognised Buster's photograph in the newspapers, alerted Scotland Yard but the message was intercepted by the officers who were arranging for Buster to give himself up. Fearing that the credit for his arrest would go to others, they passed a message back to Buster and Derek Glass, warning them to keep away from Harrods. Derek

Glass therefore telephoned the store and asked for the suits to be delivered to a false address, and when they refused he slammed down the receiver.

The hand-over of the £40,000 was to take place at East Dulwich station. Bill Jennings, who had been a frequent visitor to the house at Wraysbury, volunteered to take it. His presence irritated June, who thought that the £90,000 had gone to his head. He used to turn up wearing hand-made crocodile-skin shoes and a tailor-made shot-silk suit — all in imitation of Bruce: but where Bruce, she felt, could carry off such sartorial embellishments, Bill only looked ridiculous.

He was all the same a loyal and reliable friend to Buster — and one who because he had his own whack could be trusted with £40,000, which Buster had counted out in torn, worn, mouldy, Scottish and ten-shilling notes. Bill came to Wraysbury and set off to take the money to the other side of London.

In the meantime the intermediary, X., had met the Flying Squad officers to take them to East Dulwich station. They had bad news. Rumours of the agreement had reached their superior officers who had ordered them to call it off. They had found it difficult to explain the "find" of £50,000 in the telephone box and wanted no more deals of the kind which had been done with Alf. "Tell Buster to go abroad for a year or two," said the Flying Squad officers. "We'll see what we can do when the scream dies down."

X. immediately went to a public telephone box to call Buster and stop the money. Buster told him that it was too late — the money had already gone — so X. returned to the police officers who offered to meet the £40,000 and escort it to a safe place. The offer was declined and the policemen departed, repeating their advice to Buster to go abroad.

When X. was sure that he was not being followed, he made his way to East Dulwich station where Bill was waiting with the money. X. drove him away in his van to a house in South London, and on the following day the money was returned to Buster less £500, the price of the overnight stay.

The time had come for Buster to find out whether the Germans would keep their promise and help him leave the country. It was almost a year now since he had last spoken to Karl at the time of Sigi's departure and he was somewhat ashamed of having held back their £250,000 for so long. But Karl, when he spoke to him, sounded relieved rather than angry. He promised to arrange his passage to Germany by the same route that Sigi had taken, and to lay on plastic surgery once he was there. He agreed with Buster that June and Nicky should remain in England until the operation had been performed and a passport obtained in his new likeness.

On the day of his departure, Buster dressed up as a merchant sailor in blue denim trousers and a donkey jacket, packed two suitcases, counted out £5,000 of his money and set off with Bernie Carton in a van with the £250,000 packed in a crate behind him. They stopped outside St Katharine's dock; at mid-day the gate opened and a docker came out to take him into the restricted area of huge brick warehouses. Buster carried his suitcases; the docker and Bernie Carton carried the crate until they reached the gangplank of a Belgian freighter. Now Bernie Carton departed and Buster was taken on board by the chief engineer who hid him in the hold and told him to stay there until the boat left London. He was there for twenty-four hours, in which time he had nothing to eat except a sandwich and a thermos of tea.

It was misty as they docked in Antwerp. A man and a girl, both German, were waiting for Buster in a Mercedes: they drove him to a hotel where he had a bath while the girl ordered him breakfast. When Buster came out of the bathroom wearing a suit, the man, who spoke English, handed him a British passport in the name of Jack Miller. It was an amateur forgery — merely Buster's photograph stuck into another passport and the impression of the official stamp pushed through with a pin.

They set off for Germany in the Mercedes, reaching the border that afternoon. Buster was afraid that his fake passport would be recognised, but the car was waved through without any examination of their documents and sped down the motorway towards the Rhine. The man and the girl spoke in German which Buster could not understand, but he gathered that she was urging him to drive faster because she was expected at a cocktail party.

They reached Cologne by seven and drove straight to the Excelsior Hotel. They parked the car: the German girl ran ahead while Buster followed with the man. They went into the hotel and there, standing in the foyer, was a woman of around thirty in a long, silver evening gown. She was introduced as Hanne Schmidt, and he as Jack Miller: she smiled at him and in excellent English apologised that she could not stay with him now because she was on her way to a reception, but that she would see him the next morning and discuss all the arrangements that were to be made.

The German took Buster back to the car and they drove away from the centre of the city. After two rough nights on the freighter Buster was exhausted. He was taken to a small hotel on the outskirts of Cologne where he went straight to bed and fell asleep. The attractive girl in a ball gown who had met him at the Excelsior Hotel, Hanne Schmidt, arrived at eleven the next morning. She had a brisk, business-like manner and immediately asked what they could do for him. He asked for plastic surgery, a false passport, a Swiss bank account and a passage for himself and his family to Mexico City. She told him it could all be arranged.

The German who had met him in Antwerp now drove Buster and Hanne Schmidt back into the centre of Cologne where they had lunch in a restaurant and later coffee in the Excelsior Hotel. Hanne asked Buster to tell her about his family, and he described June and Nicky, but their conversation was constantly interrupted by the telephone which Hanne answered in different languages.

Later that afternoon a man appeared wearing jodhpurs, a turtle-necked sweater and a monocle. Hanne introduced him as the doctor who would operate on Buster's face. Tea was sent up to the suite, after which they all drove out towards the Zoo to the clinic, which was where the doctor introduced Buster to his wife. She owned the clinic, and Buster complimented her on its cleanliness and modernity. The doctor then took him into his office where he measured his face.

"And why do you want to change your appearance?" he asked Buster.

"He is a friend of the Party," said Hanne Schmidt, after which the doctor asked no more questions.

Buster spent the night in the clinic, but the next morning the doctor came to him to say that the operation could not go ahead. His wife had seen that there was nothing wrong with Buster's face and had forbidden it: since she owned the clinic, there was nothing he could do. Shortly afterwards Hanne arrived and was apparently angry with her friend. She herself drove Buster across Cologne to another clinic in a large house on the outskirts of the city. Buster was immediately struck by the contrast between this clinic and the other: while the first had been light and clean, this was dark and dirty — and the elderly Russian doctor who was introduced to him was evil-smelling and shabbily dressed. He examined Buster's face and made various suggestions in German which Buster only half-understood, but was too frightened to question and so went obediently to a bed in a private room.

The operation took place next morning. A Belgian nurse who spoke some English gave him two brown pills in place of breakfast "to stop the bleeding", and then led him to the operating theatre, a small room with a lamp and a basin. The Russian doctor injected Buster's nose with a local anaesthetic, and while he was waiting for it to take effect, measured his chin for an ivory implant. The plastic implants for his nose were already prepared, and the Belgian nurse explained to him that when inserted on either side of the bone, they would make his nose look larger and flatter. As she spoke Buster could feel the doctor's knife cut the skin down the side of his nose. A small chunk of flesh was cut off the tip; then the knife came up under the flesh to prise it away from the bone; the implants were pushed up under the flesh and the skin stitched together again.

The second operation was performed the next morning. Again there was no pain, but the sensation of the doctor's knife scraping away at his bone while the doctor whistled to the classical music on his portable radio, was almost more horrible than pain. He only stopped whistling to show Buster the chin implant which he had carved out of a block of ivory and drilled with holes through which the flesh could grow.

The day after this second operation Hanne fetched Buster from the clinic and drove him to the flat of a woman outside Düsseldorf where she had arranged for him to convalesce. Her name was Annaliese von Lutzeberg, and she was the widow of a Prussian aristocrat who had been killed in the Second World War. It appeared from their conversation that she was a friend of Hanne's mother, and she had a spare room which was used by her nephew who was now studying in Munich.

The flat was pleasantly placed overlooking woods, but Buster's convalescence did not go well. As the anaesthetic wore off the stitches on his nose and chin had grown painful, and the wounds did not heal but became inflamed and swollen. Two days after the operation Buster squeezed his nose and pus poured out, so Annaliese telephoned Hanne and she came from Cologne to drive him back to the clinic. She spoke angrily to the Russian doctor who the next morning cut open Buster's nose to drain the poison from the wound. The Belgian nurse, who with a colleague was holding Buster's head, explained in her broken English that his body was rejecting the implants and they would have to be removed. The Russian doctor took hold of a large pair of tweezers and groped around under the skin of Buster's nose to get a grip on the plastic. The pain, as he pulled them out, was so acute that Buster wanted to scream; but he preferred to suffer silently than show weakness in front of women.

Buster now lived for some weeks in the flat of Annaliese von Lutzeberg, waiting for his face to heal. The fugitive gangster and the Prussian aristocrat evolved a pleasant routine: Buster would rise first and make breakfast of coffee for Annaliese, tea for himself and rolls and boiled eggs for them both. When it was ready he would knock on her door and say "Frühstück ist fertig, Frau von Lutzeberg," and when she appeared he would say "Guten Morgen", because Hanne had told him that he must learn German in case she could only obtain a German passport. These two phrases, however, were the limit of his knowledge and practice: thereafter they would speak English, which Annaliese spoke badly but better than Buster spoke German.

It was Annaliese who told him that Hanne was acting for Otto Skorzeny — the war-time commander of Hitler's commandos who had rescued Mussolini during the war. Skorzeny and his wife had an estate in Ireland, where Annaliese had been to stay, and a villa on Majorca; but they lived mostly in Madrid, and so Hanne, who was the daughter of one of his wartime subordinates, acted for him in Germany.

Though astonished that this former Nazi should lead the organisation which had financed the Train Robbery, Buster was in no position to be fastidious about the antecedents of those who were caring for him so well; for Hanne continued to visit him in Annaliese's flat, and when the swelling in his face had subsided she sent her own hairdresser to cut his hair. She drove him herself to Cologne for the passport photograph to be taken and returned the next day to burn the negative in front of him.

Buster now waited for the passport which was to be obtained from the Passport Office in London in the name of his relatives. To pass the time, Buster would take Annaliese's dog for walks in the woods, cook his own lunch in the flat — usually fillet of pork and mushrooms, because he was still on a protein diet — and in the evening talk and drink wine with Annaliese or Hanne. Sometimes the three would go out to a restaurant or a film such as

My Fair Lady: and there were evenings when Annaliese was out and Hanne would sit and drink wine alone with Buster. She told him stories about Skorzeny: how once, on a trip to Morocco, he had bumped into a rabbi who had cursed him, whereupon Skorzeny had drawn himself up to his full height and said: "If I were to dispose of you, you would be the seventeenth rabbi on my list." During the war her father had suspected him of experimenting with a prototype gas gun on the prisoners in the Dachau concentration camp. She also told Buster that the young subordinate officer, a friend of her father's, whom Skorzeny had told to bury the Nazi treasure in the Alps around Berchtesgarten had been killed before he had returned; and that after the war, when Skorzeny was supposedly regaining his physical strength in the mountains, he was engaged in a fruitless search to find it again.

In return Buster told Hanne about the Train Robbery. She listened, fascinated, making him go over every detail, and became angry with him for removing his gloves at the last moment, and for not making sure that the farm was cleaned up after them. She seemed to equate the audacity of the robbery with the audacity that had been the hallmark of Skorzeny's career. She appeared delighted that the money had been stolen from British banks, but grew angry when Buster once suggested that it would be easy to steal the precious stones which surrounded the statue of the Virgin in Cologne Cathedral.

He accepted whatever she said, for Buster's feelings for Hanne Schmidt had grown from gratitude to genuine affection; and Hanne too seemed to have succumbed to "Jack's" undeniable charm. As a favour to a friend she invited him to invest in a Spanish property company run by Skorzeny which was developing a tract of the coast in Alicante. Buster sent for £10,000 from the Swiss Bank account into which most of his money had now been paid from England, and became a partner under a false name in what he hoped would be a profitable concern.

In spite of his fondness for Hanne and Annaliese, Buster missed his wife and child, and was frustrated by the time it was taking to obtain a passport. Hanne had made him promise never to telephone England from the flat: but there were times when he would go out to Düsseldorf airport and call June from there. Once, when Hanne was away, he arranged for June to come over for a couple of days. Derek Glass was to take her to Heathrow airport and Buster was to meet her at Düsseldorf.

Unfortunately June, who had hardly been abroad before, let alone on an aeroplane or with a forged passport, was so nervous that she mistook the departure time for the Flight Number on her boarding card. She waited for Flight 09.00 to be called over the loud speaker; and it was not until ten o'clock that she went to an official and was told that her plane had left an hour before with one passenger short.

She was advised to take a flight to Cologne, and travel from there to Düsseldorf by train; but she was in a quandary, because though the airline offered to contact Buster at Düsseldorf airport, it meant giving them his name. In the end she reasoned that if he heard the name Jack Miller called out, he would know that only she had given it; so she asked them to give the message that she was flying to Cologne, and when she arrived there she was met by Buster sadly shaking his head.

June was unimpressed by the plastic surgery — she thought it made little difference to his appearance; and Derek Glass, who came out on a separate occasion, thought it was a disaster. He said that the ivory implant made his chin curl round to meet his nose like Mr Punch, and that people in the street stopped to stare at him.

No sooner had he said this than Buster too imagined that everyone was staring at him; and when Hanne returned he told her that it would have to be changed. He therefore returned once again to the Russian doctor, had the implant removed, toned down, and sewn back into the skin.

Though there was never any question of paying Hanne for these services, it all came to nothing because the Passport Office in London seemed to have realised that the application was a false one, refused to issue the passport by post, and almost certainly sent the photograph to the police. Since Buster insisted upon a British passport, Hanne advised him to find other friends or relatives who would take out passports in their own names and then change the photographs. This was arranged in London, and at the beginning of March 1965 two passports arrived at last in the names of Jack and Pauline Ryan — the same Christian names as Buster and June had used in Wraysbury. The photographs were changed and Buster took them to Frankfurt where he obtained visas to enter Mexico.

By the end of March he was ready. Before he left Hanne helped him buy two silver chalices which he engraved with the words "Annaliese from Herr Miller", but when the time came to go Annaliese was away so he left them on her dining-room table with a thousand marks to pay for his board and lodging. His extraordinary sojourn in Germany had come to an end, but his parting with Hanne was not final, for through his partnership with Skorzeny in the Spanish property company they would keep in contact with one another, and Hanne promised to visit him in Mexico.

He left alone in a taxi. At Düsseldorf airport he met June and Nicky who were brought out to Germany by Derek Glass. The four caught another flight to Brussels where Buster's indispensable friend parted from them and returned to London, while Mr and Mrs Ryan with their daughter Katie boarded a Sabena flight to Mexico City.

10. The Good Life

Jimmy White, the quiet, middle-aged ex-paratrooper who had been brought in by Bruce as the Train Gang's Quartermaster Sergeant, remained in England and for three years escaped arrest. A solitary thief, not known to work with either firm, he should have had a good chance of remaining undetected altogether, yet was known to be one of the Train Robbers almost at once — first by other criminals and then by the police. The day after his return from Leatherslade Farm, a group of men purporting to be Flying Squad officers broke into his flat and stole a brief-case containing £8,500 of the money and his passport.

A second misfortune came when Brian Field's relatives dumped the luggage containing £101,000 in Dorking Wood only a mile or two from the site where Jimmy had bought a caravan and hidden £30,000 in its panelling. The Surrey police, in checking up on new arrivals in the vicinity, had come to the caravan and found the money. Jimmy had left perfect prints on the ply-wood and was therefore identified at this early stage as one of the gang which had robbed the train. Two days later, on Thursday 22 August, his photograph appeared in the papers along with those of Bruce and Charlie; and a few days later his wife Sheree's followed. She was described as a woman 5 foot 2 or 3 inches tall with "an olive or Mediterranean-type complexion" who would be travelling with a baby aged six months and a poodle called Gigi.

There now started many months of suffering for them both. Friends in Clapham with whom they had been hiding wanted them to leave at once. All Jimmy's other friends and acquaintances to whom he appealed dithered between terror and greed. An old jail-mate charged him £3,000 to spend a week in his garage, sleeping on the back seat of his car, using a bucket as a lavatory and feeding on an odd sandwich or bottle of milk.

There was only one man who voluntarily offered his assistance — a stocky, middle-aged thief who was known as "the Professor". Jimmy had worked with him in the past, and admired his talent for impersonation whereby with a minimal prop like a cap or a scarf a Cockney costermonger would be transformed into a City gent; but he knew that behind the act there was a cunning and remorseless greed, and that if he now offered his help, it was only to get what he could of the money from the train. In the end, however, he could not refuse it because no one else would take them in. He gave himself and his family into the hands of the Professor who insisted at once that they must separate to reduce the risk of detection.

Jimmy was sent north to Mansfield in Derbyshire where he was hidden in the house of a council worker. He paid another £3,000 for this board and lodging, but at least the couple were decent people and he lived in relative comfort. Sheree and the child were taken by night to an army camp outside London where she was hidden by a woman whose husband was posted abroad.

Late one night, after she had been there for a month, the Professor returned. Imagining that he had come to take her to Jimmy, Sheree got dressed; but he told her that he had come for the baby. At first she refused to be parted from her child, but the Professor insisted that since it was known that she had a baby it was dangerous for the two of them to stay together. He was going to take Stephen to his father, and in "a day or two" the family would be reunited in a safe place.

With great reluctance Sheree agreed and the Professor disappeared with her child into the night. She remained at the army camp; the "day or two" became weeks; and when eventually she was driven to a house in Kent, neither Jimmy nor the baby was there. Her new hosts told her that both were safe and well, and that any day now she would see them; but week followed week and she remained alone. She became hysterical and threatened to give them all up to the police if they did not take her to Jimmy and Stephen, so she was taken by night back through London and north to Derbyshire. There, in the council house near Mansfield, she found Jimmy — but not her child.

Each had thought Stephen was with the other. Sheree was

distraught, and Jimmy realised at once that the Professor had kidnapped the child not so much to save his family from detection, as to keep a hold over them until he had bled him dry; for all the time he had been in Mansfield, Jimmy had been paying out thousands of pounds to the Professor for the different people who were said to be hiding his wife and child.

For three weeks Jimmy and Sheree remained in Mansfield sending messages to the Professor to produce Stephen, but there was no response. They suffered doubly because they were trapped: outside the law, they could not call upon it to help them, and knowing this the Professor had only to hold the child to obtain their money. They would gladly have paid it to recover their son, but Jimmy knew that without money they were finished. No one in the underworld does something for nothing: a thief obeys only the stick of violence or the carrot of cash. Disinclined by nature to use force, Jimmy decided to call the Professor's bluff; for if Jimmy was arrested for robbery, he could implicate the man who had harboured him. He therefore drove down to London with Sheree, and the most "wanted" couple in Britain sat down on the front doorstep of the Professor's house in Kentish Town and refused to move until they had their baby.

They got what they came for. The Professor took them to a basement in Camden Town where an elderly woman handed Stephen back to his mother. Sheree was so happy to have him back that she hardly noticed his condition, but Jimmy observed his grey skin, filthy clothes and the lifeless expression in his eyes.

The White family now returned to Mansfield, and since the council worker had agreed to continue to hide them, they were free at last of the Professor. Jimmy decided to use some of the stolen money to buy a hill farm of around 140 acres through the mother of their Derbyshire friends and both families went to live there. He was sitting in a pub in the neighbourhood when he heard the news of the thirty-year sentences. He had to leave to hide his distress, and while his friends were sent off to different prisons around England, Jimmy settled down to the hard life of a hill farmer.

He enjoyed the practical work of raising and caring for stock; and both he and Sheree got on well enough with their Derbyshire friends. He paid for their living expenses; the farm was in their name, and Jimmy had asked the husband to take care of £10,000 of the stolen money. One evening in August of 1965 — almost the second anniversary of the robbery — he overheard a conversation on the telephone extension between this man and his brother-in-law who happened to be a policeman. "What have you been up to?" the brother-in-law asked. "The betting shop tell us that you've been placing bets of £500. Now where do you get that kind of money."

Jimmy knew only too well: he came down the stairs in a rage but there was nothing whatsoever he could do but pack some suitcases and set off on the run once again, leaving everything he had built up behind him.

With Sheree and his son Stephen, he fled to the south coast — first to Romney and then to Littlestone in Kent. Here they changed their names to Bob and Claire Lane, and for a while led quiet, untroubled lives; but both knew that time was against them. When they had arrived in Kent only £7,000 remained of the stolen money: the rest had gone in the caravan, and the extortionate expenses of life on the run. Since their photographs were still posted outside every police station, and occasionally printed in the newspapers, Jimmy could never get a job: with some of the remaining money he bought an old Land Rover and a trailer, hoping to pick up odd jobs towing sailing dinghies to and from the sea; but this did not make them a living, and at the eleventh hour Jimmy made up his mind that he would have to go abroad.

It was not just the need to make a living which led him to this decision; for almost three years now he and Sheree had lived fugitive lives, and the pressure upon their minds had become intolerable. As Jimmy looked out to sea from Littlestone, the idea of just sailing away from it all became irresistible: he already owned a dinghy, but that was not large enough to cross the Channel, so he started to search for a larger vessel and found what he wanted in a converted lifeboat. The owner wanted £7,000 — the sum with which they had arrived in Kent — but Jimmy now had only £3,000.

On 10 April 1966 the *Sunday Express* published yet again the photographs of those wanted for the Great Train Robbery: Bruce, Buster, Charlie, Ronnie and Jimmy. Two friends Jimmy had made from the crew of the Dover lifeboat recognised him: one did nothing about it but the other told the police. A few days later he was arrested at his home in Littlestone.

In many ways Jimmy was relieved that his life on the run was over — to wake up from a nightmare, even in a police cell. He voluntarily gave up the £2,000 found in his possession, as well as the dinghy, the Land Rover and the trailer. He also told the police about the £6,000 hidden behind the stove in the caravan which up until then had not been found.

He was tried in June 1966, at Leicester Assizes. Although he began by pleading Not Guilty in the hope that the evidence against him would be weak, it soon emerged that he too had left prints at the farm as well as on the caravan, so he changed his plea to Guilty to robbery, and the prosecution accepted his plea of Not Guilty to conspiracy. The judge, Mr Justice Nield, sentenced Jimmy White to eighteen years' imprisonment — little more than half the terms given for the same crime to the other Train Robbers three years before. Time, it seemed, had subdued the outrage of the judiciary.

Buster, June and Nicky Edwards, travelling as Jack, Pauline and Katie Ryan, arrived in Mexico City at eleven at night, exhausted after their long journey from Europe. They were met at the airport by Bruce and Franny Reynolds who were both suntanned and elegantly dressed. The two men greeted one another like long-lost friends; the two women had never met before.

Bruce drove them in his Ford Thunderbird to the Hilton Hotel where he had reserved a suite. There flowers, chocolate and champagne were waiting for them — and a doll for Nicky. Buster and June were so moved that they wept. The champagne was opened and the four toasted their successful escape from England and the good life to come.

Bruce and Franny and their son Nick were now established in Mexico. The contacts which had first brought them there had turned out to be useless and for the first weeks they had been floundering on their own — speaking no Spanish and at a loss to understand the Mexican immigration laws, until Bruce had been befriended by a merchant from whom he had ordered some suits — a Syrian Jew call Joe Sachs.

Sachs had been born in Manchester but had come via Argentina to Mexico City where he had established different businesses, including the Dunhill concession for pipes and cigarette lighters. He not only befriended Bruce — inviting him to his house to meet his family and taking him to learn to play polo — but also introduced him to a good lawyer who handled his immigration. The only thing the lawyer could not do was to treat Bruce and

Franny as a married couple. Bruce's passport was in the name of Keith Miller — coincidentally the same surname as Buster had used in Germany — while Franny's was in the name of Angela Green. Officially there was nothing they could do but live in sin.

A few days after their arrival, the Edwards family moved from the Hilton to the Diplomatico Hotel to be nearer Bruce's flat; and after a week of searching through the small ads of the English-language newspaper, they found a flat of their own. It was large and expensive, with separate quarters for a maid, but it was near the Reynolds's flat and was suitably luxurious in its appointments for a Great Train Robber.

The two couples now spent most of their time together in common pursuit of the good life. It was what they had dreamed of and worked for, yet Buster and June still felt ill at ease so far from the Elephant and Castle, and relied upon Bruce and Franny to show them what to do. Bruce flourished in the sun: he had always seen himself as a playboy and now acted the part with nonchalant conviction. He was charming, witty and debonair: in shops and restaurants he had a self-assurance which Buster envied and tried to emulate. Bruce had twenty-five tailor-made suits so Buster ordered twelve for himself. When Bruce changed his Ford Thunderbird for a Cadillac, Buster bought a Mercedes Benz. At week-ends they would drive out to Mexico City in one or other of the fancy cars to try a new restaurant or watch a bull-fight which Bruce particularly liked because of his hero-worship of Hemingway. They also made longer trips to Acapulco on the Pacific coast, and when the Edwards's visas were due to be renewed, they drove north to California.

In Mexico City itself the two men started their day at Sanborn's — a café and English bookshop — where they would have breakfast and read the British and American newspapers. After breakfast they would look through the paperbacks to see if any new books had been put on sale since the day before: and then wander down to the Hilton Hotel to sit in the foyer and watch the coming and going of the guests.

They returned to their respective flats for lunch. Both Franny and June employed maids but both liked to cook themselves, for besides taking the children to school in the morning and fetching them in the afternoon, there was little else to do. Their husbands spun out the afternoons by either taking some exercise in a health club, or returning down-town to some other English language bookshops.

In the evening the two couples went their own way. Bruce and Franny liked to remain at home and get drunk — a habit they had formed while hiding in Albert Mews; and if they went to a film they would choose something like *Zorba the Greek* which they considered too sophisticated for Buster and June.

June was irritated by this condescension — particularly when it came from Franny who was only just twenty; yet Franny in some ways was right — not about *Zorba the Greek* which June enjoyed — but about their incapacity to enjoy the good life in Mexico City. June not only missed her mother and sister: she could not adapt to riches. She employed a maid — a seventeen-year-old Indian girl called Liu — because Bruce had said it was *de rigueur,* but whereas she loved housework Liu did not, so June always went around cleaning up after her. Nor could she bring herself to restrict Liu to the cramped quarters designed for a maid: she ran around the whole flat, ate with the family, and spent most of her time either playing with Nicky whom she taught her own particular dialect, or when Nicky was at school, trying on June's dresses in front of the mirror. Unused to employing servants, June paid her 100 pesos a week which was five times the normal wage, until Joe Sachs heard about it and told Buster and June that they must cut it down.

Having learnt the local dialect, Nicky was able to converse with the other children who lived in the street. She would go out and play with them, or shout at them from the balcony of their sixth floor flat to come and play with her toys in her room. One day a German woman who lived two storeys beneath them came up to their flat and explained to June that Nicky was talking to the other children "in an Indian dialect — the language of the slums". June did not realise, she said, that it was quite improper for Nicky, or any child from such an exclusive block of flats, to mix with such riff-raff and bring them into the building. In Mexico, she said, the rich and the poor never mixed.

June and Buster promised that they would do what they could to control their daughter; but their exclusive way of life had not given them exclusive attitudes. Snobbery was as alien to them in Mexico City as it had been in South London. They could think of no way of preventing Nicky from playing with the guttersnipes below — nor did they want to. They merely told Liu that in future she should not bring troupes of these little vagabonds to the flat.

In November 1965 Charlie Wilson turned up in Mexico City. He had originally intended to remain in the South of France, and had started to learn French, but his wife Pat who was quite unafraid of the "ruthless gangster" she had married disliked foreigners and foreign languages and Charlie felt she would prefer a country where English was the mother tongue. He had settled on Canada, and had applied to emigrate there under the name of Alloway; and it was while waiting for these formalities to be completed that he had decided to visit his friends in Mexico City.

Bruce and Buster went to the airport to meet him, but so successful were the alterations each had made to his appearance that for a time they failed to recognise one another. When finally they did there was an emotional reunion and Charlie was whisked off in Bruce's Cadillac to celebrate his arrival with Franny and June.

Although Charlie had known Bruce as a child, it was decided that he should stay in Buster's larger flat for the three weeks he was there. For a time this worked well: Charlie was as full of jokes as always, and a welcome addition to their limited circle. As time passed, however, and the three weeks became six, he began to irritate the others. He hated Mexico; he could not speak Spanish; he loathed the beggars in the street; and lost his temper whenever anything went wrong. He complained continuously and became morose over Christmas because while his friends had their families with them he was separated from his.

June in particular became exasperated not just because Charlie's huge hulk hung around her home for month after month, but because he openly expressed what she dared not admit to herself — a hatred of the good life in Mexico City — the flies, the heat, the snobbery, the squalor and the persistent babble of a foreign language. She was increasingly homesick, and could see no future for Nicky whose friends were either the children of American diplomats who went to the same school, but could not visit her in her home, or the urchins from the streets below.

In the end Charlie's presence irritated her so much that she begged him to leave, but before he did so Buster brought the news that Hanne Schmidt had arrived in Mexico City and had summoned him to the hotel where she was staying with her travelling companion — the daughter of a French arms manufacturer. She had brought him 9,000 dollars, the first dividend on his investment in Skorzeny's property company.

Since he was getting through his other money at an astonishing rate, Buster was glad to receive it.

He told Hanne that Bruce and Charlie were in Mexico City, and the next day they all had lunch together at Delmonico's Restaurant. Hanne asked them what they were doing in Mexico, and since that answer was nothing, she tried to interest them in schemes of her own. She proposed that they should run guns to the Peronists in Argentina; or train troops for a planned putsch in Panama — but the three thieves turned down both projects because they were not quite their line of business.

The next day when Buster saw Hanne alone again, she told him that she had not liked Bruce and Charlie: "and tell them," she said, "not to steal the jewellery which my friend has brought with her from France".

Hanne and her friend departed. Soon afterwards Charlie heard that his emigration papers were ready and left for France and Canada. Bruce and Buster were left alone once again with Franny and June to resume their tedious life of luxury and idleness. They both knew that it could not last. Buster in particular realised the rate at which he was spending the money he had transferred to Switzerland. His everyday living expenses alone came to £250 a week. With Bruce he tried to think of ways in which they could economise but came to the conclusion that it was almost impossible: in Mexico there seemed to be no middle way of life, and foreigners were only tolerated as long as they were rich.

He was also losing money in London. He heard from Bernie Carton that the final consignment of £20,000 — due to be paid through him into the bank of Switzerland — had gone astray. When they had found the man who had "lost" the money, and had gone round while he was in his bath to persuade him to give it back, their methods of persuasion had brought on a heart attack: they had left him dead in the bath without finding out what had happened to the £20,000.

Buster told Bruce that he could not keep up his life in Mexico much longer. Bruce's problems were less immediate because he had brought more of his money out of the country and had invested part of it with his friend Joe Sachs and was now a partner with him in certain ventures. He did, however, consider with Buster the possibility of taking up their old profession in Mexico but concluded quite quickly that without criminal contacts or a good knowledge of the language it would be futile.

In April of 1966, sitting in Sanborn's having breakfast, Buster and Bruce read of Jimmy White's arrest; and in June, of his conviction and sentence to eighteen years' imprisonment. The dramatic reduction in the size of the sentence convinced Buster that the time had come to reopen negotiations with the police. He was no longer in a position to return any of the money, but hoped he might still do a deal whereby they played down his role in return for his surrender.

At the end of August 1966, Buster flew from Mexico to Germany via the United States. He booked into the Excelsior Hotel in Cologne where he was met by Derek Glass who brought the news from Bernie Carton that, if Buster gave himself up, Detective Superintendent Frank Williams would treat him fairly. Williams, who was now Butler's deputy on the Flying Squad, could not guarantee what sentence would follow from this, but he thought it could be as little as five years.

Buster returned to Mexico and discussed with June the choice which lay before them — a short spell in a British prison or a life sentence in Mexico. They both decided that for Nicky's sake as much as their own they should return to London and gamble on Williams keeping his word: so they took their leave of Joe Sachs and his family, who had been so kind to them all; and at the airport said farewell to Bruce, Franny and Nick Reynolds. Then the three Edwardses boarded a plane for Frankfurt: the good life had lasted little more than a year.

At one in the morning of Monday 19 September 1966, Bernie Carton called Detective Superintendent Frank Williams to say that Buster Edwards was ready to give himself up. Williams telephoned Tommy Butler but Butler, who was unaware of the preliminary negotiations, discounted it as a hoax.

When Williams arrived at Bernie Carton's house, Buster was waiting for him. He had prepared a written statement in which he denied taking part in the robbery. He stuck to this story when he faced Butler at Scotland Yard, and it formed the backbone of his defence. He said that Jimmy White had come round to his flat in Twickenham and offered him £10,000 to help clear up the farm. They had gone down there together, taken the money that had been left in the kitchen, torn off the wrappers (upon which his fingerprints had been found), and later had fled leaving the job undone.

At the committal proceedings at Linslade Magistrates Court, Frank Williams kept his side of the bargain. "Answering Mr Salmon," the *Daily Telegraph* reported, "Superintendent Williams agreed that since his arrest Edwards had denied he took any actual part in the robbery of the mail train at Cheddington, Bucks., in August 1963, when £2,600,000 in notes was stolen. Superintendent Williams also agreed that it was right to say that Edwards had asserted he did not go to Leatherslade Farm, Oakley, Bucks, hide-out of the train robbers, until after the robbery. He also agreed there was no other direct evidence connecting Edwards with an attack on the train."

The trial was held at the Nottinghamshire Assizes on 8 and 9 December 1966. The prosecution produced evidence that a newly painted Land Rover had been seen outside the flat in St Margaret's Road on the Wednesday before the robbery; that Buster had been living there under the name of Glass; that on the Monday following the robbery the estate agent had been telephoned by Mr Glass and told that he was leaving the flat and emigrating to Persia. They also reproduced the evidence of finger-prints on the bank-note wrappers and a palm print on one of the Land Rovers. Jack Mills, the train driver, was called to give evidence. He looked pale and unwell, and he described how he had not worked for nine months after being coshed during the robbery, and even then only did shunting work for the next year and a half. He said he had been in good health up to the time of the raid "but since then I have felt pretty awful". His right hand trembled as he gave his evidence.

Buster's Defence Counsel, Mr Bernard Caulfield, QC, told the jury that they should not imagine that "this person who has successfully eluded the police for over three years was a master criminal". He dismissed the idea that the flat in St Margaret's Road had been used to plan the robbery. "Do you think this mammoth operation in Buckinghamshire is going to originate from one of four flats in a Victorian house in a busy road in an outer suburb of Greater London?"

The jury found him guilty, and Mr Justice Milmo passed sentence. "You have been convicted on overwhelming evidence of a crime which shocked every person in this country," he said. "You played for high stakes and punishment must, in the public interest, be severe. I deal with you on the footing they you were in on this at a very early stage indeed, but nevertheless that you were not one of the leading planners, or a leader in the matter at all. I deal with it on the footing that you were, in the hierarchy — if that is the proper word to use — somewhere below White." He therefore sentenced Buster to twelve years' imprisonment for conspiracy to rob, and a concurrent term of fifteen years for robbery. It was three times what Buster had hoped for, but half of what the others had received.

Charlie Wilson arrived in Montreal knowing no one but carrying £2,000 and 7,000 US dollars. He opened a bank account, rented a flat, bought a car and paid a deposit on a two-acre plot of land in Hudson Heights near Rigaud, about thirty-five miles from Montreal, on which to build a ranch-style house.

By the summer of 1966 he sent word that it was safe for his wife Pat and the three girls to join him there. They flew out on a false passport in the same name of Alloway, and in Montreal the whole family was reunited for the first time since Charlie's arrest more than three years before.

Almost at the same time Bruce, Franny and Nick Reynolds turned up in Canada. Like Buster, Bruce had found that the cost of living in Mexico at the standard he had chosen far exceeded the income from what remained of the stolen money or any salary he could earn on a visitor's visa. He had already decided that it would be impossible to become a thief in Mexico, so when he was down to his last £30,000 he made up his mind to go north and see how Charlie was getting on in Canada.

He had set off in his Cadillac with Franny and Nick, driving up the Pan American Highway through Texas and the Southern States of the USA. They covered five hundred miles a day, stayed at motels and kept an ever-open bottle of vodka for Franny and of Jack Daniels for Bruce. They spent some days in Washington and New York, sight-seeing like ordinary tourists: they crossed over into Canada on their passports in the names of Keith Miller and Angela Green.

While Franny and Nick remained in Toronto, Bruce drove to Montreal and made contact with Charlie. He was impressed with his way of life in Rigaud and together they investigated the possibility of another airport robbery — this time of US currency being flown back to the United States from Montreal airport; but the more they looked at it, the less feasible it became, and in the end they abandoned it.

Bruce and Franny decided to stay in Canada but thought it wise not to live in the same city as Charlie. They took a train to Vancouver, and once on the west coast made up their minds to settle there. Franny in particular loved the empty, mountainous country, and the great distance between Britain and British Columbia made them both feel secure.

They faced two problems; the first was that they had tourist visas, which were only valid for three months; secondly their passports were in different names. Bruce therefore sent to England for new ones in the name of Firth and flew to Brussels to collect them. Back in Vancouver he took a job as a trainee estate agent, rented a house and applied for an immigrant's visa.

He knew that by doing this he was taking a risk because it was unusual to settle in Canada in this way; but it was better to try than to return to Europe and apply through a Canadian Embassy. While they waited for their application to be vetted, Franny settled into their new life — happy to be among people who spoke the same language; but as the weeks passed with no reaction to their application for immigrant status, Bruce became anxious and finally went to ask what was causing the delay.

The brusque treatment he received from the officials confirmed his fears that they were suspicious of him: he went straight home and told Franny and Nick to pack their suitcases. They took a plane to Montreal where they told Charlie what had happened: Charlie offered to hide them, but Bruce knew that if the immigration officials had discovered his false identity, the police would soon be after him, so with Franny and Nick he flew back to Europe to hide once again in the South of France.

By the end of 1967 Charlie has reason to feel safe in his new life in Canada. Pat was established as a suburban wife in Rigaud with two dogs and her own Volkswagen; his children were happy in their Canadian school and he himself had embarked on a more-or-less legitimate business venture.

He met a Polish priest who wanted to build a new church and Charlie persuaded him to join in founding an investment company which would hold the funds of various Roman Catholic parishes, paying a modest rate of interest, and reinvest them in Switzerland at a profit. This profit could then be used to build his church. Charlie had heard of an old priest who had been given charge of various church funds and had ended up with a million dollars in his own name. His long-term aim was to do the same sort of thing himself; in the short-term he talked of building a special hotel for priests and nuns.

In the meantime he too became anxious about his money from the Train Robbery which still remained in London. He telephoned the friend in London who had charge of it, and asked how much was left. The answer was £30,000 — considerably less than he had supposed. He asked him to bring the money to Canada; and some weeks later this London gangster arrived in Montreal with ten thousand pounds in Bahamian dollars. He stayed in Rigaud for a few days, and told Charlie how much of his money from the robbery had been lost in bad investments.

There was little Charlie could do but accept what he said: he realised that he was lucky to have even this last £10,000 which had been in the hands of other men for four and half years. He helped the racketeer buy some bullets for his revolver and the two friends parted amicably at the airport.

After his departure, the Wilsons felt they had broken their last ties with England and prepared to live out their lives in Canada; but England had not broken its ties with Charlie Wilson. At eight in the morning of Thursday 25 January 1968, as Charlie was preparing to take his daughters to school in the Pontiac, there was a knock on the door which he opened to find Chief Superintendent Tommy Butler and fifty officers of the Royal Canadian Mounted Police.

Charlie was flown back to London, handcuffed to Tommy Butler. Butler, who was due to retire from the police force some months before and had only been allowed to stay on to continue his hunt for the missing Train Robbers, exulted in his triumph. The robbery of a train, which had swallowed so many lives, had possessed his too. Charlie's re-arrest was the first of three jewels he wished to set in the crown of his career: Bruce and Ronnie Biggs were the other two, and he felt sure that in time he would be tipped off about them, as he had been about Charlie's London friend who had been followed to Rigaud by the Canadian Police. He sat smiling in the plane which flew them back to London, courteous as always to his prisoner like an old-fashioned schoolmaster with a mischievous boy.

The plane landed at Heathrow Airport, and Charlie was driven from there back to prison — not to Winson Green from where he had escaped, but to the High Security Wing at Parkhurst, on the

Isle of Wight, where he was met by Gordon, Roy, Tommy, Jim Hussey and Roger. Pat tried for a time to stay in Canada but eventually returned to London. When Charlie was asked whether he wanted to escape he referred his friends to Pat; she said she could never again face a life on the run, so Charlie resigned himself to serve his sentence.

Tommy Butler hoped that the sensational publicity provoked by Charlie's arrest would force the last two Train Robbers out of hiding. There were rumours that Bruce was in the South of France, which gave Tommy Butler the excuse to go there to look for him. Photographs of Bruce and Franny, taken in Mexico, had been found in the Wilson's house in Rigaud, so he had a better idea of what they looked like.

These jaunts abroad, together with his apparent passion for publicity, and above all the postponement of his retirement as head of the Flying Squad, caused some resentment among other police officers. Frank Williams, his deputy, who had hoped to secure his own succession by bringing in Buster, had miscalculated the effect of his deal: the evidence he had given in Buster's favour, which had led to a lighter sentence, had only annoyed his superiors who now considered him unsuitable to succeed Butler as head of the Flying Squad.

The rumours that Bruce was in the South of France were, of course, accurate: he had been living in a villa in St Maxime since his return to Europe from Canada. He used it as a base to try and recover some of his money which had "disappeared" in England, but met with little success. Friends came to visit him — particularly the loyal Harry Booth — but by the summer of 1968 Bruce realised that he would have to move back to England himself both to recover money that was due to him and to earn some more. He remembered in particular what the Ulsterman had told Buster and Gordon: that if they pulled off the Train Robbery, he would tell them about an even larger sum of money. Bruce planned to go to Brian Field, who had now been released from prison, and through him find the Ulsterman.

Franny went ahead. She flew to London in August 1968, and returned to the same house in Albert Mews where they had hidden four years before. The friend through whom they had bought it had in the meantime lost the lease in a game of cards; but he arranged for Bruce and Franny to rent it. Once she was established, she sent word to Bruce who returned via Dublin to London.

Bruce only intended to remain in England long enough to set up another robbery, get another substantial sum of money, and then leave again — this time for New Zealand: but from the moment he set foot in his native country nothing went well.

It proved impossible to find Brian Field who after his release had apparently changed his name and then disappeared. Bruce was not especially concerned. He was convinced he had established a reputation as one of the greatest thieves of all time, and assumed that not only would the very best information come his way but the finest thieves would want to work with him.

The opposite turned out to be true. While Butler still led the Flying Squad, Bruce was a liability. No competent professional wanted the additional danger of working with the world's most wanted man: but just because of his celebrity, Bruce was besieged by all the scruffy, amateur, incompetent crooks in London. Harry Booth did what he could to help him, but he had good reason to be cautious. His legitimate business had been a success. For five year now he had gone straight, owned a nice house and a new car, and had well-spoken children at private schools.

Down to his last few thousand pounds, Bruce prepared to work with what he could get — petty, unreliable thieves — who reminded him every time he saw them of the taut, tight team which had robbed the train and was now in prison. They at least retained a certain dignity — caged at vast expense, like rare tigers — while he who was so proud, so conscious of his role, was thrown back among the vermin of London's underworld.

The fight had gone out of them both. Franny had set her heart on a new life in Vancouver: when they had to flee from there and once again live out of a suitcase, she lapsed into a depressed, lethargic state of mind. To return from the sunny, glamorous years in Mexico to the same mews house they had hidden in years before, and now count the money she spent on groceries where once they had drunk only champagne, was a wretched end to an extraordinary adventure. And it was the end. As if courting capture, Bruce began to go to parties and clubs where he would let it be known that he was the Great Train Robber. For so-called security he avoided some of his most trusted friends, and yet he revealed his identity to people he hardly knew: Mary Manson first heard that he was in London when the daughter of a friend rushed

in to her mother to say that she had been to the same party as
Bruce Reynolds.

In October 1968, alarmed at last by his own recklessness, Bruce
decided that it would be best to move his family out of London.
He rented a house, the Villa Cap Martin, overlooking the sea in
Torquay on the Devon coast. It was a square, white house with a
veranda which reminded him of the South of France where in
better times he had lived the good life. He used it as a base from
which to travel to London on business, but he was at home with
Franny and Nick at six in the morning of 8 November when
Tommy Butler and his team of Flying Squad officers came to the
door. It was opened by Franny who on seeing Butler ran back up
the stairs to the bedroom. Butler followed her, and walked in on
the man he had been hunting for more than five years.

"Hello, Bruce," he said. "It's been a long time."

And Bruce replied: *"C'est la vie."*

He was driven from Torquay to Aylesbury where he was
charged with the familiar crimes of conspiring to rob the mail and
robbing Frank Dewhurst of 120 mail bags. He then had a meeting
with Butler in which the Chief Superintendent persuaded him to
plead guilty, saying that he would not bring charges against
Franny, Harry Booth or any of the others whom he knew had
helped him.

He was tried before Mr Justice Thompson at the old Assize
Court in Aylesbury on 14 January 1969. The prosecution outlined
the case against Bruce: his prints had been found on the
Monopoly board and the bottle of tomato ketchup. His defence
counsel offered his client's plea of guilty, expressed his contrition
and reminded the judge how Bruce had enabled the police to
recover £5,500 of the stolen money — all that remained of
£90,000.

Mr Justice Thompson, in sentencing Bruce, said that "it would
be wrong for me to give any encouragement to the idea that
successful avoidance of arrest for a period entitles a criminal to a
reduction in sentence". The only different circumstances in
Bruce's case were that he had pleaded guilty and expressed regret
for his crime. "I shall make the same kind of reduction in
sentence as I believe would, in like circumstances, have been made
by the judge at the main trial. I sentence you to twenty-five years'
imprisonment."

In the public gallery Franny burst into tears as Bruce was led from the dock, while at the back of the court Tommy Butler held an impromptu press conference. He told reporters that Bruce, who with Charlie Wilson and Ronnie Biggs had been one of the ringleaders, was the last of the fifteen men who had robbed the train.

"Does this mean," a reporter asked him, "that this is the end so far as the Train Robbery is concerned?"

"No," replied Butler curtly. "Got to catch Biggs first."

Ronnie Biggs was now the only known member of the Train Gang still at large. The unlucky amateur had outlasted the professionals, and with Stan Agate's £20,000 added to his whack, he had also finished up with the largest sum of money. Most of it, however, he had left in London when he fled to Australia, and as with the other Train Robbers, what he had stolen was stolen in turn from him. The friends who were "minding" it in London sent some out in irregular instalments, hidden in the pages of magazines, but soon after his family had joined him in Adelaide, the supply started to dwindle and then dry up altogether.

Unlike his former friends, Biggs was not tempted to return to crime. Instead he took over a bankrupt residential hotel called the Grange Guest House, but it continued to lose money and Ronnie took a second job as a roofing contractor to cover their immediate expenses. Charmian gave birth to a third son, and shortly afterwards Ronnie got word from England that he was known to be living in Adelaide. He fled to Melbourne and settled as Terry Cook in the middle-class suburb of Blackburn. He was joined by Charmian and his children, but life for them all was hard: although £30,000 of Ronnie's stolen money was supposedly still in London, it was no longer being sent out to him, and he realised that they were unlikely to see any of it again. Before the robbery Ronnie Biggs had been making his living as a carpenter, and now he returned to the same trade.

Despite their difficulties, both he and Charmian flourished in their newly adopted country. Not only had the sun bronzed their pallid British skin, and the swimming toned up their pleasure-loving bodies, but the easy egalitarian atmosphere of the Australian suburbs had disentangled the social inhibitions that they had brought with them from England. It added perceptibly to their happiness that on Hibiscus Road Ronnie was admired and respected as a carpenter when in Redhill he had been relegated to the lower levels of English society.

For these same reasons he liked the Australians—their easy-going manners and chirpy, slangy language. In a sense he was relieved that the money from the robbery was gone, and he was glad that it had been largely spent on his escape — not just from a prison cell in Wandsworth but from the less tangible imprisonment of English life. But his escape was not absolute: he was pursued not only by Scotland Yard and Interpol but by his own image in the popular press throughout the world. Public fascination — both indignant and admiring — in the Train Robbery itself had been sustained by Charlie's and Ronnie's sensational escapes. When Charlie was caught at the beginning of 1968, and Bruce at the end, the whole story was re-heated for public consumption and Ronnie's photograph appeared once again in newspapers not just in England but in Australia.

In March 1969 Franny Reynolds's story, which had been published in the *Sunday Mirror* in England, was serialised by a woman's magazine in Australia with a photograph of Ronnie Biggs. A disc-jockey in Adelaide, the son-in-law of the woman who had worked with the Biggs in their seaside guest house, recognised him and told the police. They tried to trace him, but uncovered instead various other British gangsters who were hiding out in Australia: on 16 October, therefore, they had his picture shown on television and seeing it Ronnie realised it was only a matter of time before their neighbours recognised him.

Tired of running, he now felt like giving himself up; but Charmian persuaded him to flee. He left the next morning and at seven that evening Charmian came out of her house to find it surrounded by policemen with drawn revolvers. While Ronnie hid out with an old friend from England, Mike Haynes, Charmian was arrested and charged with illegal entry into Australia; but she had a skilful lawyer who claimed that she had been coerced by her husband to make the illegal entry, and for the sake of her children demanded bail. It was granted, and Charmian promptly signed a contract with Sir Frank Packer's chain of newspapers and television stations to tell her story for £65,000.

Ronnie remained in hiding with the Hayneses until the end of January 1970. He then decided to move to Brazil which had no extradition treaty with Britain, and once there to send for Charmian and the children. Charmian was smuggled to the Haynes's house to say good-bye: she brought £2,000 of the Packer money and parted with promises of eternal love. On 5 February

Ronnie boarded the liner *Ellinis* bound for Panama and Southampton with Mike Haynes and his wife who had booked a passage. Once in the cabin, Ronnie removed Mike Haynes's photograph from his passport and substituted his own.

On 23 February the *SS Ellinis* docked in Panama and Ronnie disembarked as Mike Haynes. He spent the day in Panama with a girl he had met on the boat; and when he flew to Caracas a few days later he was met by another. He was already making use of his attractiveness to women. The girl in Caracas wanted him to stay, and offered him a room in her flat, but Ronnie was determined to make for Brazil. After three weeks in Venezuela he took a plane to Rio, and only six weeks after leaving Melbourne he was lying under the Sugar Loaf mountain on the Copacabana beach.

Ronnie Biggs rapidly adapted to life in Rio. He basked in the beach-combing life and indulged his life-long loves of jazz and lechery. He found work as an odd-job man with a Swiss stock-broker who lived near the statue of Christ the redeemer, and a month after his arrival rented a small flat in the rue Siqueira Campos, paying the rent in advance from money sent to him by Charmian. When his visa ran out he took a bus down to Argentina and re-entered Brazil as a tourist for another three months.

He missed Charmian and his children, but it was agreed that the children should complete their education in Australia and that Ronnie would return to visit them there when they all felt it would be safe. In February 1971, Ronnie heard from Charmian that their eldest son Nick had been killed in a car crash. He was so stricken by the news that he was inclined to go to his family at whatever risk of arrest, but Charmian herself dissuaded him. "It is hard enough losing Nicky," she wrote, "but if I lost you my life would become totally worthless. I'd have nothing left to live for. Whatever you do, Ron, don't come back."

To take her mind off the death of Nicky, Charmian enrolled as an undergraduate at the University of Melbourne. At the end of her first year she passed her exams with honours and won a Commonwalth scholarship to pay for her fees. Ronnie's distractions were less worthy, but in a sense they too fulfilled a latent potential. He discovered the pleasures of smoking pot; it affected him almost as a mystical experience — particularly in

Detective Superintendents Gerald McArthur (left) and Malcolm Fewtrell leaving the court at Linslade

Above left: Detective Chief Superintendent Tommy Butler returning from Canada in 1968

Above: Detective Chief Superintendent Frank Williams, just before his retirement in 1971

Left: Mr. Justice Edmund Davies

Opposite top left: The money found in Jimmy White's caravan

Opposite top right: Bruce Reynolds leaving Linslade Magistrate's Court in 1968

Opposite below: Bruce Reynolds and John Daly, with their wives

Rene Wisbey with her daughters Lorraine and Marilyn

ster Edwards

don Goody

Roy James

Jim Hussey

Roger Cordrey

Bob Welch

Tommy Wisbey

my White

Ronnie Biggs photographed by the author in
Rio de Janeiro, 1976

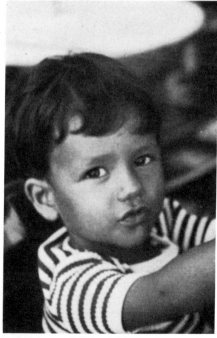

Ronnie's son Michael Biggs

Mrs. June Rothery
19, Keswick House
Crawford Road

London S.E.1. / ENGLAND

Dear June,

I received with many thanks your kind letter of
17th March 1971 but only on April 3, 1971. I personally
returned just this day from a very long - five months stay
in Germany, I had to undergo a very serious operation and
I was very lucky to come through. I was operated on the spine
and, of course, it will take many more months till I completely recover.

Please, giv my best regards to your family, and I am grea~
you especially and waiting for your kind news.

                                    Yours Sincerely,

Fragments of a letter from Otto Skorzeny to June Edwards in her maiden name conjunction with the lithe, enthusiastic sexuality of Brazilian women. He moved from one to another, ending with a passionate Indian girl called Raimunda.

And yet parallel to his enjoyment of this busy paradise was a persistent and growing home-sickness — not just for Charmian and his two remaining children but for England itself. He longed for British beer, British tea and British custard. The very freedom of Brazil which in one sense intoxicated him, in another exasperated him. There was no pleasure in conquering women who were open cities; no joy in drinking up in bars which never closed. His body sometimes longed to escape from unremitting warmth and sunshine to the cold, wet November nights of London.

One evening at a party Ronnie met a young Englishman of Russian extraction called Constantine Benckendorff to whom he confided that he was the infamous Great Train Robber, that he was not entirely happy in Brazil and that if he felt he would get generous parole he might give himself up to the British police. Benckendorff promised that when he was next in London he would try and find out what could be done; he also said he would find a journalist who would pay Ronnie some money for another chapter in his un-ending story. Benckendorff returned to England in September 1973: it was not until Christmas that he came across a journalist called Colin Mackenzie who worked for the *Daily Express*.

Mackenzie arrived in Rio on 30 January, 1974, and Ronnie met him at his hotel. He told Mackenzie that he was tired of running; that he had had a good run for his money but that he felt his life was empty without either his wife or his children. He said he intended to give himself up and hoped that by doing so he would earn the maximum parole. To provide himself and his family with some money, Ronnie agreed to be interviewed by Mackenzie in exchange for £30,000 from the *Express*. If the material was made into a book, Ronnie and Mackenzie would share the proceeds.

On the morning of Friday 1 February, Ronnie came to Mackenzie's hotel for the first working session. With him was another girlfriend called Lucia who was photographed with Biggs by Bill Lovelace, the *Express*'s staff photographer. He started to tell his story. Later in the morning they ordered drinks from the hotel's room service. Shortly afterwards there was a knock on the door: they opened it to see, not a waiter with a tray, but the tall figure of Chief Superintendent Slipper of Scotland Yard. He pushed his way into the room followed by Detective Inspector Peter Jones, the British consul, and a Brazilian policeman in plain clothes. "Nice to see you again, Ronnie," said Slipper. "It's been a long time."

Slipper, one of the last of the Train Robbery squad to be serving with the Metropolitan Police, was now a senior officer in the Flying Squad and had been tipped off by the *Daily Express* that Mackenzie and Benckendorff were going out to see Ronnie Biggs. He had followed them intending to take Biggs back to London on the next flight, but he had miscalculated by under-estimating Biggs's power over women. Ronnie was taken into custody by the Brazilian police who refused to be rushed in making up their minds about what to do with him; while the Indian girl, Raimunda, had no sooner heard of his arrest than she declared that she was expecting Ronnie's child.

This happened to be true; but even if it had not been true it would have been a shrewd move, because in Brazil there is a law that the father of a Brazilian child cannot be deported. Raimunda had a natural talent for publicity, and rapidly everyone in Rio de Janeiro became aware of her condition. Ronnie was transferred to jail in Brasilia: Chief Superintendent Slipper returned to London without his prisoner to face the exasperation of his superiors and the ridicule of the press.

The press in general feasted on the whole episode. Mackenzie and Lovelace swallowed the dishonour of inadvertently betraying Biggs and cashed in on their scoop. In Australia the Murdoch group of newspapers flew Charmian to Rio where the whole tangled melodrama of love and law was played out before their flashing cameras. They made good pictures — the loyal, middle-aged Australian housewife with a genteel bow in her carefully done hair sobbing at the side of the sunburnt Train Robber, while his wild, dark-skinned mistress raged with possessive passion. Indeed it seemed as if the insignificant couple from Redhill had been devoured by papier-mâché puppets made from the pulped paper of earlier editions. Biggs, Charmian, Raimunda and Slipper had no relation any more to the theft at Bridego Bridge; they were character actors playing out a farce for their public.

Charmian returned to Melbourne, chastened that she had left her husband chained to another woman by bonds of sensuality as well as necessity. Ronnie himself was eventually released from prison and allowed to remain in Brazil under severe restrictions. He could not work, and once each week had to sign on at the central police station in Rio de Janeiro. In due course Raimunda bore a son, and left him in his father's care while she flew to Geneva to take up a well-paid contract as a strip-tease dancer.

Ronnie as usual fell on his feet. He took a flat in Sepetiba, about twenty miles from Rio, but whenever he came to the city he stayed with a cultivated intelligent Argentinian woman, divorced from her husband, who shared his enthusiasm for jazz and literature. He spent his days on the beach, or in the cafés nearby, clutching his little son who was his safe-conduct, and talking nostalgically about British beer and British custard to any journalists, tourists or sailors who were passing through.

11. Prison

Those of the Train Robbers who had received the initial sentences of thirty years in prison had reacted with mixed shock and incredulity. At first they assumed that these penalties were the expression of some private vindictiveness in the Welsh judge, and would be reduced on appeal; and when their appeals were dismissed many still had hopes that a public outcry would be raised on their behalf. What Mr Justice Edmund Davies had described as "a sordid crime of violence" and the Appeal Court as an "act of warfare against the community", they still saw as an extravagant caper, and it was true to their gambler's optimism that they assumed their fellow-countrymen would share their view rather than that of the judiciary. "Don't worry," Rene Wisbey said to Tommy when she saw him after the appeal, "they can't leave you in that long. The country won't stand for it."

Certainly there was wide-spread indignation that men who had stolen money from a train should be more severely punished than murderers, rapists and spies. A Church leader, Dr Soper, described the sentences as "miserable, dreadful and un-Christian", and doubtless many of his congregation agreed; but neither moral outrage nor sneaking sympathy were enough to alter the ineluctable process of the law.

The Train Robbers too learned better than to rely on the fickle public, and most of them almost immediately planned to escape. Even as the black maria drove him through the gates of Strangeways Prison, Gordon's vulpine eyes were sizing up the height and thickness of the walls. Charlie Wilson, Jim Hussey, Bob Welch, Tommy Wisbey and Ronnie Biggs all set to work to plan their escapes, and the prison authorities, well aware of this, immediately placed them under stringent, almost inhuman, restrictions covered by Rule 43. In Shrewsbury, for example, Bob Welch was kept alone in his cell for twenty-three hours out of twenty-four. He was allowed no contact with other prisoners, no radio or newspapers; and he exercised alone in the prison yard. The meals pushed through the door of his cell were the only events to punctuate the day.

When their wives came to visit them, they were not permitted to embrace their husbands: either there was thick glass between them or three or four warders stood by their table to listen to what was said. These restrictions only reinforced the Train Robbers' determination to depart. Gordon had already planned one escape from Strangeways when the news came of Charlie's abduction from Winson Green; he was placed under Rule 43 which kept him in his cell throughout the day and night with only an hour's exercise in the prison yard.

He was not released from Rule 43 until the spring of 1965 when he returned to the tailoring workshop which was outside the prison walls. Sitting next to him on the bench was a local Liverpool thief who befriended him; and one morning, standing side by side in the workshop pissoir, asked Gordon: "Do you fancy going?"

"Of course I do," said Gordon.

"Well look up there."

Gordon looked up at the asbestos roof.

"If you make it worth my while," the other thief said, "I can get up there and drill it out for you."

In the weeks which followed, the Liverpudlian started the long drawn out process of stealing tools from the workshop, waiting until the hue and cry had died down, and then slipping into the lavatory to drill one hole each day. In the meantime Gordon sent out word to his friends to be ready on the outside of the prison. By July a circle of small holes had been drilled through the roof, and a rope and a hack-saw blade to saw out the circle were prepared. All Gordon required was a day when the visibility was poor: then suddenly, as he sat on his bench in the workshop, a posse of prison officers arrived and took him back to his cell. They searched him and found nothing, but he was put back on Rule 43 and the next day heard that Ronnie Biggs had gone from Wandsworth.

This second escape made the prison authorities almost

hysterical. Although in a more reflective mood they realised that any prisoner with money could always bribe others to help him escape, the audacity of both these abductions seemed to suggest that the Train Robbers were only one operational arm of some superhuman criminal conspiracy that was stronger than the state. No ordinary prison seemed able to hold them. A high security wing was being built at Parkhurst on the Isle of Wight but was not yet complete; and so Gordon, Tommy and Roy were transferred to Durham Prison, a dank fortress in the north of England, where the Chief Constable called in the Army to help guard them. He told the press that tanks, or even tactical nuclear weapons, might be used to help the Train Robbers escape.

The military commander deployed more modest weapons to guard the three London thieves, stationing soldiers with machine guns on the walls. The measures were intended to be precautionary, but to the Train Robbers they seemed like an added punishment heaped onto their thirty-year sentences. The soldiers outside their windows shouted obscenities at them, and kept their radios on all night which, together with the light burning in their cells, prevented them from sleeping. It hurt them too that the army was being used to guard them, for it seemed to imply that they were disloyal subjects when in fact they were passionately patriotic.

Inside the prison too the warders seemed to them to administer their punishment wth particular spite. They were served their food from a trolley one by one, so that for all but the first it was cold. They were only allowed to exercise in a small, inner yard and after some months they started to yearn for the sight of grass and trees. As a protest against this last restricton, they refused to go out at all, but the only result was that for five months they never once went into the fresh air but breathed only the fumes of urine, faeces and disinfectant which are the salient smells of a prison.

Tommy suffered most from these restrictions because he was less controlled than either Gordon or Roy. Gordon, after the failure of his second attempt to escape from Strangeways and his transfer to Durham, had given up trying and resigned himself to prison life, accepting all the petty injustices and degradation with a certain stoicism, and censoring from his mind all thoughts of life outside. Roy too was as calculating in his approach to his confinement as he had been towards crime. From the start of his sentence he had refused any help from his mobster friends, and the cyanide they had sent as an alternative: he had realised at once that a life on the run would deprive him just as effectively as prison of all the things he valued — his friends, his family, and above all motor racing. He also calculated — correctly as it turned out — that as time passed civic and judicial outrage would diminish and some means be found for an earlier release.

Late at night, on 5 February 1966, Gordon, Tommy and Roy were taken from their cells in Durham Prison, bundled into the back seats of three Jaguars, and driven in convoy by detectives of the Flying Squad to Nottingham. There they were joined by another fleet of cars containing Jim Hussey and Roger Cordrey. From Nottingham Tommy was driven to join Bob Welch in Leicester while the rest drove south again, skirted London and finally reached Parkhurst Prison on the Isle of Wight at a quarter past three in the afternoon.

In the new security wing there were television cameras rather than machine-guns mounted on the walls. Beneath the block there was a garden where the prisoners could grow their own vegetables, and within it cells which were relatively light, spacious and comfortable. Thinking that they were to remain there for the next seventeen years, Gordon, Roy, Jim and Roger — who were later joined by Charlie — settled down to make the most of prison life. Escape was almost impossible, and they had lost the will to try. The very monotony of life inside meant that time had lost its meaning: they had visits once a fortnight from their wives or brothers, but once the visitors had gone the grey waves of institutional life closed over them.

Those whom this living entombment made frenzied were quickly dosed with Librium and Valium; others distracted themselves from despair by concentrating on the small luxuries which could make their life more tolerable. They saved up their paltry earnings from the prison work-shops to buy belly of pork which Charlie would cook with vegetables from the garden on the landing stove. They preserved their bodies in good condition by weight-lifting and exercises; indeed in many ways their incarceration saved them from the physical ravages of everyday dissipation and the passing of time was less apparent in their appearances than in those outside. Only their skins gradually became grey from the lack of sunlight. It was as if they were pickled in vinegar.

In Parkhurst, as in the other prisons where they found

themselves, the Train Robbers tended to stick together. They formed a loyal nucleus, and their very celebrity set them above the other prisoners. The members of the two different firms who before the robbery had been so suspicious of one another, and after had sought to save their own skins, now became permanent friends. It had increased their respect for one another — as well as their self-respect — that not one of the gang had collaborated with the police. No one had grassed; no one had turned Queen's evidence; no one resented the lesser sentences given to Buster and Jimmy White. They all tried to bear their fate with competitive stoicism, and most of them — particularly those in Parkhurst — succeeded, negotiating the middle way of prison life by neither provoking the authorities nor collaborating with them.

There were times when this balance broke down. On one occasion a convict at Parkhurst was dragged away during a visit by his wife because he was swearing. Interference with a visit was a breach of the unwritten rules of the prison, so he barricaded himself in his cell. The prison officers decided to starve him out: they left him for three days without food, but food was secretly passed to him through his window from the next cell by Gordon. He swung a tin across on a line, containing some bread and soup; at the end of the three days it was seen through the television cameras on the perimeter wall and the next morning Gordon was called before the Governor — the first time this had ever happened to him — which so enraged the other prisoners in the the high security block that they too barricaded themselves in their cells.

At midnight they started banging their metal plates against the bars on their windows: Roy joined in with set square and biscuit tin and taunted the prison officers from the window of his cell. The convicts in the main prison heard the commotion and they too started to bang and shout. The prison authorities called out the engineers to break down the doors. Since all the doors opened inwards, and were jammed by prisoners beds, this meant hacking through concrete with sledge-hammers and crow-bars. As each cell was conquered its inmate was given a beating. Roy waited for his turn to come. He heard the thump of the sledge-hammers and saw the crow-bars appear through the plaster. When the door was down, seven men crowded into his cell. The first hit him with a blow which threw him back to the wall and onto the ground.

There was only room for two at a time to kick Roy's prostrate body. He managed to crawl under the bed, terrified that they would damage his eyes and he would never be able to race again. From the bed he crawled through the door and down the corridor, being kicked as he went until finally the warders stripped him and flung him naked into an empty cell. He was left there for the night. His eyes were so swollen that he could not open them, and his teeth had cut holes through his lips.

When Roy returned to his cell, he found that his letters and photographs had been torn to pieces; that the wires of his gramophone had been wrenched out and an apple tart stuffed into the mechanism. He was told that he was to be charged with assaulting the warders; when he was brought before the visiting magistrates, he produced his blood-stained clothes and asked how a single man of his stature could have sustained such injuries attacking seven prison officers. He was convicted of assault and lost forty-two days remission with fifteen days on bread and water.

In quieter times Roy was allowed to work as a silversmith. The others too developed hobbies: Charlie became an accomplished painter; Bob Welch and Jimmy White both made intricate model boats for their young sons, and Jim Hussey learnt German and Spanish. Bruce pursued his literary interests. He became librarian at Parkhurst, and used this position to read as much as he could, but he never pursued a coherent course of study: he knew from his past experience that he needed all his wits and concentration simply to survive a life that seemed designed to break his spirit, without the added strain of working to pass examinations. This led to a somewhat haphazard ingestion of fact and theory into his able and omnivorous intellect; and though his familiarity with Flaubert and Wittgenstein set him apart from the common convict, it made him more isolated and vulnerable on a human level. When he was transferred from Parkhurst to Maidstone Jail, he was not given duties in the library but made to clean floors. It was a severe humiliation for the "youngest major in the British Army". *C'était la vie.*

Buster, by contrast, was as much one of the chaps in prison as out of it. In Wormwood Scrubs he was the boss of table four where all the top convicts would sit together, an unofficial oligarchy tolerated by the authorities because they kept the other prisoners in order. He ran the illicit trade in prison "canteens" — buying hard-earned prison money for twice its face value to buy cigarettes and fresh food. He was joined at the Scrubs first by Bernie Carton: and then by Gordon, who failed to recognise Buster because he had lost so much weight; and finally by Jim Hussey. This was the group which sat at table four and monopolised the prisoners' stove, leaving bowls of water simmering all day to reserve the rings for their evening meals.

The two who suffered most from their imprisonment were Tommy Wisbey and Bob Welch. They were both by temperament more nervous and excitable than the others and Bob was in continuous pain from a twisted cartilage in his knee. Tommy suffered because he would not submit, and had not learnt the cunning compromise of outward comformity combined with inner defiance; he could quickly become hysterical with outrage and self-pity, and would blind himself to the paradox that the decidedly inhuman conditions under which he was held were imposed because he planned to escape. Certainly, he was driven to try and escape by the length of his sentence; but that was not the fault of the prison governors whom he defied with hunger strikes and roof-top demonstrations. He also misunderstood the public attitude to the Train Robbers: many were entertained by their antics, and thought their sentences too long, but few felt sorry for thieves who got away with £2,500,000.

Like defiant children Tommy and Bob would not accept that others could see through them. Just as at the trial they had almost come to believe in their own alibi, now they were equally convinced that they were harmless victims of a vindictive state, and experienced sincere indignation that they were watched by warders twenty-four hours a day. Yet no sooner were they transferred to the security wing of Leicester Prison, than they joined with some of the most notorious criminals in Britain to plan an escape.

The prison walls at Leicester were among the highest in Britain — over fifty feet on the inside with a drop of seventy feet on the outside — and as an additional precaution against the kind of escape made by Biggs during exercise, a barbed-wire compound had been constructed within the prison yard about twenty feet from the wall, which could only be entered by two doors leading into the prison; and while the prisoners took their exercise prison officers walked up and down outside the barbed-wire fence and television cameras scanned them from the wall.

One of the High Security prisoners, sentenced to life imprisonment for robbery and murder, was a brilliant carpenter; and with the Governor's permission he began to construct a long cabinet to be placed in the passage which led to the door leading out into the prison yard. Ostensibly it was a row of lockers to store their weight-lifting equipment and PT vests; in reality it could be quickly dismantled to form four eleven-foot ladders which could be joined to make two twenty-two-foot ladders, one to reach the top of the steel struts of the barbed-wire fence, the other to reach from these struts to the top of the prison wall.

The plan was as follows: on the appointed day they would exercise as usual but while returning through the passage leading to their cells they would overpower the two warders who guarded them, take their keys and unlock the door into the yard. Bob Welch would go into the yard and distract the cameras by going to the second door to tie it shut with a strand of wire. Meanwhile the others would dismantle the lockers, take the ladders out into the yard, climb to the top of the fence with one and lower the other onto the top of the wall. They would have a seventy-foot rope made of sheets which would take them to the foot of the wall where their friends would be waiting for them.

Bob Welch and Tommy Wisbey sent word out to Frank Munroe who promised to arrange to hide them, and had a gun sent in, while Eddie Richardson — another of the escape committee — made his own arrangements. A date was decided upon which coincided with a home football match for Leicester City; they intended to lose themselves among the returning crowds from the stadium.

The day arrived. It was sunny with a clear sky, and everyone was in a benign mood — especially the warders whom the high security prisoners had treated with particular consideration in the preceding weeks. They exercised as usual, watched by the two warders who were with them. When the period was over they went back into the passage to put away their equipment. As soon as the door from the yard was locked they seized the two warders, bound and gagged them. While the others began to dismantle the lockers and assemble the ladders, Bob took the keys from the warder and unlocked the door into the yard. Once he was out there he looked to make sure that the warders between the fence and the wall had gone back into the prison buildings; then he sauntered towards the second door into their compound, followed by the television cameras on the wall.

While the others crept out behind him with the ladders, he began to tie the latch of the door with wire. A warder's head popped through the window above him. "What are you doing out there, Bob?" he asked.

"The flies," said Bob.

"What do you mean. . .the flies?"

"All the flies are biting us to pieces and I'm trying to keep them out."

"What are you talking about?"

Bob turned and saw that Eddie Richardson was already on the top of the fence lowering the second ladder towards the wall. He went to the ladder, followed by the cameras. Immediately the siren sounded and warders came tumbling out by the prison wall, but they were locked out of the inner compound and could only watch impotently as the convicts waited to escape. But the second ladder was heavy and on the first attempt it fell short of the prison wall; they drew it back for a second try but the seventy-foot rope which was attached to the end fell loose and was grabbed by the warders who pulled the ladder down. There was nothing more they could do: the escape had failed.

The warders still could not get at the prisoners, and the prisoners would not let them into the compound. They stood facing one another through the barbed-wire fence, the prisoners shouting oaths and obscenities to vent their frustration and disappointment — even when policemen armed with rifles, alerted by the siren, appeared on the prison walls — until suddenly the sky clouded over. It became black and started to pour with rain.

Bob turned to Tommy and said: "You know what it is? The Guy up there. . ." — and he turned his eyes towards the heavens — "the Guy up there is telling us something. He's sorry we didn't bring it off."

The man who went through the greatest mental torment as a result of the Great Train Robbery was not a Train Robber at all. It was little consolation to Bill Boal that this had been recognised by the Court of Criminal Appeal which had quashed his conviction for robbery and replaced it with one of receiving and a sentence of fourteen years: for having had no certain knowledge that Roger's money was stolen, nor any control over it, he felt himself innocent of even that minor charge. Alas for Bill Boal, his case had, as the

Appeal Court recognised, "become obscured by the totality of the weight of the evidence against the others".

His misfortunes were compounded by his pugnacious, eccentric and prejudiced personality. Like Dreyfus he was miscast as a martyr, but where Dreyfus had had Zola to fight for him, Bill Boal stood alone. Even when he stood convicted of the robbery itself, the Train Robbers were so tied by their code which forbade any collaboration with the police, and so engrossed in self-pity, that not one of them attested to his innocence; and the barristers decided that it would be inappropriate for Roger to swear to his friends' innocence if he would not go on to say who was guilty.

Bill's first hopes were pinned on a hearing at the Linslade Magistrate's Court at which Hart and Co., the London loss assessors, sought an order for all monies recovered by the police. Their action, in November 1964, was resisted by Roy James and — for the £318 taken from his wife — by Bill Boal. Bill was brought to court and in the course of the hearing made an erratic and impassioned plea that not only had he been wrongfully convicted, but that he had not had a fair trial. The prosecution had used invented evidence against him. His own counsel had threatened him at the last minute that if he persisted in calling Roger to the witness stand he would withdraw. "The prosecution have had their pound of flesh," he said, "but it was taken with a dirty and jagged knife. . . . If I had been a traitor to my country, Mr Justice Edmund Davies might have been more lenient and sympathetic. I am neither a robber, a traitor, a conspirator or a receiver. Edmund Davies says I am a liar. He himself must examine his whole and ambitious self."

The Magistrate, Mr Leach, told Bill Boal that they were not there to discuss or argue "whether you are guilty or not and we can't listen to that sort of argument". He granted the order making over all monies recovered to the loss assessors who were acting for the banks.

In October of 1965 Bill Boal resisted the order of the loss assessors for the Anglia car that he had bought in Bournemouth. This enabled him to bring Roger to the witness box who for the first time stated that Bill "did not know anything about it until after it happened. He only came into it then because I needed someone to use and I used him". Even Tommy Butler, who with his experience and intuition must have known that Bill had had little or nothing to do with the robbery of the train, gave evidence that "nothing connected with the Train Robbery was found in the car". If he had hoped at the time of the original investigation, that the danger of seeing Bill condemned would force Roger to implicate all the others, he now saw the outcome of his miscalculation.

Bill's wife Rene did what she could to help her husband by writing to the Home Secretary and her Member of Parliament. She suffered as much as he did from the tragic turn in their life, for the wrongful conviction not only deprived her of her husband's companionship but without the breadwinner the family was reduced from modest sufficiency to outright destitution. Rene lived on National Assistance and was often hard pressed to find the fare to visit Bill in prison. She also found it hard to bear the full burden of bringing up their children because hitherto Bill had cared for them — cutting their toe-nails, whistling bird songs to amuse them, and tap-dancing in the corner of the living room on Christmas Day.

When she went to visit Bill he would only talk about his case. She was more fatalistic than he was about the likelihood of redress, but followed his every instruction, writing letter after letter, until the time came when she wished he would resign himself to the injustice. She saw the effect of their hopeless petitions on his state of mind: he was lonely, emotional and obsessed. He so hated to be treated as a Great Train Robber by the other prisoners that he refused to leave his cell, and when he sensed that his wife had given up hope Bill started to use his son David — an intelligent boy who went on to study German at Sussex University — as his agent to the outside world. He continued to scrawl appeals to the European Commission of Human Rights, and statements to the Official Solicitor, in which truth was jumbled with his paranoia and prejudice.

"My trial, my appeal, also the further attempts to suppress my rights is a disgrace and makes a farce of Justice by my persecutors. Note: I will not entertain Jewry to involve themselves with me under any circumstances. The solicitors, also Mr Simes, QC, are well aware of my likes, also dislikes. I want nothing to do with Jews. Is this why I was not allowed honest representation?"

In the summer of 1966 Bill Boal was moved to the Grendon Psychiatric Prison in Buckinghamshire for observation. He appeared to be suffering from nothing but an irrational belief in his own innocence, so he was transferred to Wormwood Scrubs in

London. Although this was more convenient for his family, Bill loathed the Scrubs and chose to spend much of the time in solitary confinement. His only contact with other human beings was with the prison officers and his family: then suddenly, in 1970, Rene Boal was told that her husband refused to see her. She wrote to the governor of the prison to ask after her husband and was told that he had been admitted into the prison hospital suffering from influenza and a high temperature. "I am now informed," wrote the governor, "that he is much better and progressing satisfactorily and is expected to be returned to the Hall within the next few days."

On 13 April Bill was readmitted to the hospital suffering from dizziness, double vision, vomiting and persistent headaches. He was unable to coordinate his movements, so other prisoners had to carry him to the lavatory. The prison doctors treated him for a duodenal ulcer but his condition did not improve. When Rene went to visit him, Bill hardly seemed to recognise her and was slow in answering her questions. Seeing how ill he was, she started once again to badger the Home Office, her Member of Parliament and even journalists to have him released on parole, for Bill had now served more than half his sentence, but the authorities refused.

More than a month after he had been admitted into the prison hospital for the second time, the prison psychotherapist began to suspect some sort of brain disease. On 26 May Bill was examined by a consultant surgeon: on 12 June he was sent to an outside hospital for nervous diseases in Maida Vale : three days later they opened his skull to find a malignant brain tumor. Part of it was removed but nothing could be done to save his life.

Only now that he was comatose and dying was Rene told she could have her husband back; but since her house in Burnsthwaite Road did not have a bathroom, let alone the facilities to nurse him, Rene left him in the hospital where ten days later he died. His body was buried by a Catholic priest in a pauper's grave, attended only by his wife, his sister and his three children.

The pain and anguish of the women and children, caught in the tragic aftermath of the Great Train Robbery, seemed to them quite disproportionate punishment for the crime. Instinctively they felt that just as we cannot give monetary value to human life, so we should not put a price on human suffering — which the judge seemed to have done by interring their husbands for the core of their lives because they had stolen £2½ million. Perhap she had assumed — remote on his bench — that men so brutal in their treatment of an old train driver would be equally unprincipled when it came to family life; for in many ways the punishments he imposed were easier on the men than the women. The Train Robbers themselves had chosen to risk imprisonment, and once resigned to it could enjoy the companionship of their comrades and the coddling consistence of institutional life.

Outside, their wives were suddenly isolated in a whirlwind of notoriety with only terrified brothers and cousins prepared to help them. Because the Train Robbers, by their nature, had been dominant men, these women had been the obverse — timid, dependent, fluffy, domesticated girls who had left every major decision to their husbands. Now, without the physical warmth or psychological support of their menfolk, they were expected to organise and coordinate lawyers, alibis and escapes as well as arrange their own lives and bring up their children.

Some of them could not take it; others clung on for a while: Gordon's fiancée, Pat, who had been so loyal to him in the witness stand, despite the revelations of his infidelity in Leicester, continued to visit him in prison, carrying messages to and fro; but when it became clear that he would never escape Gordon himself decided that she must marry another man. It was not altogether an unselfish decision: as long as she continued to visit him, he thought of her as his and was tormented in his fantasy by frustration and jealousy which only added to the anguish of his imprisonment. He explained this to her on the back of a Christmas card, after which she ceased to visit him.

Franny Reynolds had every intention of remaining faithful to Bruce with whom she had lived since she was sixteen years old. Yet as the years passed the power of a Svengali that Bruce had exercised over her personality made her more vulnerable to loneliness and insecurity. She was still in her early twenties: she would be forty before she could expect him back. She met another man, and in 1974, six years after Bruce had been sent to prison, they were divorced. She was the second Allen sister to have abandoned him, and Bruce felt bitter that she did not stand by him: but he was older now and more understanding. There was no talk of escape and revenge.

The remaining wives and girlfriends stood by the train robbers throughout their years in prison. Jimmy White's wife, Sheree, went to live in Hastings to bring up their son as best she could and prepare a home for Jimmy's return. Pat Wilson did the same for her three girls — relieved, like June, to be back among her family in London, and helped to some extent by the substantial sum of money she had been paid for her fanciful revelations in the *News of the World*.

More extraordinary is the story of Jim Hussey's girlfriend, Gill. The eighteen-year-old daughter of a South London bookmaker, she only met Jim shortly before he went to Germany, and their friendship only flourished after his return. Her parents, who knew Jim — and knew that he was a thief — were strongly against the liaison, but Gill was an independent and forthright girl and thought she saw through Jim's diffident, thuggish manner to a better man. Even after the Train Robbery she was so infatuated that she accepted an offer of marriage which Jim felt able to make now that his future was secure.

His arrest for the Train Robbery confirmed Gill's parents' suspicions. Their house was raided by the Flying Squad searching for the stolen money, and so they told their daughter that either she must give up her unsavoury boyfriend or leave home. She left home and went to live with Rene Wisbey and travelled with her for the trial at Aylesbury.

The thirty-year sentences came as a devastating shock to a young girl who had committed herself irrevocably to a man from whom she would be parted now for twenty years. On her first visit to Jim at Walton Prison in Liverpool she simply sat behind the screen with tears streaming down the cheeks of her pretty face saying: "I'm all right, don't worry, I'm all right". And even Jim, who was strongly possessed by that masculine ideal of the stiff upper lip common among thieves, was shaken and white in the face. He told her that she must treat him as dead. "It'll be best for both of us," he said, "if you forget about me and make a new life for yourself."

Ostensibly Gill agreed, but for the next year she continued to visit him once a month, and to write to him once a week, until about a year after he was sentenced Jim had a long letter smuggled out to her in which he said it was hopeless to continue. Like Gordon, he wanted to save himself the torments of frustration and jealousy, but when Gill had read his letter she went straight to the Post Office and sent back a telegram which read: "Letter received. Don't be ridiculous. See you next week. Love Gillie."

Gill had not only left her parents' house because of Jim, she had also stopped working for her father in his betting shop. She got a job instead in a dress shop; then as a waitress in a Piccadilly restaurant; and finally on the administrative staff of a model agency. This was a responsible position which entailed travelling abroad, and she remained there for six and a half years. She went out with other young men, but none of them affected her love for Jim Hussey until she met one who was like him. He was not a thief, but he was tall and had many of the same mannerisms. As a result Gill stopped seeing Jim Hussey.

Her lover — Jim's law-abiding *alter ego* — wanted to marry Gill, but although Jim had been in prison now for six years, and was expected to remain there for another fourteen, she felt reluctant to take a step that would make their breach final. Eventually she fled from the dilemma to the United States. She stayed in Maryland with an American girl who had worked for one summer in the restaurant. She remained there for a year, and she came back to England with her mind made up. She would not return to her lover: she wanted to see Jim again.

It was not easy to arrange. Self-respect is all-important to a prisoner, and Jim felt a residual resentment towards Gill who had at first refused to abandon him and had then gone off with another man. He had exchanged letters with her sister, for example, only on the condition that Gill was never mentioned: but while Gill had been in America Roger Cordrey had been released on parole. He promised to act as an intermediary, wrote to Jim, and some weeks later Gill received through the post an impersonal Visiting Order. There was no letter or message, and when she went up to Hull Jim appeared almost cold — talking to her politely about her year in the United States: but on subsequent visits he was quite unable to keep up this posture of indifference. All the former affection and attraction reasserted itself; they started writing to one another again, and by the middle of the 1970s it was agreed between them that as soon as Jim got parole they would be married.

In the case of Bob Welch, two women suffered from his crime and its consequences: there was his wife Pat, who lived with their dog in Islington; and a girlfriend, Jean, who had worked at the New Crown Club and had borne him a child.

In many ways Bob was like Dr Jekyll and Mr Hyde: he was a

nervous man, and on business could be vindictive and violent, but when it came to his dealings with women he was always courteous and kind. He had never been able to dispose of his barren wife, yet nor would he abandon Jean, particularly since she had borne him a child. When her existence became apparent in the course of the trial, he had told his family to tell his wife that she had been invented to provide him with an alibi.

For the first few years of his imprisonment, both women came to visit him — Jean on Special Visiting Orders. It often entailed a journey of seven hours for a twenty-minute visit, but the two women remained so devoted that they never missed an opportunity. Yet both were quiet, domestic creatures who were totally ill-suited to a solitary life. The strain of their condition began in both of them to have an effect on their mental state.

The first symptoms of Pat's breakdown were noticed by the other wives to whom she talked in riddles which they could not understand. She then started to imagine that wherever she went people pointed to her as a Train Robber's wife, and to disguise herself she had her beautiful auburn hair dyed black and smeared her lips with scarlet lipstick. Shortly after that she had her hair cut short and the stubble dyed blonde. Then, just six years after Bob had started his sentence, she came to ask for a divorce because she loved another man.

Bob was quite happy to grant it, and the formalities were quickly completed; but messages came in to the prison to say that the lover she intended to marry did not exist. He was a phantom young man who had sprung from her fantasy. The divorce proceeded all the same, and for some years after the final decree Bob heard nothing from her until late one winter night he was taken from his cell in Parkhurst to the telephone. It was the duty officer of a mental hospital in Newcastle. Pat had been found barefoot and destitute, wandering around the streets of the city. Bob immediately arranged for a friend to go north to see to her, but it was two months before the hospital felt she was fit for release. She came back to London and started to write to Bob again as her "darling husband". She had forgotten they were divorced.

Jean at least had the child, but she too began to deteriorate under the strain of living alone. She had moved to a pleasant house in Essex, bought by Bob's friends with the money from the robbery, but because she had decided to stick by Bob she could never go out with other men and so spent most of her time alone. Her life was centred around her visits to him in prison; yet when the time came, the weeks of anticipation together with the hours of travelling put much too much pressure on both of them as they sat face to face for half an hour surrounded by prison staff. She suffered to see him suffer from the pain in his leg, particularly as he attempted to conceal it by being seated when she arrived and remaining on his chair until she left.

She particularly hated the journey to Parkhurst which involved taking a train to Portsmouth, a ferry to the Isle of Wight and then a bus or a taxi to the prison. One day, in 1972, she arrived at Waterloo station and found herself incapable of getting on to the train. In a state of nervous panic she ran from the station, clutching her child with one hand and a bag with the other. She took a taxi to Bob's sister who lived in Islington, and the next day was sent by her doctor to the psychiatric unit of a hospital where she was put on tranquillisers and anti-depressant drugs.

In the months which followed Tommy's arrest, Rene Wisbey lost a stone in weight. She was a pretty, extrovert, fun-loving woman — and some said that her extravagance and self-indulgence had pushed Tommy into crime — but however spoilt and selfish she might have seemed in the past, she faced the lonely twenty years with considerable courage and never for a moment considered deserting her husband. She had Gill to live with her, and during the trial kept up the spirits of the other wives with her Cockney good humour.

She had one continuing advantage over them: Tommy had left his money with one of his brothers who used part of it to buy a small house in a pleasant South London suburb and pay Rene a regular allowance which enabled her to live quite well. When Tommy went on hunger strike in Leeds, she had to fly back from Majorca to persuade him to eat again. She also went out with her family and friends, and occasionally with other men. When one and then another of these escorts became fond of her and asked her to marry them, she turned them both down without hesitation. Tommy remained her husband.

In spite of her more resilient personality, she also suffered — particularly to see Tommy fighting his hopeless battles against the prison authorities; and it caused her added anguish to see her two daughters mocked at school for being the children of a Train

Robber. Shortly after Tommy had been sentenced, when Marilyn was nine and Lorraine seven, she found them playing in the school corridor instead of the playground to avoid being teased by the other children.

Even when they were not openly derided, their classmates would find ways of getting at them for being the daughters of a convict father. Once Lorraine formed part of a group of girls who began to tell one another about their fathers' professions. "What's your Dad, Lorraine?" they asked, knowing quite well that he was in prison.

She did not reply but the other girls persisted. "Go, on, Lorraine. Tell us. What's your Dad."

Lorraine looked her little friends in the face and said, "My Dad's fuckin' handsome."

Both girls grew up to be vital and attractive young women. By the autumn of 1971, when Lorraine was sixteen and Marilyn eighteen, they both had boyfriends and Marilyn had established a reputation as a folk singer in the pubs of South London. On the night of 6 November she was due to appear at a pub in Brockley, and Rene had arranged a party — including Roger Cordrey and one of his sons — to go with her. On the way home the grown-ups went in one car and the young people in another: the second skidded on the wet road and crashed into a concrete lamp-post. The driver, Lorraine's boyfriend, was killed outright: Lorraine was taken to hospital in a critical condition.

For two weeks she hovered between life and death. Tommy was brought to her bedside from Parkhurst. He was allowed ten minutes with his wife who simply sobbed in his arms, and then returned under escort to the Isle of Wight. A day or two later his daughter died. Her funeral took place on 29 November in Camberwell Cemetery. There were one hundred and ninety-six floral tributes from their relatives, friends and Tommy's professional associates including John and Barbara Daly, Buster and June Edwards, the Richardsons and the Krays; but no number of flowers could mitigate the grief of Rene and Marilyn Wisbey, who went through the funeral in a state of shock and in the weeks which followed sank into a state of lethargic depression. Marilyn could not answer questions and gave up caring for her appearance: Rene never left the house. Both women felt that the only way to escape from their depression — and the despair which afflicted Tommy in prison — would be for Rene to have another child; but if they waited for Tommy to return, she might well be past child-bearing age.

Rene considered an application to the Home Secretary, Reginald Maudling, to be allowed a "conjugal visit", but she knew it would be refused; nonetheless she suffered the indignity of having her private anguish printed in headlines over the front page of the *News of the World.* She did what she could in other ways to rouse herself from her torpor. She went to work as a barmaid, but both she and Marilyn knew that only another child would make up for the loss of Lorraine. Marilyn was under psychiatric care, but she had a boyfriend and a year after her sister's death she decided that if her mother could not have a baby, then she would. In 1974 she gave birth to a boy and called him Jonathan.

The knowledge that their wives suffered in this way without their husbands there to comfort them was the most subtle torment that the Train Robbers, like other convicts, had to undergo; but almost as insidious was the treachery of their friends.

When June Edwards had agreed that Buster should give himself up, she had expected to lose him for three and a half years: his sentence of fifteen years, though half of what the others had received, meant that he would be away for ten. For the first time since the age of fifteen, when she had first met Buster outside the Regal Cinema in Kennington, June was alone — obliged to earn her own living, bring up her daughter, and act as an outside agent for Buster's affairs.

She went to work with Derek Glass in the Nicolette Wig Factory in the Old Kent Road, which had been set up with part of Buster's whack from the Airport Robbery. It was notionally a partnership between Buster and his friend, but Derek Glass treated June like any other employee; they quarrelled about money; the work was tedious and unpleasant; and finally June ceased to go. Without a job the only money June now possessed was £1,200 she had saved for a deposit on a house in Kent. She was determined not to spend that on everyday living, and too terrified — as a Train Robber's wife — to open a bank account, she gave it for safe-keeping to another of Buster's oldest friends, Gus Brown — the fellow thief whom Buster had helped on numerous occasions, particularly after his arrest for the bank robbery in the West End.

In spite of what his way of life had brought upon them, June remained passionately loyal to Buster. Throughout his years in prison she never lost an opportunity to visit him and never went out to a pub or restaurant unless chaperoned by Rene Wisbey or the wives of other friends; yet more exacting than this determined fidelity was her necessary preoccupation with Buster's business interests; for with paltry education, a meagre vocabulary and a limited experience of life, June had no confidence in her own abilities and became quite terrified when forced outside her own immediate environment.

Some years after his first incarceration, Buster asked her to fly out to Spain to see Otto Skorzeny. After the quarrel with Derek Glass, and the subsequent loss of their interest in the wig factory, the £10,000 invested in Skorzeny's property company was their only remaining asset. There had already been a letter from Skorzeny, sent to June in her maiden name at her sister's flat, suggesting that someone should be sent out to Spain to collect the dividends due to Buster, and to inspect the development. It was agreed that June should go with Gus Brown, and together they flew to Madrid.

Otto Skorzeny was immediately recognisable, as he came towards them at the bar of their hotel, by the scar on his cheek and his immense size. As he introduced himself, in excellent English, he towered above them; and though his manner was friendly and confident, he failed to overcome June's natural timidity.

That evening Skorzeny took them both to dinner in a restaurant, treating them always with great courtesy and charm; and the next day drove them from Madrid to Alicante to show them the estate being developed by his company. He drove fast, talking all the while as they went along — saying that he had had a great respect for both Hitler and Churchill; that many of the stories told about Hitler were untrue; that people said Hitler was an idiot, but how could an idiot have governed Germany so well? June, who at this juncture knew nothing of Skorzeny's past, listened in silence, clutching the sides of her seat as the car squealed around corners of the twisting road. Once, when the car hit a bird, she screamed out loud: Skorzeny looked at her in amazement.

In Alicante all three were booked in at the same hotel; and the next morning were taken on a tour of the estate. Since June was quite unable to understand anything Skorzeny said to her about Buster's investment, she asked him to address himself to Gus

Brown; and when it came to the payment of a second dividend —
some £1,400 — she asked that that too should be given to him for
safe-keeping.

From Alicante Skorzeny drove them to Malaga to catch a plane
back to London. Before they departed, he asked June to give his
best wishes to "Jack", of whom he had heard so much, and to
bring him to Spain for a holiday on the estate as soon as he was
released from prison.

Soon after they got back to England, Gus Brown vanished —
taking with him not only the £1,400 that Skorzeny had given him
for Buster, but also the £1,200 which June had saved towards a
house in Kent. When June went to visit Buster, she described as
best she could the visit to Skorzeny and told him of the perfidy of
his friend.

Buster was pained and disillusioned. The good life promised by
limitless wealth had proved to be a chimera; now even friendship
— that basic component of human happiness accessible to the
simplest and poorest man — had been rotted by the values of his
profession. The robber had been robbed; the liar lied to. There
was almost no one now he could trust but his wife.

Sometime after this June was summoned to Brown's Hotel to
have tea with Hanne Schmidt. They had already met in Mexico,
but June was nonetheless overawed by this brisk German
girl who made no allowances for her intellectual limitations
but talked in rapid bursts about Buster's business interests. June
understood very little, but for fear of appearing a fool she
pretended to take it in and attempted to extract from the torrent
of talk the message she was to take to Buster.

The gist of it was that the property in Alicante was now
developed, and Otto Skorzeny felt that if he could find the right
buyer at the right price he should sell it. He wanted Buster to give
him power of attorney so that a sale could be effected without
delay.

All this June repeated to Buster when she next visited him in
Wormwood Scrubs. She showed him the documents that Hanne
wanted him to sign, but now mistrustful of anyone at all Buster
told her to fly out herself to Madrid and propose an alternative —
that Buster's shares in the company be made over to her.

On this second trip to Spain June was accompanied by another
friend of Buster's called Bill O'Brien with a clear understanding

that no money was to pass through his hands. They took a morning flight and Skorzeny came once again to their hotel. He took them to lunch at Horcher's restaurant, and June, who by now had read of his legendary exploits during the Second World War, sat in awed silence next to him; but Bill O'Brien — a more urbane man than Gus Brown — was able to keep up with Skorzeny's conversation, and talk to the various friends of Skorzeny who crossed the restaurant to greet him and ended up sitting at his table. It was then that June found herself next to the American who, she was told, was an editor of *Reader's Digest* and could speak a variety of different Chinese dialects.

He could as well have been speaking in one of them to June. The conversation which hummed around her was in several different languages — German, Spanish, French — but even when it was in English, it was almost incomprehensible to this unsophisticated wife of a Cockney thief. She did not understand anything of what the people were saying around her; their talk became a monotonous hum which, together with the wine she had drunk with her lunch, made her feel so drowsy that eventually she sat back in her chair and fell asleep.

Later that afternoon she went with Otto Skorzeny and Bill O'Brien to Skorzeny's office where the two men discussed business. It appeared that it was impossible to transfer the actual ownership of the shares into June's name; but if Buster preferred it, June could hold the power of attorney. Different papers were drawn up which June was to take to him in prison: then Skorzeny took them to dinner, and the next morning June and Bill O'Brien flew back to London.

She returned to the same difficult, lonely life as before. There was as yet no further dividend from the real estate in Spain and so June had to find work. Remembering how happy she had been running a tea trolley on Waterloo Station, she found a similar job with Rene Wisbey serving as a barmaid. The basic pay was modest but the tips were good and everything she could save she put aside for the house in Kent. She was determined that Buster should not return from prison to the same kind of wretched flat that they had lived in before the robbery. Little by little she scraped together enough to pay the deposit on a pretty, detached house in the Kent countryside, and then borrowed money to pay the balance and furnish it with fitted cupboards and a three-piece suite.

She found it hard to pay the interest. She desperately needed the money which Gus Brown had stolen from her on their first visit to Spain, and went around Buster's friends in South London telling them what Gus had done and demanding restitution; but Gus Brown had left London altogether — some said to Honduras — and no one seemed to believe that a Train Robber's wife could be destitute.

June borrowed more and got deeper into debt. Her troubles started to affect her health. She became withdrawn, depressed and subject to paranoia. It seemed that she and Buster had been entirely abandoned by all their friends. Then one evening an unknown man turned up at her mother's flat with a fat envelope for June containing £500. It came with the compliments of Gordon Goody.

12. Release

John Denby Wheater earned full remission on his three-year sentence and was released from prison in February 1966. He went north to manage a laundry belonging to his family in Harrogate. Brian and Lenny Field also earned full remission and were set free the following year. Brian Field, as we have seen, changed his name and disappeared.

In 1967 Parliament passed the Criminal Justice Act under which, in Section 59, a Parole Board was established to consider the release of prisoners after they had served one third of their sentences. Roy James's calculation that they would not have to serve twenty of their thirty years had proved correct; but the system, in spite of its sensible and humane intentions, left the actual date of a prisoner's release to the discretion — some would say the caprice — of the Board.

On February 1970, the driver of the train, Jack Mills, died in Crewe. An ordinary, almost Victorian working man, he had for years been the shuttlecock of the public debate over the Great Train Robbery. Rewarded for his brave struggle against masked men with £250 from the Post Office, he had been put on light duties at full pay by British Railways. When Charmian Biggs's story, for which she had been paid £65,000, was serialised in the *Sunday Mirror,* some rival newspapers contrasted her good fortune to the paltry sums paid to Mills; and the *Daily Mail* launched an appeal on his behalf which raised £34,000. With some of this money Mills bought a comfortable, centrally-heated bungalow in Crewe; but shortly after he had moved into it he died.

The cause of his death was chronic lymphatic leukaemia

complicated by bronchial pneumonia, and the West Cheshire
Coroner saw no reason to hold an inquest. "I am aware," he said,
"that Mr Mills sustained a head injury during the course of the
Train Robbery in 1963. In my opinion there is nothing to connect
this incident with the cause of death".

Despite this statement it was generally believed that Mills's
death was the delayed consequence of the blow on the head at the
time of the Train Robbery. The controversy was reanimated on 21
February of that same year when *The Times* published a letter
from Peta Fordham, the wife of the barrister who had defended
both Gordon Goody and Ronnie Biggs, and the author of a book
on the Train Robbery. She wrote that Mills had admitted to her
that his worst injury was sustained, not by the cosh, but by hitting
his head against the wall of the cab as he fell. When Mrs Fordham
asked him why he had not told this to the Court, and why he
would not repeat what he had said to a reporter — that they had
treated him "like a gentleman" — he "became very agitated and
said: 'Oh please don't ever repeat this as I have been warned that
my pension would be affected if this came out'."

Mrs Fordham also said that she had offered Mills a
consultation with a leading neurologist which he had refused. She
concluded that "all those in the 'know' in the underworld (and
certainly the convicted men themselves) maintain that (his
assailant) was a man who was never on trial but who slipped
through the net. . . . This, if true, is surely the supreme irony of
the thirty-year sentences."

Two months after the publication of this letter, Detective Chief
Superintendent Tommy Butler followed Mills to the grave. Aged
only fifty-seven, it was as if, after his compulsory retirement the
year before, he had had nothing else to live for. He died with his
task unfulfilled. His quest to catch Ronnie Biggs had failed;
indeed the day he died the *Sun* published the first episode of an
account of the Great Train Robbery, purportedly written by Biggs
while hiding in Melbourne. Butler had not been succeeded by
Frank Williams as head of the Flying Squad; Williams left the
Metropolitan Police and took a job as chief of security for Qantas
Airlines.

Roger Cordrey was released in April 1971. He had shuffled
through prison as he had shuffled through life — quiet, cunning,
humorous and unrepentant. For a time he went to work in his
sister's flower shop to satisfy the Parole Board that he had regular

employment; but as soon as the danger of a return to prison was lifted, he went into more dubious enterprises of his own. He was determined never to get caught breaking the law again, but he knew that there was a great grey area of legitimate dishonesty, and an army of timid people who longed to swindle their employers or the Inland Revenue.

Buster Edwards and Jimmy White came out of prison in the same week in April 1975. Jimmy went to live on the south coast with his wife Sheree and his son Stephen, now a boy of twelve. He took a job as a roofing contractor, the same job he had had as a young man at the start of the Second World War. He was now fifty-five years old, and impatient to pick up the skein of his life; but it was many months, for example, before his son would address him as "Dad".

Buster had considerably changed. Where before he had been cheerful and easy-going — even in the most adverse circumstances — he was now irritable and impatient. The boss of table four in Wormwood Scrubs brought his despotic manner back to the council flat in Vauxhall. It was exacerbated by the change in June who in the course of the ten years he had been away had developed an independence and self-sufficiency. She was no longer prepared to go along with whatever Buster should happen to decide. He wanted her, for instance, to give up her job as a barmaid, because it hurt his pride to have his wife at work, but June refused. She had grown to enjoy the jolly life behind the bar with Rene, and valued the independence of earning her own living. Nor could Buster afford to keep her: though loathe to admit it, he had no money at all and like Roger and Jimmy White was forced to return to the profession of his early youth, selling flowers at a stall outside Waterloo Station.

A further cause of Buster's unpleasantness was a certain remorse — not for his crime but for the suffering he had caused to June and Nicky with nothing now to show for it. He punished those who caused him pain: he snapped at June and became exasperated if she did not immediately grasp what he said to her; with Nicky, now fifteen, he was formal and remote. He loved her more than anyone, but was too inhibited to embrace her as his child.

Above all Buster felt wretched that he was free while most of the others were still in jail. Though none of them had ever expressed resentment that he had received half their sentence, it troubled him all the same that he who had been one of the prime movers in the robbery, had coshed Mills and had lived the good life in Mexico City, should now be free while his friends still mouldered in prison. It also meant that he was lonely. Bernie Carton was still in prison, and so Buster had no friends to drink with or talk to about the problems of everyday life. The liberty he had longed for now seemed so filled with difficulties and disappointments that he sometimes thought back with nostalgia to the simpler life in Wormwood Scrubs; yet to realise that he missed prison — that he wished himself apart from his family again — was so horrifying that he started to stun his thoughts with drink.

One afternoon in August he went into Harrods in Knightsbridge and stole £65 worth of clothes. He was immediately apprehended, taken to court, and sent back to prison for six months.

That same month, August 1975, the first of those sentenced to thirty years — Roy James — was released on parole. He was thirty-seven years old and had served twelve years of his sentence. Throughout this time he had preserved intact his determination to be a champion racing driver, and his first objective now was to find a sponsor, for he was in no position to finance his own re-entry into the sport. The friend who had "minded" his money had long since told him that it had all gone on legal expenses and "unfortunate investments". All that had been salvaged was a flat for his mother.

Roy knew quite well that the friend had appropriated the Train Robbery money for his own use — he later saw him driving around in a large BMW — and he could quite easily have asked some of his heavy friends to "persuade" him to return it; but alone among the Train Robbers Roy regretted his past — not from any moral remorse, but for the way in which it had ruined his promising career. He was determined now to have nothing more to do with crooks and to live entirely in the world of motor racing.

The motor racing world responded to his passion. That very season he was sponsored by Lola and drove one of their Formula Atlantic cars, but he was too impatient to make up for lost time, and at Silverstone, in a test drive, he crashed the car at 130 m.p.h. Roy escaped with a broken leg, but the car was a write-off. He wrote off another car — a Renault 5 — at a saloon car race in Malory Park, and started the 1976 season in a Formula Ford

1600. He won one race at Brands Hatch and came second in another, but in the last race of the season crashed again.

This failure to make a come-back in racing exacerbated his general bitterness. Although he had only served between one third and one half of the original sentence handed down by Mr Justice Edmund Davies, he continued to resent the apparent injustice where lesser sentences were given for rape and murder. Among the most intelligent of the Train Robbers, Roy also had the greatest capacity for self-delusion: he discounted his earlier crimes from the equation of this apparent injustice, and was suffused with self-righteous indignation against the perfidy of the friend who had spent his stolen money.

He had more cause, perhaps, to be disappointed in Micky Ball who since his release from prison for his part in the Airport Robbery had changed his name and had prospered. Now he who had once been Roy's greatest friend, and whom Roy had helped when he was down on his luck, did nothing for him in return.

Jim Hussey was released on 17 November 1975, and on Christmas Eve he was married to Gill at the Epsom Registry Office.

They too had no money. When Jim had first been arrested, most of his whack had been left with a man called Toby — a friend of a friend of Frank Munroe. Some of it had been paid out to cover his expenses during the trial, and Gill had had her fares paid when she went to visit him in prison. She had also bought an Austin 1100, but as the years went by Jim had found it more and more difficult to discover just what had become of his money. Frank Munroe had had too much on his plate to be able to keep a close watch on his "investments", and Toby always reassured him that Jim's money was safe.

In 1967 Gill decided that she wanted to open a children's clothes shop in Croydon. She needed £5,000 to buy a lease. Jim sent out instructions for the money to be paid to her, and she received a first instalment of £500 to pay the deposit, but when she asked for the balance she was told that there was nothing left. Toby confessed that he had invested the money in a car-hire firm, a costume jewellery business and two bookmakers, all of which had gone bankrupt.

Now that Jim was out of prison, he contemplated "paying a visit" to Toby to "persuade" him to pay some compensation for these ill-chosen investments; but like Roy, Jim had too much to lose by turning heavy again. Not only could he go back to prison for eight more years at the flick of a magistrate's finger; he also had a brisk, bright wife who, while not particularly fastidious about the handling of stolen goods, had no intention of losing the husband she had awaited for so long.

Their marriage was a success. Unlike Buster and June, they had no memories to live up to and no previously established relationship which would suffer from a change. They faced the same problem of masculine pride: Gill left her well-paid job at a model agency, but she soon had to find another one because Jim had some trouble finding an occupation compatible with his dignity as a Great Train Robber. For a time they planned to run a restaurant in Soho: the lease was in Gill's name, the management would be in Jim's hands and the finance come from his friends, but the police threatened to oppose the licence to sell alcohol so Gill and Jim abandoned it; Gill took a job selling radio telephones and Jim went into a favoured business for former thieves — a partnership selling second-hand cars.

Gordon came out of prison two days before Christmas 1975, and went back to live with his mother in her small cottage in Putney. She had had cancer and a stroke since Gordon had "gone away", but was still able to care for her huge son on whom she had doted all his life.

From here Gordon made an audit of his assets — not just the money from the Train, but the proceeds of thefts of earlier years. He had been exceptionally lucky in that the man he had left in charge of his affairs had remained loyal to Gordon over the years of his imprisonment. Although many thousands of pounds had been paid out to lawyers at the time of the trial and the appeal, £3,000 had gone towards the planned escape from Manchester, and his mother had been paid an allowance all the time he was in prison, around £20,000 had been invested in property — mostly sleazy rooming-houses in Fulham, Putney and South London — which was now worth around £100,000. Moreover some diamonds which Gordon had bought with the proceeds of the Airport Robbery, and which had lain in a safe-deposit box ever since, had gone up in value and were now sold at a substantial profit.

There had been losses, and like the widow who searches for the single silver piece, Gordon went after £20,000 which had been appropriated by the friend in whose house he had originally buried the money. He had moved from Barnes into a large house in Norwood where he must have thought himself safe until Gordon was to be set free in 1984: but once he realised that Gordon would be released on parole, he had moved again in a hurry. None of the neighbours, whom Gordon questioned about his "old friend", seemed to know where he had gone, but one thought it could not be far because his children still went to the same school.

To discover if this was true, Gordon drove to the school and questioned the children as they left the playground. They confirmed that the boy and girl were still there, so Gordon had only to study the voters list at the public library to find the name and address of his false friend.

The house he went to that evening was more modest than the first, but still far beyond the means of a manual worker. When the owner opened the door to find Gordon he turned pale. "I've been expecting you," he said.

Gordon entered their living room. "What are you going to do to my children?" the man asked. "You've been hanging around the school looking for them."

"I wouldn't hurt your children," said Gordon, "but I'm not so sure about you."

There followed an angry argument, with the wife screaming that her husband was a sick man, while the husband himself showed some bravado, saying: "What are you going to do about it? Call the police? Shoot me?"

"No," said Gordon. "I'm not going to shoot you. I'm not going to tell you what I'm going to do, but it's going to happen . . ." And with that veiled threat, he departed.

His friend was right, there was little Gordon could do, with seven more years on parole; and much as he loved money, he loved freedom more. English life had changed for the better in the thirteen years he had been away: the rigid distinctions in dress and manner between one class and another had given way to an informality he enjoyed, if only because he could save on the tailor-made suits and wear scruffy jeans and a T-shirt.

There was no question now of a silver-grey Jaguar: he drove instead a battered old van to see to his various enterprises — the rooming-houses, junk shops and whelk stalls. He remained unashamedly avaricious, as he had always been, and when fined for drunken driving asked for time to pay: yet when June Edwards had been desperate for money, it was Gordon who had sent her £500.

He was now forty-six years old, but dressed and behaved as if he was ten years younger — a Rip van Winkle who had slept through those thirteen years in prison. He still exercised his fascination over women, and had a sequence of intelligent and attractive girlfriends, but he seemed unable to form a permanent bond. He was unsettled. On the one hand he yearned to move out of the criminal milieu into respectable and sophisticated circles of society, yet knew they would only admit him as a passing curiosity with the label of "infamous Great Train Robber" tied around his neck. On the other he was drawn to indulge his rapacious instincts in the underworld he knew, dreaming of the day when he would realise his assets and retire to the Canary Islands.

Tommy Wisbey remained in prison for three months longer than Gordon, and Bob Welch for six. Tommy was more fortunate than most for not only did he come back to a wife and home, but as with Gordon there was still something to show for his share of the stolen money. He had left it in the hands of one of his brothers, and though there was no actual cash, there was the house in South London and various miscellaneous investments, such as the freehold of a betting shop, which brought in a dribble of income.

On the other hand, Tommy had deteriorated more than the others. The constrictions of prison on his uncontrolled temperament, and the anguish surrounding the death of Lorraine, had destroyed his spirit. He was vague now and frustrated by the sense of anti-climax that followed the euphoria of his first return. It was impossible to pick up where he had left off. Rene had changed. Like June, the years of enforced independence had given her a will of her own. She was not now prepared to be meek and naive: she too insisted on continuing to work behind the bar. Nor would she let Tommy go out on his own at night with the vague excuse of "business". She had met too many married men in the years he had been away to be taken in.

Marilyn resented her father's first attempts to assert his authority in the cosy home which she and her mother had made around the baby Jonathan. She was nineteen and a mother, yet Tommy tried to treat her as a child; he felt that Rene, who was by nature soft and indulgent, had spoiled Marilyn and more than a decade too late tried to resume the role of father. Rene and Tommy had quarrels which sometimes drove him to lash out at her with his fists: and yet as the months passed the two gradually became accustomed to a new balance of power, were reconciled and in September 1976 gave a large party in the Norbury Hotel to celebrate their silver wedding anniversary.

Bob Welch came out of prison on 14 June 1976 — the last of those convicted in Aylesbury to be released on parole. This, together wth the perpetual pain that he had suffered in his leg, left him the most rancorous of them all. He returned to live near New Cross with the gentle, docile Jean who, as soon as Bob was back, recovered from her state of depression.

Like Jim and Gill, Bob and Jean had no earlier life together to overshadow the present, and after an initial period of polite reserve, they settled down happily to family life. Bob was always courteous to Jean and gentle with his son, so that both imagined him incapable of violence; yet when Bob discovered what had happened to his money from the train while he had been in prison, his anger and resentment transformed him once again from Dr Jekyll into Mr Hyde. He had left it in the hands of a friend called Colin who was not a thief himself but lived on the fringes of the criminal world. In the early years, Colin had paid out money for the lawyers, had bought the house in the country for Jean to live in and had given her ten pounds a week to live on. Whenever he came to visit Bob in prison, he had assured him that his money was well invested and would be worth twice as much when he came out.

After a time, however, Colin had come less often to see Bob in prison and would make evasive answers to Bob's questions about his money which, because of the presence of prison officers, were inevitably oblique. Bob had asked Frank Munroe to help: Frank was assured that all was well, and sent word to Bob to that effect. Yet when Bob asked Colin to buy his mother a bungalow and a colour television, nothing was done. Worse still, Bob's wife, Pat, was persuaded to move to a rented flat so that Colin could sell her house. Jean was also moved from the house in the country to a much smaller one in London and her allowance was stopped. She was forced to live on National Assistance or on what Bob's mother could afford to give her. When Bob's mother died she left £2,000 to her son, which had to be used to help him in prison.

Bob himself had been kept in ignorance of these developments because the women did not want to add to his suffering and frustration. It was only when he came out that he was told, and he was put into such a rage that late one night he slipped a knife into his sock and paid a visit to Colin in his large, comfortable house . . . . As a result they came to an amicable understanding whereby some of what had been taken would be repaid just as quickly as the goose could lay the golden egg.

Bruce and Charlie remained in prison, waiting for the Parole Board to set them free. Buster was released for the second time and went back to the flower-stall outside Waterloo Station. It was not a job he wanted for the rest of his life, but he was happy to do it for the time being: he and June decided to sell the house in Kent and remain where they had always lived, in the back streets of South London.

He was happier too because his friends were out of prison. He went early each morning to buy flowers from the new market at Nine Elms, then stood by his stall selling them to the busy commuters. The chaps hooted and waved as they drove up West to the drinking clubs in their BMWs and Mercedes Benz. Once it was known he was there, old friends dropped by to see him. Bill Jennings came along just long enough to tell Buster he was skint and then, with "we must have a drink some time", he was gone. There was gossip about the other Train Robbers. Frank Munroe had been in touch with his friends from the second firm: he too said he was penniless. John Daly was said to be living on the dole in the West Country. Alf Thomas and Gus Brown had disappeared.

On Sundays Buster himself would go up to the drinking clubs and gossip with the thieves, pick-pockets and racketeers. Although crime was booming, they all complained that times were hard. Gangsters now grassed and got away with it; sentences were longer; and Scotland Yard had been purged by the new Commissioner of the Metropolitan Police, Sir Robert Mark — it was less easy now to find an officer who would do a favour in return for a drink. Gangs like the Krays and the Richardsons had been smashed by the police, and new young firms had taken their place.

Buster watched it all from the side-lines like a retired footballer who had once played in the First Division. Certainly, if it had not been for Nicky and June, he would have gone back to thieving, because for him it would always be the only life worth living. As it was he held back, and thought of other ways to make money —

for money was still what he and all the Train Robbers wanted. Roy in particular needed £25,000 to remain in racing; all the rest wanted stakes to set themselves up in some sort of legitimate business, and the only one with any money — Gordon — pretended he was destitute.

There was one obvious source of income — their memoirs. Ronnie Biggs, Charmian Biggs, Pat Wilson, Franny Reynolds and Sheree White had all been paid substantial sums for their stories; even John Wheater had written two articles in the *Sunday Telegraph*. A German magazine now offered Roy several thousand pounds simply for a photograph; but they all knew that if some sold themselves separately, they would spoil the market for the others — particularly Charlie and Bruce who were still in prison.

It was then that Gordon introduced them to a South African property dealer and ex-mercenary called Gary van Dyk whom he had met through the buying and selling of houses in Fulham: van Dyk persuaded them that if they banded together and made him their agent, he would negotiate a high enough price for their combined confessions to bring each a worthwhile whack; and towards the end of April 1976 he presented himself at the London offices of W. H. Allen and Co.

Part Three Corroboration

13. In Pursuit of Proof

At the beginning of this book I described how I came to write it, and why I was convinced that the Train Robbers' story was true. I had hoped nonetheless to discover in the course of my researches some corroboration of Skorzeny's involvement. I was encouraged by an article in *Le Monde* on 5 November 1976, entitled "Gangsterism and the Extreme Right", in which Bernard Brigouleix described how one of those arrested for the spectacular robbery of the Société Générale in Nice had connections with European fascism where, "however strong its internal rivalries, and however diffuse its organisation, the tendency is more towards coordination and internationalisation. Madrid in particular is again a centre. This presupposes the means, as does the working of a certain number of mutual aid societies which try to provide throughout Western Europe for the needs of former members of the SS and the old henchmen of Italian fascism, all driven out of their respective countries at the Liberation".

This information was consistent with what the Train Robbers had told me, and fitted the known facts about Otto Skorzeny. Descended from officers in the Austro-Hungarian army, he had been born in 1908 into "the solid, once comfortable Vienna bourgeoisie".[1] He grew up into "a giant of a man with slate-grey eyes and dark, springy hair";[2] and because there was no future in the Austrian Army he trained as an engineer. As a student he practised the duelling traditional to ·the officer class and was slashed on the left cheek which left a scar from his temple to the

---

[1] Charles Foley, *Commando Extraordinary*, Longmans, Green and Co., 1954. p. 16.
[2] William Stevenson, *The Bormann Brotherhood*, Arthur Barker, 1973, p. 117.

corner of his mouth. He wrote his thesis on "The Calculation and Construction of the Diesel Engine" and after graduation became a partner in a construction company, married and, according to the authorised version, settled down to a quiet domestic life.

Secretly, however, he joined Ernst Kaltenbrunner and Adolf Eichmann in the "German Brotherhood", a Nazi Fifth Column organisation. He was later to be accused of burning Synagogues in Vienna; he was certainly active in the *Anschluss* under cover of the Gymnastic Club. When the war started in 1939, he entered the Waffen-SS as an officer cadet and was posted to the 1st SS Regiment, "Leibstandarte Adolf Hitler".

After the war Skorzeny was to claim that the Waffen-SS was merely an elite corps of the German army, and certainly by 1945 it had developed into a force whose chief purpose was to fight the war; but in 1939 the Leibstandarte was Hitler's Praetorian Guard which swore a personal oath of loyalty, bravery and "obedience unto death".[1]

He fought on the Russian front, reached the rank of SS-Obersturmführer (1st Lieutenant) and was awarded the Iron Cross, and in December 1942 was chosen to form the kind of commando units which were being used so effectively by the British in North Africa. He began to plan sabotage in the Middle East which would cut off the Allied oil supplies but none of his plans came to fruition until Hitler himself selected him to rescue Mussolini from the government of Marshal Badoglio.

This operation was Skorzeny's one undoubted success. After weeks of undercover intelligence work it was discovered that the deposed dictator was held in a winter sports hotel at the top of the Gran Sasso mountain in the Apennines. The only access to the hotel was by a funicular railway which was held at both ends by the Italian army. Skorzeny and his men crash-landed onto the mountainside in gliders and stormed the hotel. Mussolini was set free and, with Skorzeny, was flown from the plateau first to Vienna and then to Hitler, his deliverer, in the Wolf's Lair in East Prussia.

This "Liberation of Mussolini" did much to raise the Nazis' morale. It brought Otto Skorzeny Hitler's gratitude and esteem which led in turn to a leap into the aristocracy of the Nazi Movement no less spectacular than the assault on the Gran Sasso. He

[1] George H. Stein, *The Waffen-SS,* Cornell University Press, 1966, p.285.

was taken up by Himmler and Bormann, and it was possibly at this stage that he met his second wife, Ilsa Schacht, the daughter of the (former) Minister of Finance and Plenipotentiary for War.

While Germany's political and military strength was waning on almost every front, Otto Skorzeny fought on with immense enthusiasm as if convinced that his brand of audacity could win the war. Bolstered by the prestige of his one successful operation, he plundered other regiments of their best men and equipment. He was given *carte blanche* by Hitler — in particular a signed statement that "Sturmbannführer Skorzeny has been directly charged by myself with secret and personal orders of utmost importance. All personnel, military and civil, will assist Sturmbannführer Skorzeny by every means and will forward all his wishes." The results, however, were less spectacular than the means at his disposal. When Admiral Horthy of Hungary was suspected by Hitler of preparing a separate peace with the Allies, Skorzeny and his men, through a mixture of force and guile, took the Regent's Palace in the centre of Budapest; but he failed to find Tito in the Balkans, or to alter the outcome of the Battle of the Bulge by sending saboteurs behind the lines in American uniforms.

As the war drew to its close, Skorzeny acted as the operational arm of those leading Nazis who intended to survive their inevitable defeat. Bormann sent him to retrieve a lorry-load of secret documents, but these were captured by the advancing Russians. Walter Schellenberg, the chief of Military Intelligence since the arrest of Admiral Canaris, and his deputy Reinhardt Gehlen, were planning to exchange immunity from prosecution by the Americans for the intelligence and resistance networks which Gehlen with Skorzeny had set up behind the Russian lines. When Skorzeny was told to form a last redoubt in the Alps around Berchtesgarten, Schellenberg and Gehlen sent their records to be hidden behind the "ring of steel". Walther Funk, Schacht's successor as Minister of Economics and President of the Reichsbank, also appeared with the State Treasure to add to the gold and jewels which the Nazis themselves had brought to bury in the mountains.

It was here that Skorzeny and an elite of SS officers waited for the end. On 30 April 1945, Hitler killed himself in Berlin. For some weeks afterwards Skorzeny remained hidden in the Alps, assisting the more notorious Nazis to make good their escape via

Italy to Spain and South America. Skorzeny himself then surrendered to the Americans. There was little evidence that he was guilty of specific war crimes, and his very size — together with the scar on his cheek — made it unlikely that he would have escaped detection had he chosen to leave. It is probable, too, that like Gehlen and Schellenberg, Skorzeny had already reached some understanding with the British and American Secret Services. He was tried as a war criminal at Dachau, but the charges of shooting American prisoners-of-war and ordering the assassination of Eisenhower could not be proved against him. The prosecution case collapsed when a British agent, Forrest Yeo-Thomas, gave evidence for the defence that the Allies too had disguised their men in enemy uniform.

Skorzeny was acquitted, but was held for a time for "de-Nazification". He was allowed out of prison every now and then to visit his family, and was followed by Allied agents in the hope that he would lead them to more notorious war criminals. On 27 July 1948, Skorzeny escaped in the boot of a car from the camp where he was held. He returned to the Alps around Berchtesgarten — purportedly to regain his health, but quite possibly to look for the buried treasure. Shortly afterwards his father-in-law, Hjalmar Schacht, who had been classified as "a major Nazi offender" and sentenced to eight years in prison, was released and "almost overnight he was directing a major West German bank of which he soon became president".[1]

Skorzeny himself now went to Buenos Aires and then Madrid where the governments of both Perón and Franco were sympathetic to fugitive Nazis. In Madrid, as in Vienna before the war, Skorzeny set up a legitimate business and "passed himself off as a businessman with a somewhat eventful past who was now more interested in money than in an adventurous life".[2] In reality he and the former Luftwaffe pilot, Hans Ulrich Rudel, set up ODESSA, providing former members of the SS with money, plastic surgery and contacts in South America. Their operations were international, but then so too were their clientele, for by the end of the war "foreigners outnumbered native Germans in the ranks of the Waffen-SS. Of the thirty-eight SS divisions in existence in 1945, none was exclusively German and at least

---

[1] William Stevenson, ibid. p. 117.
[2] Angelo del Boca and Mario Giovana, *Fascism Today,* Heinemann, 1969, p. 81.

nineteen consisted largely of foreign personnel . . ."[1] The scattered remnants of "possibly . . . the largest multinational army ever to fight under one flag" now re-formed into a conspiratorial mutual-aid society with branches all over the world. When the former chief of the Gestapo in Lyons, Klaus Barbie, was arrested in 1972, "he named Otto Skorzeny as the chief of the network called Die Spinne . . ." which could "command the loyalty of 100,000 fascist sympathizers in twenty-two countries" and was "funded by Nazi investments".[2]

When Perón was overthrown in 1955, many of the ex-Nazis whom he had employed either fled the country or went underground. An attempt was made to use Ireland as a new base of operations: Skorzeny bought an estate near Cork, and "Skorzeny and two representatives of a German and Swiss bank had protracted talks with members of the Irish Government," promising "to transfer considerable sums of capital to aid its economic development".[3] This venture failed, largely because the traditional antagonism of the Irish towards the English did not extend to sympathy for ex-Nazis. Skorzeny himself, who "had expected a demand for his services as a guerrilla expert",[4] was forced to sell his estate because of the antagonism of his tenants.

The more notorious war criminals were thus forced to live incognito in the unhealthy and uncivilised corners of Paraguay, Bolivia and Brazil. Madrid remained safe for Skorzeny, Rudel and the other more "respectable" ex-Nazis. They were invited by Franco to look upon Spain "as their second fatherland", and Skorzeny took him at his word. He entertained his friends in Horcher's restaurant (Horcher had been a protégé of Goering) which was patronised by many of Franco's cabinet, and it was here that he took June to lunch. He was given a Nansen passport and used it to travel from Madrid all over the world. In 1951 he attended a conference of European Fascists (the "European Social Movement") in Malmö in Sweden. "From that time on the presence of Skorzeny was reported in Cairo, Malmö, Tangier, Buenos Aires and Rome, as well as in many German and Austrian towns."[5] In July 1960 — three years before the Train Robbery —

[1] George H. Stein, ibid. p. 154.
[2] William Stevenson, ibid. p. 154.
[3] Denis Eisenberg, *The Re-emergence of Fascism*, MacGibbon & Kee, 1967, p. 19.
[4] William Stevenson, ibid. p. 141.
[5] Angelo del Boca and Mario Giovana, ibid. p. 81.

he was seen in Bonn at a meeting between Hans Ulrich Rudel and Sir Oswald Mosley.[1]

In 1971 Skorzeny developed cancer of the spine. He was operated on in Germany but died in Spain on 5 July 1975. His body was cremated in Madrid at a ceremony attended by a mixed gathering of Germans and Spaniards. Afterwards his ashes were flown to Vienna where in the suburban cemetery of Doebling they were buried in his family plot.

It was to Vienna that I now went in pursuit of proof that Otto Skorzeny's organisation of former Nazis — whether called Die Spinne or ODESSA — had financed the Great Train Robbery: for the publishers had suggested that I should go to see Simon Wiesenthal who through his centre for historical documentation relentlessly pursues Nazi War Criminals whom the rest of the world has forgotten. As it happened W. H. Allen had published a book he had written so it did not prove difficult to arrange an appointment.

Simon Wiesenthal was a younger and more vigorous man than I had expected, and seemed to regard me with a certain coldness and suspicion as if he and an Englishman were not necessarily on the same side. He went on opening his post as I told him that I had reason to believe that Otto Skorzeny and his organisation of former SS had financed the Great Train Robbery, and for a time after I had finished he seemed to think that I was playing some practical joke. Even when I had assured him of my sincerity he was incredulous: it was inconceivable, he said, that Skorzeny would have descended to common crime, and anyway he would never have needed to raise money in that way because the Nazis had had their buried treasure, and his business in Spain was a success.

I persisted, and in my presence he telephoned a contact in the office of the West German public prosecutor who specialised in Skorzeny and had tried to have him charged wih various war crimes. He too felt unable to believe my story. Simon Wiesenthal, who had by now become friendlier, made photocopies of some of his documents which related to Otto Skorzeny, and told me the names of police and intelligence officers in other countries who might know more: but it was clear at the end of the morning that

---

[1] Denis Eisenberg, ibid. p.40.

my journey to Vienna had failed to produce the confirmation I sought.

There was another possible source of corroboration—Ronnie Biggs. Although his escape from Wandsworth Prison was made with the help of an English convict, his own account of his subsequent passage abroad, which appeared in *Biggs: The World's Most Wanted Man* by Colin Mackenzie, made it sound remarkably like Buster's: he had gone by Tilbury rather than St Katharine's dock, and the plastic surgery was done in Paris rather than Cologne, but he was cared for by "the organisation" which was perhaps Skorzeny's network of neo-Nazis.

Biggs was in an ambiguous position in regard to the book. The other Train Robbers loathed him. The reason they gave was that he had "named names" in Mackenzie's book: one gangster who had appeared in its pages had sworn that if ever he saw Ronnie again he would tear his arm from its socket and beat him to death with it. The Train Robbers animosity, I suspected, came more from their irritation that the least significant member of the gang had had the most publicity and the least punishment. They were particularly determined that he should have no share in the proceeds of our book because, they said, he had had so much already: the publishers, on the other hand, felt that just because of his notoriety he should be included, and early in the negotiations Gary van Dyk had volunteered to fly out to Rio de Janeiro to persuade Biggs to cooperate with the venture.

He took with him a release from the publishers which, if Biggs signed it, would enable us to use his name without fear of libel. The inducements were a certain sum of money and a letter from Bob Welch on behalf of all the Train Robbers asking him to help for the sake of old times. Gary returned ten days later with his task accomplished. He was full of the pleasures of Rio, and insisted that if ever I decided to go out and interview Biggs, he would come with me: but when, in February 1977, it was decided that I should go, Gary had disappeared to Portugal in pursuit of a sensational story about Angolan mercenaries, and I flew out to Rio alone.

I was met at Galeao Airport by Ronnie Biggs himself with his two-year-old Brazilian son, Michael, and his most recent girlfriend, the German-Argentinian divorcee called Ulla Sopher. Biggs was taller and thinner than I had expected him to be, but he had the same smirk I had seen in many of the photographs: he greeted me in a quiet, reserved manner and we drove in Ulla's Volkswagen to my hotel. There the mistress departed with the child while Ronnie and I sat down to talk business.

The offer I had brought from W. H. Allen was this: some money had already been paid to him by Gary van Dyk for signing the release; more would be paid to him just for talking to me; and more still — considerably more — if he could substantiate certain aspects of the story by which we meant, of course, the Skorzeny connection. In an amused Cockney-Australian drawl Biggs opened our conversation by saying that he would rather have nothing whatsoever to do with the book. Since I had just finished a journey of five thousand miles to see him, this slightly depressed me, but he went on to say that for the sake of "the Train Gang", as he called them, he would cooperate and he would cooperate wholeheartedly for the larger sum of money.

"What the publishers want to know," I said, "is whether you have anything to say which is not in Colin Mackenzie's book."

"Much more," he said, "about my life here in Brazil."

"What about the robbery itself?" I asked, "and your escape to Australia?"

He looked at me oddly. "There is something I *could* tell you," he said, "but the Train Gang wouldn't like it."

"I think they would want you to tell me everything," I said with a significant look in my eye. "After all, they themselves have kept nothing back."

He laughed. "Indeed they have not," he said. "They've kept nothing back."

"So why should you?"

"My worry is this, Piers. That if I tell you now what I know, they might send someone to rub me out."

"They need never know."

It took me some time to persuade Biggs that he could trust me to keep his secret: he remained reluctant to tell me what he knew, yet realised that our negotiations could hardly proceed unless he did. "All right," he said at last. "I'll risk it. You want to know about that German business, don't you? Sigi at the farm, and all that?"

"Yes," I said. "And if the same people helped you escape."

He laughed again and looked at me down his nose with a sneer. "The trouble is, Piers, there aren't any Germans."

"How do you mean?"

"You're being conned, my old friend. It's a put-up job."

"How do you know?"

"I was at the farm, wasn't I?"

"Yes, but . . . but perhaps you didn't see him? And they didn't tell you?"

"Look, Piers, you don't have to believe me if you don't want to, but I kcow it's a con because that South African guy, Gary van Dyk, came out here to tell me what to say! But I'm a reformed man, you see, and I'm not prepared to do it. It just shows you, doesn't it? Thirteen years in prison, and they're back at it. Whereas the only one who didn't do time is the only one who's straight."

I was silent — aghast, confused and unable to think of anything to say. Ronnie studied my consternation for a few moments and then, with a cold smile, stood to take his leave. "We'll talk again tomorrow," he said, "and see what we can work out."

He departed and I lay back on my bed to think over what he had said. It was late. I was tired and hot, and my thoughts raced round in confusion. I could not decide whether or not to believe Biggs, for the implications of either course seemed equally unpleasant. If what he said was true — that the whole Skorzeny connection was a hoax, invented by Gary van Dyk and perpetrated by the whole gang — then the publishers had paid a large sum of money for a stale story. If, on the other hand, it was Biggs who was lying, the implications were even more alarming. At best he wished me to disbelieve the Skorzeny connection so that he himself could break it to the world and reap the benefit: at worst he was still in the care of Skorzeny's organisation and had been told to persuade me that it did not exist.

The more I pondered this last possibility, the more convinced I became that this was the explanation — for it still seemed inconceivable to me that June had invented her meeting with Skorzeny in Madrid, or could have discovered that he was a friend of the *Reader's Digest* editor who spoke fourteen Chinese dialects. I suddenly realised how thoughtless and foolhardy I had been to come to a country known to be a nest of ex-Nazis. Clearly Biggs had been saved from extradition not because of his child, but because of neo-Nazi influence in government circles. The woman who had been with him at the airport, Ulla Sopher, a German-Argentinian with blonde hair and blue eyes, was part of their network. All the strands of the story came together to form a noose around my neck. I expected at any moment the ageing stalwarts of ODESSA to burst into my room, knock me unconscious, and later drop my body from a private aeroplane high above the Matto Grosso. When eventually I fell asleep that night over the whirr of the air conditioner and the gurgle of the refrigerated bedroom bar, it was the last slumber of a condemned man.

The next morning I awoke refreshed, and a little more optimistic that I would see my family and my country again. My only hope, I decided, was to convince Ronnie Biggs and Ulla Sopher that I believed their story about the hoax. I met them after breakfast, and when Ulla had once again left us Ronnie and I resumed our conversation of the night before sitting at a café on the Copacabana Beach. We both inveighed against Gary van Dyk — I for the hoax, and Ronnie because he had only paid him half of what had been promised by the publishers. He added that Gary had given him only a most cursory briefing about the German connection.

Gradually, in the course of the morning, I began to believe that Biggs was telling the truth. Most convincing of all was his fear that if ever I told Gary or the Train Robbers that he had "grassed" on them, they would send someone out to kill him. "There are plenty of guys in London," he said "who'd just love to come out here and do me for a thousand quid and the ticket."

I assured him again that I would never reveal what he had told me, and the more convinced I became that he feared for his life, the less anxious I became about my own. I was still perplexed by his motive for exposing the hoax, for I could not believe that he would risk his skin simply to demonstrate that he was an honest man. It soon revealed itself. When he saw that I believed him, Ronnie sought to persuade me that without the German connection his account of his experiences with the inexhaustibly licentious women of Brazil would be vital for the success of my book, and was therefore worth double the sum of money that the publishers had been prepared to pay if he could have confirmed the Skorzeny story.

I took it upon myself to decline his offer on their behalf, and spent two more days in his company as a tourist rather than a writer. Biggs seemed glad of the company of an Englishman, and when the time came for my departure I found I had grown fond of this small group of expatriates composed of Ronnie, Ulla and their friends. They drove me to the airport. Ronnie said how much he envied me returning to the cold, wet weather of London in February — how he hoped that one day he would be pardoned and could return — and he made me promise to send him a parcel containing custard powder, mixed spices and Lyons Quick-Brew tea.

In the plane, on the long journey back to England, I considered what I should do next. I now believed that what Biggs had told me was true — that the German connection was a hoax. Though it still astonished me that June Edwards had lied so thoroughly, a number of facts fitted this new hypothesis. John Wheater, for example, had gone to extraordinary lengths to get vacant possession of Leatherslade Farm without paying the balance of £4,500 — an insignificant sum if Bruce had had £80,000 from Skorzeny. They had also stolen one of the Land Rovers when it would have been safer to buy it. Roger had been caught with £142,000 which when multiplied by seventeen came close to the total sum of money stolen. His explanation had been that Frank had asked him to "mind" some of his whack, but knowing now the kind of man Frank was supposed to be, it seemed highly unlikely that he would have left £50,000 with Roger. And why did not Sigi telephone Germany from Buster's flat and arrange his own escape — an easy task, one might have thought, for the organisation which could abduct Charlie Wilson from Winson Green prison.

The problem I pondered now was how to get them to admit it. The first possible course of action upon my return would be to confront the Train Robbers with what I had learnt in Brazil. If I did this, however, they would be likely to "front it out" and say that Biggs was the one who was lying. It was also possible that Biggs's fears were justified — that if they knew he had grassed they might send someone to Rio to "do" him. The second option was simply to tell the publishers that they had been deceived, and leave them to accuse the Train Robbers of breach of contract; but here again it would be a matter of accepting Biggs's word against theirs. It would be no easier to prove their story was false than to prove it was true.

The third possibility would be to get one of them to admit the hoax. This seemed almost impossible: they had stood together over the robbery itself and were unlikely to betray one another now. It was also quite clear that if the story was a hoax, the trust which I had thought had grown up between the writer and his subjects was itself part of the deception. I was just another sucker being robbed not of his money but of his reputation, and the more I thought of this, the more angry I became and the more determined to be as cunning and unscrupulous as they had been to get at the truth.

As it happened I had arranged to visit Bruce Reynolds in Maidstone Prison on the Tuesday after my return. This was my chance. I knew how vulnerable and isolated a man becomes whose only contact with the outside world is through occasional visits or cryptic letters. Bruce in particular suffered because he was sensitive, intelligent and highly-strung. I had also observed, on previous visits, that he felt some resentment against the others for proceeding with a book before he was released on parole. By the time my plane had landed at Heathrow, I had made up my mind that Bruce would be the weak link in the chain.

I reported to the publishers in London that the Skorzeny connection was probably a hoax, and the following day travelled by train to Maidstone with a tape-recorder in my mackintosh pocket. The prison was in the middle of the town and reminded me half of a hospital, half of a boarding-school. I was let in through the gates with the usual group of wives and girlfriends. By the time Bruce was admitted to see me I was already seated at a small table in the large visiting hall.

He was thin, pale and nervous but managed within the prison regulations to appear smartly dressed in grey flannel trousers, a blue and white striped prison shirt and a navy-blue cashmere cardigan. We started to talk about the robbery they had planned at Weybridge and moved on to Leatherslade Farm. "What I can't understand," I said, "is why you left to Field and Mark the cleaning up of the farm."

"In retrospect that is a good question," said Bruce. "but at the time it was left to different people to do different things. It was Buster and Gordon's responsibility via Brian Field that this would be done. The guy was getting enough money for it."

"Why didn't you buy the farm?"

"It should have been bought. What I found out was that Lenny Field was trying to be in the action without putting any money up."

"Why didn't you put the money up?"

"Well, who was going to buy it?"

"This brings me to one of my anxieties," I said. "You are meant to have had eighty thousand quid from the Germans. How on earth did you spend that eighty thousand quid?"

"You would be surprised how quick it goes when you are trying to organise something like this. There are people wanting wages . . ."

"A hundred pounds a week for fifteen whacks for three months comes to £19,500."

"Yes, but that is adhering to the £100 a week. Roger had a lump sum — had had £5,000 and we gave him another £5,000 before."

"He said he paid it back."

"Did he? I didn't know . . ."

At this point I shook my head and sighed. "I've now got everybody's transcripts," I said, "and the whole business of the German thing is unbelievable."

"What do you mean 'unbelievable'?"

"When I first heard about it, I thought that if Buster and Roger had spent months sitting dreaming up something to flog a dead horse in terms of a story, then this would be it, but I thought we'd go along with it. I've now got all the interviews and it doesn't stand up."

"Well, I'm in a position, Piers, of being tail-end Charlie. I was brought into it when I didn't want to be brought into it."

"I think they are being unfair to you, because they are out. If the publishers think they are being conned. . . . You know what happened to Clifford Irving. He got some years in prison for that. I don't know who is behind it, but I think it is very unfair on you. You are mad to get involved with a man like Gary van Dyk. He is a pure con man. And he doesn't see things through."

"Well, you know what I know. A friend of mine came out and said to me that they were going ahead with something and was I in it? We had all agreed that we wouldn't do anything until we had got out. The way it was put to me was virtually blackmail. 'If you are not in it, you don't get anything.' So I went along with this, and I said, 'O.K. Tell them that I don't want to be fucking in it.' I was very upset about this. If it was going to be a question of a show down, I would meet them on Putney Heath with Purdies. They are gambling with my liberty. I had Roy up here. . . . My principal thing was that I didn't know Gary from Adam. I've got little faith in Gordon and he's Gordon's man. I know what

Gordon is like: I know his vices and I know how impressionable he is. I told Roy it would be a rip-off. Gary comes from South Africa, and it is impossible to discover the guy's provenance in any way. How the hell did they meet him? Eventually I agreed to meet him. I listened to him and he was quite personable. He answered all my questions . . . so once I saw that it was all going to be tied up properly, naturally I'm interested . . ."

As the conversation continued, Bruce became even more candid about the hoax, complaining that he had been placed in an impossible position by the others. He had never been told, beyond the sparsest outline, what he should say about the Germans: when I had asked him on an earlier occasion whether Sigi could speak English or not, he had had no idea what the others had said and could only flounder. He had also been upset to think that his friends in Mexico City, who were Syrian Jews, would read the book and think that he had worked with a Nazi.

Bruce seemed relieved, now that the truth was out, but like Biggs he would not take upon himself the onus of admitting the hoax. All he would do was give me a note for Buster, written on the back of a Kit-Kat wrapper. "Jack," it read. "Things won't work as they are. Keith."

When I got back to London I telephoned Buster and arranged to meet him that evening at a pub on Holland Park Avenue called The Mitre. It was months, now, since I had first met the Train Robbers and in the course of my researches I had made varying personal judgements about them. Buster, who had been the most inventive and energetic in deceiving me about Skorzeny, was paradoxically the most likeable and dependable of the whole gang. While most of the others showed some of the nastiness and paranoia which we traditionally associate with crime, Buster was more like a "noble savage": within the limits of his predatory profession he was generous, loyal and brave. He had worked the hardest on the book, had always kept appointments and had come up with three times as much information as the others — some of it apparently invented but some of it presumably true. When he came in through the door of the pub I could not bring myself to feel angry with him because I knew that he must have seen this job, like the Train Robbery itself, not as a cold deception but as a profitable practical joke.

I told him that by comparing the transcripts I had realised that the German connection was a hoax. I had put it to Bruce, Bruce had admitted it, and I had the confession on tape. Buster blustered until I gave him the note I had brought out of prison. He read it quickly and then tore it into tiny pieces. He knew now that it was futile to deny the deception. He admitted to me that Horst, Karl, Sigi, Klaus and the £80,000 had been invented. Charlie's abduction from Winson Green Prison had taken place more or less as he had described it except that there had been no pistols or handcuffs and his abductors were not Skorzeny's men but gangster friends from London who felt that they owed him a favour.

"But how on earth did you pick on Skorzeny?" I asked.

"Because the rest is true," said Buster. "All that about Hanne and the property company. That's perfectly true."

The story he now told me went as follows. The robbery had not required any finance. Roger had not asked for a guarantee, there had been no wage of £100 a week and no antagonism between the firms. Jim Hussey had been to prison in Germany for picking pockets at the *Oktoberfest,* but he had only worked with the second firm before the Great Train Robbery. The inner circle of the first firm had robbed a security van in Chelsea shortly before the Train Robbery which had provided quite enough money to buy the Land Rover and the Army lorry.

Their whacks, after the robbery, had been around £150,000 each. Roy had not driven Sigi to London because there had been no Sigi; but had fallen asleep as he said and only returned to the farm after the others had left. A boat had been planned to take the money not to the Thames Estuary but to the London docks.

The story of Buster's journey to Germany was, he assured me, true in almost every detail. Through Bernie Carton, Buster's friend and fellow Train Robber Bill Jennings had met a man he called Brent who had promised to arrange to have his money transferred to a Swiss bank. Bill had brought Brent out to Wraysbury: June had taken an instant dislike to him, for though a Cockney crook like the others, he was unattractive to look at and boasted of the international connections he had made through his political support of Sir Oswald Mosley, the leader of the pre-war Union of British Fascists. (Brent presumably met Skorzeny through Mosley, but Buster purported to be ignorant of their precise connection.)

The services he offered Buster had covered not just the transfer of his money to Switzerland, but a forged passport and plastic surgery. The cost was to be seventeen-and-a-half per cent of all money sent abroad, £20,000 to cover services in Germany and tickets to Mexico. Buster accepted the deal.

A few days later he went to the Hilton Hotel to meet the London representative of a Geneva bank. He was introduced by Brent under a false name and was described as a bookmaker. The banker explained that the transfer of funds was quite simple; once the cash was in the hands of their representative in London, it was automatically credited to his account in Geneva. He gave Buster an account number and they settled on "Ritter" as the name in which the account would be opened. The banker then asked to see Buster's passport but was fobbed off by Brent.

In the following weeks Buster and Bill Jennings delivered their money to Brent in consignments of £20,000 and when Buster left England, £82,500 was waiting for him in Switzerland — £100,000 less £17,500 commission. The balance remained in London. As he had promised, Brent also provided Buster with a passport in the name of Jack Miller. Bernie Carton arranged his passage to Antwerp via St Katharine's dock on the Belgian freighter, which cost Buster £2,000. Brent himself with a German girl met him in Antwerp and drove him to the Excelsior Hotel in Cologne where he met Hanne Schmidt . . .

By now I was wary of believing anything at all, but this new version of events did seem more plausible. The thin characters of Horst, Karl, Sigi and Klaus fell away and we were left only with Hanne Schmidt, and Otto Skorzeny. It enabled me to believe June's story about her visits to Madrid which I had always been unwilling to doubt. Moreover it made me feel less gullible, for truth and falsehood had been woven together with exceptional skill.

Buster gave credit for that to Gary van Dyk. When Gordon as we know had come across him in dealing with his slum properties in Fulham, Gary was on the point of bankruptcy and was looking for new fields of endeavour. He persuaded Gordon, who in turn persuaded the other Train Robbers, that he should act as their agent and started to hawk this new property among publishers and newspapers. He asked a high price, because each of the Train Robbers wanted a whack of at least £10,000, but it soon became clear that no one would pay such a sum for an old story. It was then that Buster mentioned Skorzeny — not just that he had invested in his company, but that he had read on the back of a paperback edition of Skorzeny's memoirs that he was the "suspected master-mind behind the Great Train Robbery".

No one knew how this came to be written, but Gary van Dyk seized upon it as the bait he needed to hook a large sum. He persuaded Buster that it was the only way to raise money for his desperate friends, and finally Buster agreed. Night after night he and the others were rehearsed in the invented story by Gary. It was like the old days. Each came up with his own ideas: Roger would say that he had demanded a fee of £10,000. Bob Welch invented the antagonism betwweeeee zzmêe two firms.

Sitting in the pub that evening, Buster assured me that everything he was now telling me was true; but seeing the still sceptical look in my eye, and realising how hard it now was for me to believe anything he said, he promised that if I came to his flower stall the next day he would give me some documentary proof of his connection with Skorzeny.

I went to Waterloo Station around mid-day, and true to his word Buster produced a letter from Otto Skorzeny to June. He had torn it into three pieces to remove any reference to his investment in the Spanish property company. The first was the top left-hand corner with Skorzeny's name printed on the paper. Beneath it was typed June's maiden name and the address where she had been living in 1971, and then the words "Dear June".

The second scrap was a paragraph which read as follows, "I received with many thanks your kind letter of 17th March 1971 but only on April 3, 1971. I personally returned just this day from a very long — five months stay in Germany, I had to undergo a very serious operations and I was very lucky to come through. I was operated on the spine and, of course, it will take many more months till I completely recover."

The third piece of paper contained the last paragraph. "Please, giv (sic) my best regards to your family, and I am great . . . you especially and waiting for your kind news."

It was signed "Otto".

Although delighted that at last I had in my hands some documentary evidence of a link between Skorzeny and the Train Robbers, I was warned by Buster that he might well be obliged to deny what he had told me the night before. He had talked to the others who were afraid that, if they admitted the hoax, the publishers would abjure the contract. They were to meet together later that day, and with me that evening; and if the vote was to front it out and stick to the story they had originally told me, then Buster would back up his friends. "They hate losing money," he warned me again, "and they hate losing face."

I returned to Holland Park and found Gary van Dyk waiting for me outside my flat. As with Buster, I could not bring myself to be angry with him. He had a quality of hulking amiability, like that of a huge unruly bear, which compelled one to feel fond of him. We went into the Mitre for a drink, and for a time he tried to persuade me that I was mistaken about the hoax — that Bruce was mentally unstable, that the whole German connection was perfectly true: but faced with my certainty, he did not insist for long. Nor did he seem upset that I had seen through his confidence trick, but warned me that "the boys" would not own up. "You're taking away their pride," he said, "and that's all they've got left."

Gary's main worry was that once the hoax was established, the publishers would renege on their agreement. He explained that several of the Train Robbers had borrowed money from gangster friends to set themselves up in business which, if no more money came from W. H. Allen, they would not be able to repay. It clearly baffled Gary that I was so insistent on telling the truth if an embroidered story would make more money, and such was his talent for infecting others with his enthusiasm that for a moment I myself wondered why I was so scrupulous.

It was now six in the evening. Gary waited in the pub where he had arranged to meet the Train Robbers, while I went back to my flat. There I found a message that June Edwards had been calling me repeatedly throughout the day; and shortly after my return she telephoned again with a message from Buster that on no account was I to tell the others that he had admitted the hoax. She spoke with such a tremulous and breathless voice that her anxiety spread to me, and as I waited for the Train Robbers to arrive I became increasingly worried that the approaching confrontation might prove dangerous. Until now my relations with all of them had been on a level of jocular courtesy, but I knew from the way in which some of them had described past episodes in their lives, that there came a point at which anger and frustration found expression in violence. In the latter stages of my researches I had come to suspect that perhaps half of them had at some time in their lives murdered other men; and though I knew that little purpose would be served by killing me, the author of their book, I was uneasy all the same.

At half-past nine Gary and the Train Robbers trooped across from the Mitre into my basement flat. The only one absent was Gordon who was in Lisbon on some errand for Gary. They sat around in silence while I started, stuttering, to explain how I had compared their different versions of the German connection and had found that they did not tally. I had put this to Bruce who had been forced to admit the hoax.

No one spoke. Buster, Roger, Roy, Tommy and Jimmy White all looked at the floor in glum silence. Then Jimmy Hussey started to talk. He said that I had got it wrong, that every word they had told me was true, that Bruce had apparently gone mad in prison. "You don't know what it does to a man, Piers, being shut up there all alone."

Bob Welch joined in. Like Jim, he was angry and upset: "I was there, Piers, I was at the farm. I saw Sigi. Now are you saying that I didn't see him? Are you calling me a liar?"

"Not a liar," I said nervously. "Just an embellisher."

We continued to argue. I refused to concede that any part of the hoax might be true, but tried to make light of their deception with such common quips as: "We all of us lie, even to our wives": for I thought it possible that at any moment one or other might take out a "shooter" and hold it to my head saying: "You'd fucking well better believe us, Piers."

The others remained silent and morose, supporting neither one side nor the other, and it was only when there seemed to be a total dead-lock which only violence could resolve that to my great relief Gary stepped forward to interpose his huge frame and calming bluster.

He proposed a compromise. The Train Robbers had told me the true story but there were aspects of it which I found incredible, and as the writer I must be free to exclude them. If, as a result, there were some gaps in the narrative, then Buster would fill them in with plausible "inventions".

We left it at that and parted friends — and to this day some of the Train Robbers might swear that there was a German called Sigi at Leatherslade Farm. I did not, however, take Gary van Dyk's advice and change the book; for even though I was satisfied now that I was near to the truth, I could never be certain and thought it best to leave the story as they had told it to me and let each reader decide upon its veracity for himself.

Epilogue

In researching and writing this book about the Train Robbers, I had hoped to learn something about the mind — and particularly the conscience — of the criminal, for it seemed to me that if thieves like the Train Robbers were always bad men with determinedly malevolent intentions, as the various judges would have us believe, then there is little we can do but lock them away to protect others, and pray for the salvation of their souls: but if, on the other hand, they are not bad men — but good or morally indifferent men led by the circumstances of their lives to steal, then something might be done to coax them into conformity with conventional notions of civic behaviour, or even alter the notions themselves to accommodate what they believe to be right and wrong.

By the time I had finished the book, however, all I seemed to have learned was that thieves were facile liars — something I knew before I started. All other observations had been undermined by their skilled deception. I have said, for example, that I suspected some of the Train Robbers to be murderers: Gordon and Buster had admitted to me that they had set off to kill the man we have called Stan Agate — the old train driver brought in by Biggs — and Charlie Wilson had told me that, after they had failed to find him, he had asked his friends to "take him for a holiday in the West Country". Now I had to ask myself whether all this was true, or another invention to add spice to their story.

In Brazil I had asked Ronnie Biggs if he knew what had happened to Stan. He could not even remember his family name: he showed the same indifference to the fate of the man he had involved in the robbery, and whose whack he had taken, as he did towards his first wife Charmian who remained in Australia. He had, however, given me details of where Stan had worked; and soon after my return to England I engaged a detective agency to track him down.

The only clues I could provide were his Christian name and the station where he had worked thirteen years before. With admirable efficiency the private investigator went to work. Pretending that he was searching for the obscure beneficiary of a client's will, he examined the station records but found that no one called "Stan" had worked for British Rail in that period: but some of the employees at the station remembered that an old man whose nick-name was "Stan" had worked as a shunter in the early 1960s and so far as they knew still lived at his home address.

Determined now to discover whether Stan was dead or alive, I drove down to a bungalow in the outskirts of a town about twenty miles south of London. The door was opened by a woman aged between fifty and sixty. I asked if Stan Agate still lived there, and if I could speak to him. She showed me into a small hall and for a moment I became anxious that if Stan was now an old man as he must be, the shock of what I was to put to him might bring on a heart attack or brain seizure, and the woman who was his wife told me as we passed through the vestibule that he had recently suffered two strokes. I might now have made my excuses and turned back, but the power of my curiosity was too great. I had to know if this was the old train driver.

We came into the living-room and there watching television was the smiling round-faced old man who matched exactly the Train Robbers' description of Stan. I sat down and in a hesitant voice explained that I had just returned from Rio where I had seen Ronnie Biggs who had asked me to come around and see how they were. After this lying introduction, there was a moment of difficult silence: then the wife started to speak. She had hoped, she said, never to hear his name again. Ronnie had been an odd-job man who had put in some new windows — the windows there (she pointed): and since their only son had emigrated to Australia, they had befriended him. When Ronnie had invited her husband to go with him as "tea-boy" on a tree-felling expedition, he had accepted but had known nothing of what was intended until he had found himself among the whole gang in Leatherslade Farm. He had refused, of course, to take part in the robbery, had never been near the track and had never had any of the money. She herself had not realised where he had been until Ronnie Biggs had been arrested: then she had confronted her husband who had admitted his inadvertent role. She had immediately burnt all the clothes he had worn that night, and from that day on she had waited — either for the police to arrest her husband or for the gang to murder him.

While his wife told me this story the somewhat senile Stan grinned shamefacedly. I was uncertain of how much he understood of my conversation with his wife; but though it was clear that he had not been frank with her about the role he had played, it was not for me to enlighten her. I had done what I had set out to do — I had established that Stan had not been murdered — and promising never to reveal their identities I returned to London.

But what was I to make of what I had discovered? Did it show that my suspicions about the Train Robbers were fanciful? Or that they had been as incompetent about murdering Stan as they had been about clearing up the farm? Had they really intended to kill this witness to their crime? Or was the expedition to murder him another invention? Were they murderers or were they just thieves? It was impossible to know.

Besides this uncertainty about what they had done, I faced a further difficulty in coming to any general conclusions about the criminal conscience. Although they all came together at Leatherslade Farm with the single purpose of stealing money from a train, they were all separate individuals with distinct identities. Certainly most of them were brought up in the same impoverished areas of London and shared a common aspiration to achieve something better, but it would be wrong to conclude from this that they all became thieves for the same reason. Different members of the gang shared the same characteristics, but the same combination was rarely found in any two: Bruce, Gordon and Roy were dandies, aspiring to banal concepts of the good life. Bruce and Bob were romantics — imaginative, sensitive, nervous. Bob and Roger were gamblers. Roger, Roy, John Daly and Jimmy White disliked violence. John and Gordon were Irish. Gordon and Charlie were unusually huge: Roy was unusually small. Roy and Gordon were unable to form mature relationships with women, and even in middle-age lived with their mothers; Bruce and Ronnie Biggs were fashionably promiscuous; Buster, Charlie and Tommy Wisbey were solid, family men. Such are the numerous factors which any twist of the kaleidoscope can form into different interpretations of the criminal personality.

It might therefore be more useful to turn to the crime itself and see to what extent it reflects wickedness. The £2½ million which they stole from the train belonged to the banks. Some of it was insured, so the final, almost imperceptible loss was to the shareholders of the banks and insurance companies who, as the Train Robbers would say, "could well afford it". Certainly it would be hard to point to any human suffering which resulted from the theft of the money itself, and because of this the Train Robbers refused to consider it wrong. They showed the same incapacity as Piaget observed in younger children to see in the simple laws of private property a general interest which they should respect.

This blindness, however, is not confined to thieves: a large number of supposedly law-abiding citizens will swindle the state, or state corporations, or other impersonal property-owning legal entities, if they think they can do so undetected; and perhaps at the same time clamour for the greater punishment of criminals. Yet it would seem obvious that we all benefit from currency, banking, commerce and trade; that the channels through which they move must therefore be protected; and that to do this there must be either heavy escorts of armed guards, or proscriptive laws with deterrent punishment for their infringement. Given that this second method has been preferred, I do not see how Mr Justice Edmund Davies could have given much shorter sentences for such an ambitious crime, and the issues of violence of which he made much during the trial had little to do with the matter. Certainly since he delivered those sentences no one has stopped and robbed a train.

From the way the Train Robbers themselves described and defended their use of violence, it seemed commendably restrained. They said that they only coshed men who resisted them, as if to say that they only ran over those who stepped out into the road in their path. That some used force and others did not seemed to stem from their physique and temperament rather than any moral consideration. Roy was small, Roger weak, and Jimmy White gentle. For giants like Gordon, Charlie and Jim Hussey violence was their *raison d'être,* and to suggest that they should desist from violence seemed as absurd to them as proposing to a Caruso that he should not use his voice.

It is therefore beside the point to argue about whether the train driver, Mills, was injured by the blow from a cosh, or by hitting his head on the locomotive as he fell, or was not injured at all but merely put on an act at the instigation of the police to persuade the public that the Train Robbers were bad men. They used what force was necessary, regardless of the damage to the man's skull, and never pretended to me that this was not so.

At first sight this seems worse than stealing the money because the one was an impersonal crime against property and the other a cruel assault on a man: yet here again one must beware of judging others by one's own standards. I myself have never in my adult existence fought with a man or woman: I share with my peers not so much a revulsion as a deep inhibition which acts in the brain to paralyse any reflex transposing anger or aggression into acts of physical violence. The Train Robbers, on the other hand, grew up in gangs where a fight was the natural means to settle a dispute, and seemed sincerely baffled by the middle-class citizen's abhorrence of violence — an abhorrence enshrined in the law and quite evidently embedded in the attitudes of Mr Justice Edmund Davies.

The Train Robbers showed a comparable distaste for verbal aggression, something which I — and perhaps even Mr Justice Edmund Davies — have had recourse to frequently in our dealings with other human beings. That is not against the law, perhaps because the law is made by those who are physically weak but mentally agile: yet to the Train Robbers and their peers an honest fight, with bruises and broken bones — even a showdown with Purdies on Putney Heath — is preferable to a verbal exchange where they with their brief education and limited vocabulary are at such a great disadvantage.

What seems cruel and inhuman, then, in the coshing of Mills is not so much the violence itself as the cowardice of fifteen masked giants leaping at an old man from the dark: this, one might think, is indisputably wrong — the behaviour of wicked men. Yet if we analyse more closely the Train Robbers and their milieu we may find that even this apparently evil act does not necessarily prove that they are wicked men. First there is their background, by which I do not mean only the context of their infancy and adolescence, but the whole sub-society of working-class South London. There is no doubt that there was and still is endemic poverty juxtaposed to conspicuous consumption north of the river. It is not difficult to imagine the young Bruce Reynolds, for example, bicycling across the Thames to London's West End where the houses were large, light and elegantly proportioned; where the shops and department stores of Bond Street and Knightsbridge displayed every variety of diverse and luxurious merchandise; nor hard to guess his feelings as he returned to the meagre tenement where his father struggled to feed his family on the wages of unskilled labour. For even now, after thirty years of a Welfare State, the squalor and poverty of London's poorer boroughs, side by side with the flagrant display of extravagance and riches in the West End, is an affront to any moral sensibility; and however true it may be that the preservation of such inequality is in the final interest of us all — that the poor will only get richer if the rich get richer still — it should not astonish a reasonable man if it gives rise to a sense of grievance not just in Piaget's children but in Camberwell's grown men.

The Train Robbers were all determined to change this inequality of condition but only for themselves. None was a Robin Hood. Even Bruce, the son of a Socialist and Trades Unionist, was consistently selfish in his drive to escape from the slums of Battersea. In the course of my researches I found almost no instance of unselfish behaviour in any one of the Train Robbers. Roy once did a milk round, after a spell in prison, and would let the children from the Council flats steal bottles of orange juice off his float; and Jimmy White, after the Train Robbery, slipped a few hundred quid to some old thieves who were down on their luck. The others, apart from the free-spending on their families and friends, and competitive extravagance at gangster "benefits", spent their stolen money on themselves.

Yet even where a thief does not act as a Robin Hood, he may still be seen as one. As E. J. Hobsbawm says of rural bandits, "whatever the actual practice, there is no doubt that the bandit is considered an agent of Justice, indeed a restorer of morality, and often considers himself as such". The same might be said of those urban bandits, the Train Robbers, who were and still are regarded with considerable sympathy, and were given much tacit support in their own circles. A small army of auxiliaries brought them information, ran errands and hid their money — not just because they hoped for some of the money itself. It astonished me to discover how little Mary Manson or Buster's friend Derek Glass had in return for the risks they took. Even total strangers brought them information, not for a whack or a drink, but because they enjoyed the discomfiture of the rich and powerful. "The crucial fact about the bandit's social situation is its ambiguity. He is an outsider and a rebel, a poor man who refuses to accept the normal rules of poverty and establishes his freedom by means of the only resources within the reach of the poor, strength, bravery, cunning and determination. This draws him close to the poor; he is one of them. It sets him in opposition to the hierarchy of power, wealth and influence: he is not one of them."[1]

Certainly there would be an insignificant amount of crime if large numbers of ordinary people did not feel themselves to be the friends of thieves — or at any rate the enemies of the police who they see as oppressive, hypocritical and cruel. The picture of the Metropolitan Police, particularly of the Flying Squad in the early 1960s, which emerges from the Train Robbers' story — some of them taking bribes to alter evidence or drop charges, and others fabricating evidence to secure convictions — may well be exaggerated, but because so many Metropolitan police officers have been convicted of corruption or dismissed from the force since the Train Robbery took place, it cannot be regarded as totally false. Between 1972, when Sir Robert Mark became Commissioner of the Metropolitan Police, and February 1976, "eighty-two officers had been dismissed following formal proceedings. A further 301 had left voluntarily during the course of criminal or disciplinary enquiries. . . . In addition forty-six officers were currently suspended, ten of them awaiting trial, twenty-four awaiting the decision of the DPP and the remaining twelve the subject of serious disciplinary enquiries".[2]

It may also be that the Train Robbers were frequently deceived by those who pretended to bribe the police, and pay large sums of money to lawyers, when in fact they pocketed the money themselves. When one of the Train Robbers' wives was wanted for questioning, she was convinced that any officer from Scotland Yard who took her in would plant on her a stolen £5 note. He said that he had to pay £500 to an officer outside the Metropolitan area to make the arrest. This incident, if true — a policeman being bribed to be honest — adds an ironical touch to the story, but it could also be part of a running confidence trick whereby thieves are fleeced of the money they steal.

---

[1] E. J. Hobsbawm, *Bandits,* Weidenfeld and Nicolson, 1969.
[2] Barry Cox, John Shirley, Martin Short, *The Fall of Scotland Yard,* 1977, p. 213.

The effect of this corruption on the moral attitudes of the Train Robbers was certainly to neutralise any bad conscience, for their immediate adversaries were seen to be equally cynical towards and parasitic on the society they supposedly served. Indeed the whole notion of society was for the Train Robbers a middle-class myth. What we see as a beehive or an ant-hill, with clearly defined roles for each bee or ant, they see as the state of nature itself with one species preying off another, and different members of the same species fighting for ascendancy and survival. Or, to remove it from metaphor, what we call civilised society and see as a reasonable and moral contract between different human beings on the same tract of land, they see as an oppressive conspiracy by the physically weak but mentally strong to impose values which further their interests.

Force, for example, is presented as immoral yet it has been and is unhesitatingly used in the interests of the state (Gordon's cosh was a truncheon of the *Guardia Civil*): as inhuman, when it is among man's most prevalent and consistent characteristics; and as uncivilised when it is common in societies of cultural abundance (Benvenuto Cellini, after all, stabbed his enemies in the back and Pushkin died from a duel). The Train Robbers would say — were they given to this kind of reflection — that by "civilisation" we really mean complexity — the web with which the clever clerks paralyse those with contrary talents and gain for themselves an ascendant position in the community.

The Train Robbers showed total repugnance for the rules and formalities of the modern state — licences, permits, taxes, National Insurance Stamps. This anarchism explains their appeal to the poor. I myself, who have everything to gain from literate values and everything to lose from savagery, find something seductive in the life and values of the Train Robbers. Like tigers or elephants they seem the last traces of an age which drew upon fundamental human qualities of courage and loyalty. Their lives as well as their liberty could stand or fall on the strength of friendship: love could mean the sharing of great luxury and great suffering. Poor youths like Buster, Bruce, Tommy and Charlie took to crime to escape not so much from the poverty of their condition as the emasculation of menial, repetitious labour for a paltry wage. Their wives responded with a savage loyalty: just as none of the Train Robbers used his £150,000 to run off with a younger woman, so few of the wives abandoned their husbands at the prospect of twenty years' separation. In a domestic context, Buster, Tommy, Charlie, Jim Hussey and Jimmy White must surely be seen as good men.

It was consistent with these values that the only authority recognised by the Train Robbers was the natural authority of a "name" — another criminal who had earned their respect through demonstrable qualities of courage, cunning and ruthlessness. The authority they rejected was that delegated to policemen, judges and Home Office officials; and here again I find some sympathy for their feelings. Certainly I have an involuntary dislike for the Courts of Law. The Judge's robes and wig seem to be the props of a primitive pretence that the Judge represents the Sovereign and the Sovereign represents God; yet certainly since the Civil War there has been no widespread belief in the Divine Right of kings, and the laws that are made by Parliament express not the will of God but either a sectional interest or a kind of utilitarian "welfarism". Adultery, which in its effect on children is often more inhuman than theft, has long since gone unpunished by the law: and even as the Train Robbers rotted in prison for stealing bank-notes, Parliament permitted sodomy which the God of the Old Testament punished with fire and brimstone.

Perhaps the most abhorrent instance in this story of the hypocrisy of the Law is the case of Bill Boal. The Appeal Court judges realised that there was no convincing evidence against him on the major charges of robbery and conspiracy to rob; yet sent him to prison for fourteen years for receiving. Perhaps Bill Boal did know, or should have known, that the debt he was recovering from Roger was paid in stolen money; but so too did the eminent counsel at Aylesbury who received fees of several thousand pounds which — under any reasonable interpretation of their favoured word "deduce" — they must have known came either from the Train Robbery or from other crimes. They would answer, I dare say, that it was not their duty to decide whether the money owed to them was stolen or not; and so would Bill Boal.

These instances of the absurdity and hypocrisy of the law are not meant to suggest that we should return to a theocratic state simply to put thieves in the wrong: the very kings and barons in whose Divine Right the sovereignty of the state was once said to reside had more in common with Buster Edwards and Charlie

Wilson than with our modern civil servants, cabinet ministers or constitutional monarch; and even if the Train Robbers were pious, believing Christians, an exhortation to render unto Caesar the things that are Caesar's would almost certainly fail. Bob Welch was the only one to believe in God whom he felt to be on his side; for when his escape from Leicester failed, and the sky darkened, he took it as a sign that God was disappointed that he and some of the most cold-blooded murderers in England had not got away.

Yet without the proposition that the law of the land expresses Divine or even Natural Law, we are left with only the public good or the well-being of society; and we cannot then describe the Train Robbers as bad men because they are antisocial, when to judge from their values, loyalties and behaviour they do not belong to our society but to another, parallel, society which exists on the same island but is more foreign than much of France and Spain. They abjure Rousseau's Social Contract; they defy Hobbes's Leviathan and as the second of Disraeli's two nations wage intermittent war against us. Thus the coshing of Mills, and the attempt to frighten Pelham, become no more cowardly or immoral than the cudgelling of an enemy sentry in the last war, or the execution of a spy. Bruce's fantasy that the gang was a platoon of SAS commandos, and that his Borstal institution was Colditz Castle, were closer to reality than he supposed; and Buster's alliance with Skorzeny was ironically appropriate. Poetically one might describe the Train Robbers as Saxons still fighting the Normans; more exactly we must recognise, if only from the evidence of this story alone, that many of them are Irishmen who feel no instinctive affection for the British state or British institutions.

And to see thieves as the shock troops of the militant poor, and to accord them combatant status, still permits us to lock them away; but it implies that we should no longer look upon them necessarily as either sinners or psychopaths but must extend to them the civility of a Geneva Convention. There is still scope for persuasion that whatever the rights or wrongs of the matter, crime does not pay; but for two reasons I am sure that this will never succeed. A thief will always see obedience to the law and collaboration with the police as a betrayal of his own kind by which he would lose all self-respect; and the love of a gamble is probably the most pertinent facet of a thief's personality. I am sure that even if the Train Robbers had known before the Robbery that only one in five would escape with his whack, not one of them would have dropped out.

As a result of the suffering they and their families later experienced, almost all of the Train Robbers would now concede that crime does not pay in subtler ways. Money, however acquired, does buy such commodities as freedom, comfort, cleanliness, light, privacy and respect — all of which contribute to contentment — but it is clear that the "good life" of which they all once dreamed turned out to be a mirage. Those who got away found that they had lost more than they gained. Only Charmian Biggs seems to have escaped in mind as well as body from the confines of her environment to the suburban Nirvana of Australia and work as an editorial assistant on the University of Melbourne Review; but Ronnie her husband sits homesick on the Copacabana beach, longing for London's damp drizzle, strong tea and custard.

It is also quite clear that the end which was supposed to justify the means was destroyed by the means. The saying that "war is hell and all its glory moonshine" is as true of the sporadic civil war between criminals and the state in Britain as it was in the real Civil War in the United States. The combatants are inevitably wounded by the conflict — not physically by shrapnel but in their spirits by treachery and deceit. As a result of the robbery, some of the Train Robbers lost their wives; almost all lost their friends. The liars were lied to; the robbers robbed. Dishonesty is contagious and indiscriminate: a small crime leads to a greater crime, a thief becomes a murderer. There is an inexorable progression from one to the other. When Gill Hussey asked Jim, who she considered so gentle and controlled, how he had come at the age of eighteen to beat up a police inspector, he had simply replied: "It's the name of the game." Buster's defence of the coshing of Mills was that he did "what had to be done". It is the logic of the profession which in criminal careers leads to cruelty and death, yet in other professions — the police, the law, and journalism — leads to equally ruthless, unscrupulous and essentially amoral behaviour. In the pages of this book I have myself broken the promise I made to Biggs that I would never reveal that he had exposed the hoax, putting him perhaps in danger of death. I have described, too, how I confronted Stan Agate, an old man who had already suffered two strokes, with an incident from his past just to satisfy my own curiosity. I did what had to be done: it was the name of the game.

The evil, then, which I had sought in the Train Robbers can be found in any one of us and has little to do with the law of the land. There was both a good thief and a bad thief on Calvary, and the good thief went rapidly to heaven. And if I return from my journey into the underworld convinced that we should obey our laws, it is not because the laws are always good, but because the power of the state is so much greater than that of those who fight against it. "Certainly an equal distribution of property is just," wrote Pascal, "but since we are unable to enforce justice, we have made it just to obey force; unable to strengthen justice, we have justified strength so that justice and strength go together and there is peace, which is the overriding good."

Appendix
What Happened to the Money

As might have been expected, it has proved difficult to discover just what happened to the £2,295,150 which was never recovered by the loss assessors. I myself am convinced that in most cases this is not because any of the stolen money is still in the possession of the Train Robbers, but because they kept no accounts and find it hard to remember what they spent prior to their arrest. In several cases the Train Robbers themselves do not know what happened to their money while they were in prison but found none when they came out. I have pointed out the exceptions to this rule in the text.

I have, nonetheless, attempted to draw up an approximate balance sheet. The figures are based upon either the memory of the Train Robbers or my own speculation.

Total stolen from the Train: £2,631,684

"Drinks" pulled out prior to the share out:

— Stan Agate	£20,000
— Joey Gray	£10,000
— Lennie Field	£12,500
— Mark	£28,500
— Roy (to buy vans)	£2,000
— Friend of Charlie's (?)	£8,000
— Left at the farm (approx.)	£684
	£81,684
17 "whacks" @ £150,000	£2,550,000
	£2,631,684

Roger Cordrey £

Car bought in Oxford	380
Given to Bill Boal	200

Taken by Bill Boal	150
Sent to sister-in-law	860
Vehicles in Bournemouth	475
Flat in Bournemouth	58
Found on Roger	116
Found in cars	134,982
Found in flat	5,910
Unaccounted for	6,869
	£150,000

Jim Hussey   £

Initial out of pocket expenses	£5,000
Legal expenses	33,000
Gill's visiting expenses	1,000
Car for Gill	500
Deposit on children's clothes shop	500
"Lost" in bad investments — car hire company, costume jewellery business, and two bookmakers	110,000
	£150,000

Tommy Wisbey   £

Initial out of pocket expenses	3,000
"Lost" in Camberwell	8,000
Legal expenses	28,000
Burnt because rotten	5,000
Cost of changing up stolen money	7,500
House for Rene in Norbury	6,000
Paid to minders	10,000
Property speculation by Tommy's brother	20,000
House for a relative	6,500
Solicitors' fees	1,000
Betting shops	15,000
Rene's living expenses over thirteen years	20,000
A relative's living expenses	20,000
	£150,000

Gordon Goody   £

Initial out of pocket expenses	4,000
Legal expenses	30,000
Minders	7,000

Prison expenses	3,000
Manchester escape plan	3,000
Mother's living expenses over thirteen years	15,000
June Edwards	500
Stolen by a minder	40,000
Invested in property	27,500
Unaccounted for	20,000
	£150,000

Bob Welch £

Initial out of pocket expenses	10,000
Legal expenses	30,000
Jean's allowance @ £10 per week	5,000
House in New Cross	5,000
Appropriated by minder	100,000
	£150,000

Roy James £

Legal expenses	10,000
Life on the run	8,500
Cost of changing up stolen money	6,000
Recovered by police at his capture	12,000
Left with Pelham	500
Cost of recovering money from Charlie's friend	7,000
House for a relative	6,000
Allowance for his mother	13,000
Given to Micky Ball	12,500
Appropriated by minder	74,500
	£150,000

Buster Edwards £

Expenses in hiding in Wraysbury	10,000
Cost of transferring money to Switzerland	17,500
Cost of escape to Germany	4,000
Invested in Scorzeny's property company	10,000
Services in Germany	20,000
Expenses in Mexico	68,500
"Lost" in London	20,000
	£150,000

Jimmy White	£
Scottish and Irish notes left at the farm for the others	16,000
Stolen with his passport in his flat	8,500
Given to old thieves	8,000
Cost of changing up mouldy notes	23,000
Hidden in the caravan	36,000
Initial payment to "the Professor"	10,000
Stolen by a minder	10,000
Farm in Derbyshire	5,000
Stock	3,000
Land Rover and boat	1,600
Money in his possession when caught	2,000
Expenses of life on the run	26,900
	£150,000

I did not talk to Brian Field, and do not know the real identity of Alf Thomas, but suggest the following disposal of their money:

Brian Field	£
Dumped by a relative in Dorking Wood	100,900
Legal and other expenses	49,100
	£150,000

Alf Thomas	£
Left in the telephone box	47,245
Unaccounted for	102,755
	£150,000

Although I talked to Bruce Reynolds, Charlie Wilson and Ronnie Biggs, I did not have the opportunity to arrive at even an approximate breakdown of how they disposed of their money. Most was spent on the run; and in the case of the first two, some was recovered at their arrest. I am prepared to believe that none of them have any of the stolen money now, and that John Daly had his whack stolen from him prior to his arrest. I have no way of knowing what happened to the whacks of the men I have called Bill Jennings and Frank Munroe.

Bibliography

del Boca, Angelo, and Mario Giovana, *Fascism Today,*
    Heinemann, 1969
Delano, Anthony, *Slip-up,* Quadrangle, New York, 1975
Eisenberg, Denis, *The Re-emergence of Fascism,*
    MacGibbon & Kee, 1967
Fewtrell, Malcolm, *The Train Robbers,* Arthur Barker, 1964
Foley, Charles, *Commando Extraordinary,* Longmans, Green, 1954
Fordham, Peta, *The Robbers' Tale,* Hodder & Stoughton, 1965
Gosling, John, and Dennis Craig, *The Great Train Robbery,*
    W. H. Allen, 1964
Hobsbawm, E. J., *Bandits,* Weidenfeld & Nicolson, 1969
Mackenzie, Colin, *Biggs: The World's Most Wanted Man,* William
    Morrow, New York, 1975
Millen, Ernest, *Specialist in Crime,* Harrap, 1972
Skorzeny, Otto, *Skorzeny's Special Missions,* Robert Hale, 1957
Stein, George H., *The Waffen-SS,* Cornell University Press, 1966
Stevenson, William, *The Bormann Brotherhood,* Arthur Barker, 1973
Tetens, T. B., *The New Germany and the Old Nazis,* Secker & Warburg,
    1961
Williams, Frank, *No Fixed Address,* W. H. Allen, 1973